The Ties That Bind

~

Abiding Fate

Also by K. R. Brehmer

A HERITAGE SAGA

The Way Back Home ~ Finding Rose

The Bend of the Road ~ Tiding Westward

The Ties That Bind
~
Abiding Fate

A Heritage Saga

K. R. BREHMER

⟩B

Copyright © 2025 by K. R. Brehmer

All rights reserved. This book or any portion thereof may not be reproduced or used in any manner whatsoever without the express written permission of the publisher except for the use of brief quotations in a book review.

Published in the United States of America by K. R. Brehmer.
First Printing, 2025

ISBN 978-0-9864340-6-8 (softcover)
ISBN 978-0-9864340-7-5 (ebook)

Cover and book design by the author.

This is a work of fiction. All characters, organizations, events, incidents and dialogues are either products of the author's imagination or are based on the historical and personal record, both long past or more recent.

So walk me over this bridge
The river's so deep and so wide.
Just walk me over the bridge, my darling,
We'll get to the other side.

Amber Marshall and Shaun Johnston,
The Bridge—Heartland Soundtrack

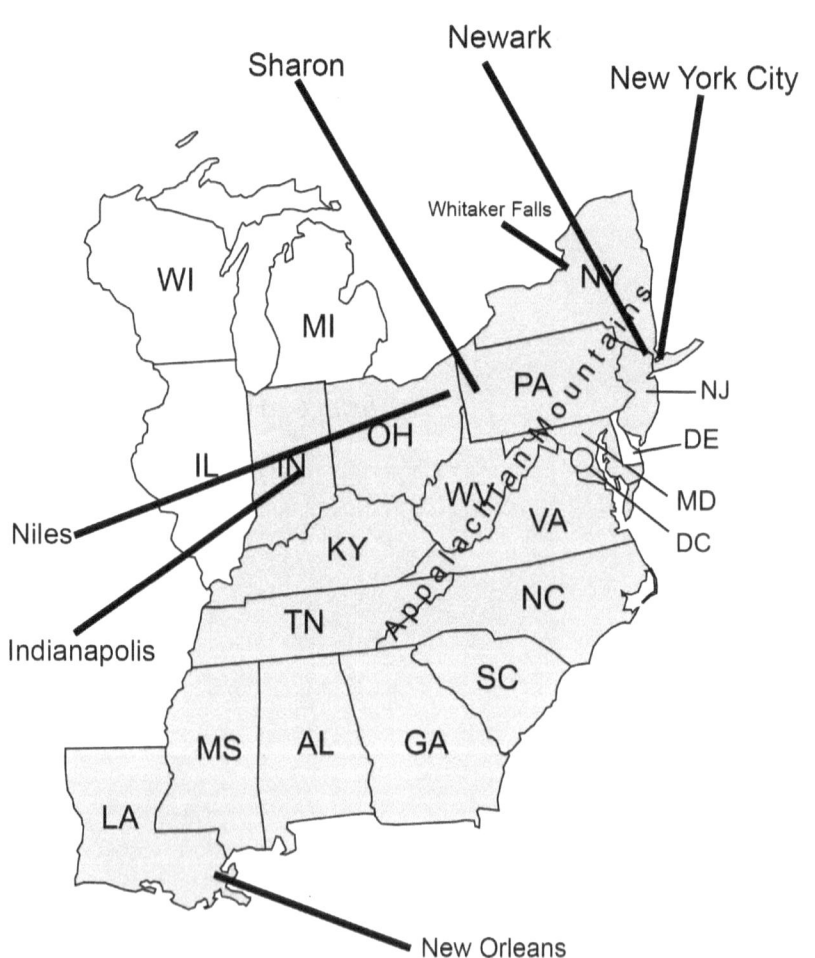

FAREWELLS

Port of Naples, Italy, August 1926

"Let's go, Antonio, I need to get on board now!" Maria yelled as she yanked hard on her brother's arm." Half dragged, he accompanied his sister as far as he was allowed to go—to the foot of the gangway and no further—then she bear-hugged him goodbye and told him they would soon be together again. The next time he caught a glimpse of her she was waving at him from the upper deck, pinned against the rail on her right and on her left and from behind by a mass of bobbing heads attached to bodies a good deal taller than her own.

The sun showed no pity in casting powerful rays down on a placid sea on a middle of August day in southern Italy, only to be reflected upwards again by the brilliantly shimmering waters of the Bay of Naples. The SS Conte Biancamano began to steam slowly away from the dock, heading at first towards the Strait of Gibraltar and from there onto the endless expanse of the Atlantic Ocean itself.

Even the intense summer heat was not powerful enough to dry the tears rolling down the faces of relatives and friends standing on shore and looking up at her. So many passengers packed together like sardines, only squeezed into a sleek ironclad steamship instead of a small tin can that comes with a key for rolling back the top. How could the ship stay afloat with the weight of so many standing on its decks? Leaning against the port side rails and each other, the distant shapes jockeyed among themselves to reach advantageous positions in which they could be seen while still seeing the crowd watching them from below. One of the smaller sized bodies that had managed to wedge itself into a coveted viewing spot belonged to Maria Conte. Her brother looked forlorn as the ship began to pull away from the dock. How she wished he could be standing there by her side aboard the shiny new transatlantic liner that had only been launched for the first time the year before. Instead, all he could do was to wave a kerchief through the air like the others around him were doing!

Aged eleven and fourteen Maria and Antonio were meant to be on their way together to finally join their long absent, but never forgotten, father in America. It would be her first meeting with Michelino Conte, her father having left behind the shores of Italy and a wife six months pregnant with Maria nearly twelve years before. For her brother it would be almost the same. Only two years old when his father left, he remembered nothing about him. The moment had finally come it seemed, to make the long awaited journey. But the port physician clearly had other ideas. He had detected a problem with Antonio's eyes while performing a routine health check before passengers were allowed to board the ship. Her brother watched uneasily, his shoulders slumping, as the doctor continued to poke and prod him. Then he was asked a series of questions: How long had his eyelids been reddish and swollen? Were they often itchy? Did he have any pain? Were his eyes sensitive to light? Had there been any loss of vision?

It was like the stream of questions was never-ending to someone about to start the next phase of his life.

"What to do you mean there's something wrong with his eyesight? How could there be? My brother's never had a health problem like that before. And he can see perfectly well. He was reading a book just last night. He is perfectly…," his livid sister now nearly shouting, "and you can tell by looking at him he's as strong as a horse." In truth, his solid appearance and Mediterranean good looks did fly in the face of unhealthiness.

"His eyesight is not exactly the problem, at least not yet," the doctor calmly told Maria. He was accustomed to emotional reactions when it came to a decision to deny boarding and knew how to handle them. "It looks like an infection of the eyes is causing the problem. I'm sorry to say, miss, but he's definitely failed the examination. No one is allowed to go aboard unless they have a clean bill of health. If we were to let him sail today with you to New York right now, do you know what would happen? Their Public Health Service officers would conduct another examination similar to our own, take one look at his eyes and discover the same problem we have found here."

"But even if they did do that at least we would be together and we could handle it there. Why not let him go anyway? Our father will be waiting there for both of us, not just me."

"Because your brother would then be refused entry by the customs based on his medical condition—possibly even trachoma in his case—and he would be sent back as soon as possible to be treated in his country of origin. That is if he were to be one of the more fortunate ones. Besides, while he was in arrivals he would be restricted to staying only on the customs island itself. There would never be a chance of seeing your father unless he was to be released. His status would not open to any family discussion. And his deportation back to Italy would be at the shipping line's expense in the end since they would be deemed at fault for allowing him to travel in the first place. That's the policy and we must abide by it."

"Still, why not let them decide?" she continued unwilling to concede just yet. "What if we promised to pay the return fare if it came to that? Then, at least, my brother and I would be going together like we're supposed to be doing now. And maybe he will be better by the time he gets there."

"You should also be aware there's also the possibility he could be detained much longer before he is sent back to Italy. The holding facilities on Ellis Island would not be the most pleasant place even for a short time. He might be staying next to illegal immigrants also waiting for deportation for reasons other than medical. There are criminals and political detainees all grouped together in the same living space. It would be a rough place to be in, one that could be dangerous for a child basically left to fend for himself most of the time. There isn't much supervision in the holding areas on Ellis from what we know about it."

By this time Maria could tell further argument would be useless. The man was growing increasingly antsy, often glancing between his wristwatch and the line of other passengers still waiting their turn to see him. Maria was also nervous in worrying the ship would be hoisting anchor soon. Then he had Antonio step to one side and in doing so added that once her brother had cleared health requirements in Italy he could sail on another ship at a later date. Ships left frequently, and the same *2a Classe Economtica* ticket from the Lloyd Sabaudo steamship line that was now in his possession would be honored at that time. There would be no additional charge under the circumstances.

But the case was not the same for Maria; she would need to purchase a new ticket since the one she had now would no longer be valid in the future. Her brother had been refused embarkation by staff whereas a decision not to board would be her own. Unlike Antonio, she had not been disqualified in failing to meet official medical requirements and she had neither cancelled nor changed her dates within the prescribed time limits. At this juncture she felt she had no choice but to continue with the voyage since their fare had been paid for by their father for this specific ship leaving on the 19th of August. To ask him to send money to pay for another ticket would mean an indefinite delay in joining him in America. Scraping together enough for a second fare would not be easy. The friend of the family travelling with them as their chaperone faced the same dilemma should he decide not to embark at this time, either depart now or lose the money. He came to the same conclusion as Maria; they should continue the journey as planned.

***

Maria, although two years younger than her brother, had kept a watchful eye on Antonio from start to finish when they left Bagnoli to go to the port. Not unusual, in fact she had a habit of doing so in daily practice. The first leg of the journey to Naples had been a trek from their mountain village down to the station in Montella. From the town of Montella they would catch the train to Avellino, the capital city of the eponymous province, and from there to Naples proper. Ever on guard for signs of a meandering attention—Antonio could appear at times to be totally oblivious of the circumstances in which he found himself—she would nudge him along with gentle prompting to keep him from going astray if he did. Just the opposite, Maria was usually alert to her surroundings and circumstance. Occasionally too alert, as her brother had experienced more than once, in jumping to conclusions and barging in when she shouldn't have done.

And all during the journey northwest to Avellino and further westwards to the sea, some sixty miles all told from their hometown, she wanted to ensure nothing would happen to hinder their safe arrival in Naples in a timely manner. They needed to stay on their toes when they arrived so they could together receive all the last *buon viaggio* wishes from those who had helped raise them over the past eleven years and in return give them their endless thanks even though it had been difficult at times. It had been far from ideal living with relatives led by a stern grandfather still they had sacrificed so much in time, energy, devotion and money to see them through to this parting moment. Maria knew they owed them an enormous measure of gratitude for all of their kindness whether or not that kindness had been with certain strings attached.

Dozing off, either literally or figuratively, would not be appropriate at this point whatsoever. However, like sometimes in the past, she had mistakenly taken Antonio's calm, sometimes almost sleep-walking exterior for a lack of proper attention to their present circumstances and had stopped to tell him so. Although he was not naturally as exuberant as his sister, he was in his own way quietly observant and mindful of what was happening about him. Perhaps even more so than Maria at times as he did not let emotions get the better of him unless pushed to the limit. And there was no lack of determination when needed, just as with his sister, but with a different level of surface ferocity and the kind of affability that made it easy to get along with people.

Nothing had been normal; nothing had been easy; nothing had gone according to plan for so long. Just maybe, just maybe the pitfalls of the past were just that, of the past and left behind them forever. There could only be a better life awaiting them ahead in America when they were at long last reunited with their father. Life in Bagnoli Irpino after their mother's premature death at the age of twenty-six had been anything but straightforward. Instead of finding solace in the welcoming arms of grandparents, aunts and uncles, it had often felt like feuding families had used the two of them as excuses to torment each other. They squabbled amongst themselves over living arrangements, money matters, responsibilities and obligations.

Divisions between their father's wealthier side of the family and mother's poorer side had come to a head when the former moaned pathetically that child support remitted by the children's father was not being fairly distributed. It was just one more instance of why the wealthier grandfather of the two deserved his nickname of "the wolf" in its negative connotation! The falling out between the two family sides had led to a poor attempt at mutual avoidance—something nearly impossible to do in a small town—while pressuring the children to do the same.

Pettiness had sunk to new lows when the two children

were separated and forced to live apart for a time with a different set of relatives. Without giving adequate thought, or possibly any thought at all, to the welfare of the two young people, the grandparents had made the arrangement based on their own personal circumstances only. These children should thank their lucky stars to have relatives to care for them was the attitude that prevailed. Of course, the wealthier group ended up having a larger say in the settlement. Nevertheless, Maria and Antonio Conte were wise enough, even at their age, to realize they had no choice in the matter. They had to live with whatever was decided. In a way you could say they were clear-eyed, much more so than most of their contemporaries, having grown up without normal parental guidance. At any rate the siblings had always kept in mind no matter how many years had gone by their living situation was still temporary. They had to be patient and bide their time a little longer until their father brought them all together as a family again. Perhaps it was the best thing that they had no conception just how long that would turn out to be. Who would have guessed twelve years would elapse since Michelino Conte had emigrated from Italy to avoid a war before he would be ready to have them join him?

Maria Conte, for her part, had from a very early age found her zone of comfort within the power of her own voice and an outgoing personality to back it up. Whenever she could she exercised her natural vocal gift whether it was at church, in school or at home—or simply when she felt like exercising her lungs by singing in the streets, forests or anywhere else. She was not shy, and used her singing and self-confidence to publicize her own presence in the small town of Bagnoli Irpino. Her belief in herself and the power of her voice were more than once used fearlessly to deter perceived transgressions. Short and sturdily built, her character reflected her stature; she was never one to stand down when confronted with ill-mannered behavior. Antonio was altogether different for he had found his distraction in food. Not only did he have a craving for tasty concoctions—a tendency towards a slightly rounded figure already in evidence—he also took great pleasure in their preparation. Cooking food, especially the art of baking, was welcomed by relatives on either side. And bottoms hastily filled seats around the dining table when Antonio announced his preparations were ready to be served. For such a young person he showed a stick-to-itiveness and talent beyond his years. Even without a recipe he had become adept at judging the kind and amount of ingredients that made what was usually a common dish into *un gusto speciale* in whichever family home he happened to be staying at the time.

***

This was one time Maria didn't feel like singing. What was going to happen to her brother now that he had been disallowed from sailing and she would no longer be there to guide him, and to help protect him from bullies? It was an eye problem of some kind the doctor had said. He would be permitted to depart at a later date in exchanging the ticket already purchased for a new one after he had undergone treatment and was cured, she recalled. The treatment might not take that long if the problem was not serious. Of course she didn't want to leave him behind but she wasn't sure she would have given up leaving at this late date even if her ticket could have been exchanged for another date without additional cost.

Their father would be half as disappointed with only one of them missing! Ultimately, it was Antonio's prompting that settled it for good; Maria must go without him or it would be like starting over again.

It was a bitter pill to swallow because at the end of their voyage Michelino Conte—the father whose only image she ever had seen was the photograph in the living room—would be standing there ready to welcome the **two** of them. She could just imagine how eager he would have been to take them both to their new home. What she couldn't imagine was what his reaction would be. In his last letter he had written of the plan once they had cleared custom formalities. A less than three mile ferry ride from Ellis Island to Jersey City and they would be at the waterfront train station. Then on the Broadway Limited—a special train of the Pennsylvania Railroad—they would be whisked away from New Jersey and headed for their new American home in the town of Sharon. Excitement dripped out of each of his words when his letter had been read out loud. Pennsylvania—the place with a strange sounding name, taking up half the envelope when written—was wide, large, and where they would be living was almost four hundred miles west of New York. How long would it take and what would it really be like when she finally got there?

There was a small chance Michelino Conte would receive forewarning of events in Italy before the ship's arrival in New York. A postcard would at least be immediately mailed from Bagnoli concisely explaining what had befallen Antonio. It would be better if it did get there first so the shock could be reduced for expectations of their reunion had been running at a feverish pace for weeks on both sides of the Atlantic. After more than a dozen years apart, it would be hard to put into words how much the two children and their father looked forward to finally being a true family.

For Antonio, it would be like meeting him for the first time since he had been only two years old when Michelino had left southern Italian shores. Like his sister, his only real recollection of what he looked like was from the photo. He had studied the details over and over throughout the years but a one dimensional depiction was just that; it didn't talk, change expressions and never moved. What his father was really like would only be revealed when they finally spent time together. As for Maria, since she had not graced the world before he had sailed off for America, it literally would be meeting her father for the very first time.

APENNINES

Principato Ultra, Kingdom of Naples, Italy, Summer 1799

On the two sides of the Apennine Mountains, a range which stretches the entire length of the Italian Peninsula—a distance of over seven hundred miles—the countryside slopes either easterly to the Adriatic Sea or westerly to the Tyrrhenian Sea. Narrower and lower in the northern and southern extremes, the range reaches its greatest concentration of higher peaks in the broader central part of the elongated strip of land with boot-shaped topography at the southern end. While these rugged crags and peaks dividing the Principato Ultra from Capitanata in the South—corresponding to the regions of Campania and Foggia as they are also called—do not compare to the grandeur of the Alps, they are imposing enough not to be taken lightly or ignored when it comes to mountaineering challenges. Campania incorporates the bustling metropolis of Naples on the Italian west coast in contrast to the many small towns and tranquil villages scattered around the province's mountainous interior. The section of the Apennine range closest to Avellino, another large sized municipality about fifty miles inland east of Naples, is called Irpinia. And situated within the Irpinia domain from north to south are a few of the more prominent Irpinian communes: Savignano Irpino, Montecalvo Irpino, Ariano Irpino and Melito Irpino at the northern end, and Cassano Irpino and of course **Bagnoli Irpino** on the southern edge of the administrative division of Principato Ultra.

Angiolo Conte and Tschüss, his working canine companion with a name stemming from Norman times, had roused themselves from resting in the shade, a small respite from the pressing heat of an early summer afternoon. With the cooler part of the day almost upon them, shepherd and his dog would soon begin slowly prodding their herd of sheep from the forested slopes of the highlands down to the fields and meadows of the *Piano Laceno* below. The hills of this part of the Apennines were cooler against the sun of midday, but the warmer Laceno plain and swampy terrain would provide better grazing grounds needed before nightfall. Bagnolese sheep, a special local breed characterized by their distinctive black and white mottled faces with long noses curving downwards, would be able to graze to their heart's content.

"What do you say, Tschüss, should we get a start with our wooly friends now?" There was no doubt that his dog was ready; he leapt to his feet with an all-business-like look in his eyes and with ears perked up ready for a command to move into action. These foolish wooly creatures were here to do his bidding. "Let's get to work then, Tschüss!" If they kept moving and with a little bit of luck, Angiolo might meet up with one of the other local shepherds roaming the countryside. Catching-up on news, tempered with a smidgen of gossip to boot, would be the order of the day if they did. Their Italian world seemed to be in turmoil once again. Wasn't it almost always the case nowadays or did it just seem that way?

Leaders rose and fell so often it was so hard to keep track of who the mighty ones were at any given time—not that it made much difference in the scheme of things whoever they were. The last word he had heard before leaving Bagnoli for the hills went something like this if he remembered correctly: Naples once again is in shambles because of harsh reprisals that had been carried out by Cardinal Ruffo—a representative of the exiled King of Naples—against Republican French interlopers who had taken possession of the city in yet another uprising.

Fabrizio Ruffo had only recently been dispatched by King Ferdinand from his location in Sicily to retake Naples from the French usurper who had a few months prior seized control of the entire kingdom. The kingdom was comprised of several southern provinces including the Principato Ultra, or Campania as it was more and more often referred to by its inhabitants, and the very same in which Angiolo and Tschüss were herding their flock of sheep. The integrity of the kingdom had been restored after only a few months of foreign occupation. But French aggression was another attempt in a long and convoluted history of land grabbing.

Southern Italy had seen many influences come and go, and all of them had left their marks in shaping and reshaping competitive allegiances. Not so long ago the region had belonged to Spain and before that, for a short time, in possession of Austria within the Holy Roman Empire. Further back it was the French and Spanish again. The conquest of southern Italy by the Normans in the 11th century was preceded by Greek colonization and harkened back even further in time, to before the advent of Christianity. Perhaps it was the ancient migration of Greeks that had passed down the trait of blue eyes quite common among present-day local communities; in fact a pair of them had spotted his friend Mario and his flock just ahead of them.

"Ciao, my friend," shouted out Angiolo as soon as he was close enough. But he had to wait a little more before receiving a greeting in return. And when he did, it came unexpectedly from unsmiling lips.

"What's with you, Mario? You don't look yourself. You haven't come down with something, have you?"

"No. Nothing like that, nothing I know about at least. Last night I lost two of my sheep," the sullen herder groused. "I'd been told there was a wolf pack praying on chickens and maybe some goats too in the area but had seen no evidence of anything like that myself until now. I guess I should have paid better attention and been more vigilant."

For as long as Angiolo could remember he had heard tales, almost sacred in nature, of the Irpinia wolves. They formed an integral part of local folklore but also constituted real threats to livestock and livelihoods at the same time. The name Irpinia itself was derived from the Latin word Hirpini, referring to an ancient tribe which contributed to the blood—now in a much diluted quantity—flowing through many of his kin and himself. Furthermore, the name Hirpini came from the word *hirpus*, which meant wolf in the Oscan language spoken by long gone tribesmen. True to their historical habits, grey wolves, sometimes called Apennine wolves, still roamed the territory; but they were seldom seen unless sought out specifically to be hunted or trapped. While the stories about local wolves may not have reached the mythical heights of the she-wolf who saved newborns Romulus and Remos, the twin brothers who founded Rome, the belief that a wolf led the first settlers to the Irpinias was equally as significant to the Italian

South. A second wolf-based legend of a miracle that occurred at a monastery on the other side of the city of Avellino from Bagnoli Irpino was also widely repeated among locals. In brief, one day at the Sanctuary of Montevergine a donkey used by Saint William for many types of work was stalked and killed by a wolf. Afterwards the saint confronted the wolf, reprimanded then tamed the animal in order to take the place of the donkey for his new beast of burden and means of transportation.

Legends and miracles aside, and even if the wolf was revered as the guardian symbol of the Irpinias, it was serious business to Angiolo and his fellow shepherds when there was actual evidence of a wolf attack on their livestock.

"Where exactly did it happen, Mario? How do you know for sure it was wolves that did it?"

"They left clear footprints in the soil softened by the light rain we had yesterday morning. You can tell there was a pack of them, not just a lone wolf. And you could also tell by what little remained of the carcasses which were scattered around with some of the bones consumed as well. No doubt about it, wolves, and very hungry ones at that."

"So, you said it happened last night. Were you still in the forest?"

"I was less than two miles away from here, at the hut in the small meadow higher up, you know at the *Piana dei Vaccari*."

"Well, with wolves lurking around the area we are going to have to take every precaution from now on. And when we bring the sheep lower down closer to town we should forewarn our relatives to alert the other townspeople. A hunting party may have to be formed to go after this pack. My brother Gerardo Conte will know what to do."

Two weeks later, just before the autumnal equinox, Angiolo brought his sheep to the outskirts of town. There had been no further incidence of wolves as far as he knew. But he had lost many hours of sleep watching over the herd, awake and on edge whenever there was the slightest noise out of the ordinary. Leaving Tschüss with two local youths he knew, he went to his older brother's residence to ask his advice. Onorio had not heard of any other recent wolf encounters either but spread the word to several neighbors to ask around Bagnoli if anyone else did. Nobody had anything to report of relevance. But just to be extra cautious, he would send word to Conte relatives on the other side of the Apennine range to see what news they had. He would let Angiolo know what their response was hopefully within a week at most. Since the weather had just started to turn to autumn-like temperatures, all of the herdsmen on either side of the mountains would soon be heading to lower altitudes. Summer may yet show its face again but only for a short spell if it did.

***

Capitanata, Kingdom of Naples, Italy, September 1799

When Luigi, the messenger from Bagnoli, delivered his news to Bovino that there had been wolf sightings and some troubles on the western side of the mountains, their eastern counterparts went immediately into action. At first it was like an agitated nest of hornets had attacked the village. It seemed like every one of the four thousand two hundred inhabitants of the small town had nothing else buzzing through their heads than the image of bloodthirsty predators on their doorstep. Like many other villages in the region of Puglia, also referred to as Apulia, in the province of Capitanata or Foggia, it had experienced ebbs and flow in population over the centuries of its existence. Set in the wooded foothills on the verge of the Daunian mountains—a segment of the eastern side of the Apennines sloping down to the Adriatic Sea—the millennia had seen Bovino's numbers suffer in tandem with the decline of the Roman Empire. Losses through conflicts with the Lombards, Byzantines and Sacracens had only been surpassed by near obliteration from the plague. But each time the village set on a hill and over eighteen hundred feet above sea level rebounded, managing again and again to rebuild and increase the size of its citizenry. Refusing to be abandoned, Bovino had for some years now been in a steady growth trend. But the fear of the past was always part of the present, and any danger, such as wolves, was quick to be met with a collective reaction.

This time, though, the anxiety produced from the report was short-lived. As far as anyone knew the presence of wolves in the vicinity had not recently been noted. They were relieved to leave the fearsome animals to their countrymen living on the other side of the mountains. And this was as it should be. Wasn't the Principato Ultra as proud to use the Irpinian symbol of a wolf as protector of its land and people as were their own citizens of their town's location in the pure air of the highlands?

However, not all of them were as unconcerned as the most cavalier of townsfolk seemed to be with their neighbors across the mountain divide. Over the years there had been plenty of interaction between the two small populations which had resulted in producing a core of bloodline relationships.

One such Bovino group with strong Bagnoli roots was the Paulone family. Gaetano Paulone had actually been born and raised in Bagnoli. But while on a business trip to Bovino as a young man he had met a young and attractive distant relative named Teresa Conte connected to a branch of the Conte family he knew well who had also been born in Bagnoli. They had plenty to gossip about since members of these two families had ties going back generations—to the dawn of oral history if accounts were to be believed—which continued to this day.

Before long Gaetano and Teresa had married and had decided to make their home together in Bovino instead of their place of birth. In some ways it was a sacrifice for Gaetano to be away from the life with which he was so familiar, but that same familiarity also had its drawbacks for someone who had spent all his life under the intense scrutiny of a small village. Helping to mitigate any lingering homesickness, though, there was a group of relations already established in the commune. Those bearing the Paulone surname would make Gaetano's adjustment to his new surroundings that much easier. And as the crow flies the distance between the two towns was under thirty-five miles so visiting his former home would not be hindered by distance.

Yet, he knew in his heart returning may not come that often since trips on a donkey, by foot, or a combination of the two, between the two places was anything but a straightforward journey given the rugged nature of the land. A thirty-five mile journey from Bovino could easily turn into fifty miles or more having to traverse through the villages of Agata delle Noci, Accadia, Anzano di Puglia, Vallata, Guardia Lombardi, Sant' Angiolo di Lombardi and Macchia Prima in order to avoid rivers, gorges or other obstacles before finally reaching Bagnoli. Many months had passed since Gaetano Paulone had paid a visit to his home town; in fact he hadn't returned since his marriage to Teresa Conte. The weather was still holding fine and he had just finished his a job repairing the stonework of a farm building west of town. His profession as *muratore* had been keeping him steadily busy and was the excuse he had used for not acting sooner.

"*Amore mio*, I think it would be a good time for me to go to Bagnoli since my friend Luigi will be returning there as well with the good news there seems to be an absence of wolves in our neck of the woods. He and I can travel together, which makes the journey safer and go by a lot faster. I promise to bring back a surprise or two along with any interesting reports from your people and mine."

"What if I need help, you know if there's something I can't do by myself? I know it's probably needless to worry too much but still I do when you are not here."

"If anything unusual comes up while I'm gone, just get a hold of one of your cousins—Salvadore or Donata, or even cousin Constanza, the wife of our friend Orazio. They'll know what to do.

We will leave before dawn tomorrow morning. Luigi needs to be back in Bovino next Sunday for his cousins wedding."

Out of bed and on their way at dawn with a sky giving just a hint of changing light, the beauty of the place in which he lived left him a little breathless. Or maybe it had something to do with not getting enough sleep the night before! But with each footfall forward it was as if everything was proceeding as expected. What Gaetano had intentionally omitted to mention to his wife was that the two men planned to take a shortcut to the station at Ponte di Bovino, not far away but in the narrow passage of the Val di Bovino on the Cervaro river. He hadn't told her because she would have become even more nervous about his leaving. The pass of Bovnio was well-known for being one of the more risky areas to sojourn through. But for two strong young men travelling together, they thought there would not be much to be concerned about.

On their merry way trudging happily along when everything changed in an instant. A band of Capitinata brigands had come out of nowhere and started to surround them. The situation was even worse than they could have imagined. The much vilified scoundrels that had so often been on the tips of local tongues and could be ruthless had now become a reality. Seven or eight of them, outdoor-hardened men who looked as if they meant business, had encircled them. There could be no thought of trying escape by running like the wind into the nearby woods outnumbered as they were. Then the tall thin one with at least a week's worth of dark stubble on his face moved forward towards them. In a calm but commanding voice they were told to empty their pockets and place the contents down on the ground in front of them along with any weapons they carried. Then take five steps backwards when that was done.

Although his tone had not been harsh his eyes were. The message was clear: no dickering, no pleading, no excuses would be tolerated. And what seemed the most strange, the whole group of robbers looked almost identical in appearance, as if they were twin brothers times four. Either they had grown used to be covered in dirt or had spent several lifetimes in the sun or had died their hair and mustaches black to match bronzed bodies, whatever it was, they were a swarthy-looking bunch of hoodlums who were menacing enough to make their point.

"Alberto," the one that had come forward turned back around again and spoke to his comrade, "pick-up our friends donations." Wordlessly, he started to do as he was told. Then the leader motioned for Alberto to search them to make sure Gaetano or Luigi had held nothing back. Convinced their pockets had been emptied, he had Alberto collect the items into a sack. Then with merely an *"Addio e grazie amici miei!"* the band of robbers vanished back into the woods as quickly as they had appeared. Traumatized, the two victims plunked down on a log to pull themselves together. So the much heralded stories and their warnings were true! Accounts of marauding bandits threatening the countryside had been passed down for generations.

But these stories usually told of them robbing mail coaches or wedding corteges or other targets where the gains would be substantial. This group of miscreants would be sorely disappointed with the meager takings from today's encounter. For only a short time they had been on a secluded stretch of a road in a narrow valley, almost a ravine actually, that could be easily mistaken for well-heeled passersby perhaps even going all the way to Naples. Some gang members, it was said, supposedly were from Bovino itself. And there were those who believed there was an altruistic motive in making the rich pay a price for what was owed to the poor but just as many had their doubts about that.

After a while Gaetano and Luigi had settled enough to be able to shrug their shoulders and exchange weak grins of those who had narrowly escaped a much greater misfortune.

Although they had lost what was of little value to many, the few *piastras* and *grana* that had once jingled in their pouches mattered to them. Should they turn back now that they had nothing but the clothes on their backs? Even if they carried on to Bagnoli, how could Gaetano keep his promise to bring back something to his waiting bride? But they had come this far already, and the embarrassment of falling into the hands of thieves could be postponed if they attained their objective, so it was onwards. Fortunately at each small village they passed through, after their story was told and retold a half dozen times, enough support was offered to keep them moving forward to their destination. It wasn't the first time that even the most removed of villages had heard of similar tales. And given the long history of bandits roaming the Capitanata, it most likely wouldn't be the last!

ANTONIO PAULONE

Bovino, Puglia, Southern Italy, 1832-1842

Antonio Paulone had already led a life divided by place from the time he was ten; he wasn't sure if he was Bovinesi or Bagnolesi or somewhere down the middle. Gaetano Paulone, his father, had met Teresa Conte in Bovino but they married in Bagnoli where they both had been born. But after their marriage, a time came when Antonio's parents made the decision to move to a town located on the opposite side of the mountains from their birth place, in deference to his wife's wishes to be close to her parents. It was somewhat uncommon in a region where such moves usually occurred only when husband and wife differed in place of origin. So Bovino in Puglia, a picturesque town situated on a hilltop with family ties to Bagnoli Irpino, became his new home too.

Beyond Teresa's parents, their motivation for making such a change had been simple: olives! A number of relatives in Bovino had for generations been involved with olive growing, olive pressing and oil extraction, planting trees of different varieties and development of new harvesting techniques and seasonal experimentation. For people like these it was said that olive oil—not blood—flowed through their veins. It was also said it would be almost impossible to find a Bovinesi who didn't have something to do with this magical fruit. Although they were still young and inexperienced, Gaetano and Teresa were ever optimistic in taking on the challenge of learning the business while calling on experience from old timers. What could be better? The air was pristine and the sunshine as undiluted as the sweat on their brows as Gaetano and Teresa started their new venture of orchard farming. The freedom to become one with the elements on a daily basis suited them to a tee.

Circumstances changed course again, however, when Teresa's uncle, who owned one of the two grocery businesses in Bagnoli—the town on the Monti Picentini side and west of the Apennines—fell ill one day. It had come out of the blue for there had been no previous sign this man in his early forties had been suffering from any particular ailment. A customer, after ringing the bell for service twice, decided to peek around the counter when he got no response and that's when she saw him sprawled out on the floor and appearing to be semi-conscious. She had helped him slowly to his feet and then to a chair in the rear of the store. Kinfolk were notified to fetch him home later that day. He began to recover a little during the following days but not sufficiently to permit running the store again. Mental faculties remaining sharp, his new role was giving advice to those working in his stead in the mornings. But most of his day was spent resting and lying down. Eventually a family decision was made to contact his niece and her husband in Bovino to see if they might be interested in taking over the business.

At this stage of their life it was not something Gaetano and Teresa had ever thought about doing or were prepared to do. But it was an offer Teresa's husband would have difficulty turning down for more than one reason. They were quite content with their life of olives in Bovino, definitely not unhappy with the town itself and loved what they had managed to cobble together so far. But the idea of a stable income to a couple about to add a new family member in the coming months was too enticing in the end to resist. Besides didn't they have the responsibility to uphold traditions of family helping family in need?

So it came to pass that their first child, Antonio Paulone, was born in Bagnoli, not in Bovino as had been expected. But all had not been lost from their time in Bovino. An interest in the olive business was retained so there were reasons for going back and forth between the two towns over the intervening years. As their son grew older he spent more and more time among the olive groves. Although Antonio felt like he belonged to both places and knew them well, much more than his brother and sisters did, his heart really laid in the shade of the olive trees.

Antonio's childhood had been politically marked by mostly thwarted revolutions and insurrections in a territory seemingly headed, by fits and starts, in the direction of a single country perhaps one day to be called Italy. The upheavals mostly towards unity were not as frequent in Campania, which continued to be dominated by the Kingdom of the Two Sicilies. In spite of old aristocracies dissolving into a more scattered and propertied society, the Kingdom remained intact. It was ironic in a way that the pro-national, widespread and secretive society, the Carbonari, had its origins in southern Italy where economic conditions stagnated. But it was often said the really great revolts always started in the South. Nevertheless, it was still worrisome to a boy growing up at a time when independent state after state—especially in the northern part of the peninsula—had uprisings quelled with the support of the Austrian army in 1831. But throughout the decade the discontent continued with insurgencies in 1833-1834 spearheaded by *Giovine Italia,* the Young Italy organization assembled by Giuseppe Mazzini.

The list was comprehensive: The Kingdoms of Sardinia and of the Two Sicilies; the Lombardy-Venetia Kingdom, a crown land under the Austrian Empire; the Duchies of Modena and Reggio, Parma and Tuscany; and those of their tiny neighbors, the Duchies of Lucca and of Massa and Carrara, when combined with the Papal States, presented a checkerboard of entities competing with each other for importance. They were also vying with other countries that were in the process of binding small principalities, duchies and other realms into larger nations that would hold greater political and economic clout as a group in the end. The thirties were a chaotic decade, with boundaries in flux and consolidation occurring at a rapid pace but not without leaving future stability in doubt as well.

***

Perhaps it was these confusing times that had played upon Antonio Paulone's thinking for a while now. In 1839, not long after he had passed his seventeenth birthday, the feeling that he was getting nowhere in his life came to a head. It was like he was trapped in a place where he had no control over his own destiny. He needed to do something about it, to talk to someone.

"Can I say something to you father before you go to work this morning?" he asked at the breakfast table.

"Is it important enough to delay my leaving for the store, son? You know the customers depend upon me being there on time to open. They'll be waiting there as usual for the door so they can get on with the rest of their morning afterwards. You know this as well as…" Antonio, already half-anticipating an excuse from a father who never seemed to leave behind his grumpiness nowadays, was in no mood to listen to a longwinded reply. "Look father, I just want to talk for a moment, not to hear another reason why you don't have the time to listen to me again," he barged in.

The corners of Gaetano's mouth seemed to drop to his ankles: "Do you know who you are talking to? This household allows no disrespect, Antonio. And it will not be tolerated now," his father continued. "You say you want to talk to me—well first you certainly will "listen" to me when I'm good and ready and that will be after I get home from the store." He rose from the table flushed with anger. But before he went out the door he turned back towards his son: "And don't forget to be at the store at three o'clock to restock and straighten the shelves then scrub the floors clean. No talking, just working!" Failure to reach his father was just one more strike against the kind of life he had been living. It wasn't the first time but he was determined now to make it the last time. It didn't take long before he began a course of action: first he stuffed an old carpet bag with as many clothes that would fit and then he grabbed a well-worn knapsack off the hook near the door and gathered some food from the larder to put in it. He scrawled a short message and left it in plain sight on a table. He went to his mother working in the garden behind their home. He told her he was going out for a while, gave her a peck on the cheek and squeezed her shoulder then returned inside for a moment to take one last look around before leaving for good.

He hadn't meant for it to be so abrupt yet he had been thinking about moving out for quite a while and had a plan already in mind. Now as he started on his way to Bovino he felt relieved, sure that once there his cousins would take him in—at least until he got his feet under him. He would send word to his parents once he was there about his ideas for expanding the olive business. Why would they refuse since it would save them from having to travel there so often, and it would relieve them, his father especially, of a son whose comportment had obviously become unacceptable? If they didn't agree with him, well then so be it; he would have to find something else to do, maybe even further away in the city of Foggia. Or perhaps he might even become a seaman off one of the small towns on the coast. There were plenty of small fishing boats that needed extra hands. Yes, a job as a mariner would suit him, he thought, and it would lead to a whole new kind of life! But one thing he knew for sure he wasn't going back to Bagnoli, to a life of broom-pushing, unpacking boxes and stocking shelves to the tune of his father's commands.

Inspired, Antonio knew the route by heart and moved swiftly on nimble legs, reaching Bovino in less than two days time. The weather remained fine and he had relished the freedom of spending overnight under the stars with no one to tell him what to do. Free as a bird until nerves began to trouble him as he entered the town and immediately walked towards the home of his cousins Concetta and Pietro. He couldn't help himself from feeling anxious because of the circumstances, although his family and theirs knew each other well and, even more importantly, had managed to stay on good terms without bickering about small things. Arguing was a trap to which many other families were prone to fall into, even the ones that were close-knit. Concetta was bent over in the front garden, pruning, planting or harvesting, he wasn't sure which, when he arrived at their home.

"It's me, Concetta, your cousin Antonio who's come to see you." Startled a bit by the interruption to her concentration it took her a moment to recognize who of her many cousins it was. But when she did he was grasped in her arms and smothered with kisses. "But you are all alone. Where are your father and mother, Antonio?"

"It is just me this time, Concetta. It was time to get out on my own. I think my parents needed some time away from me as well. Anyway, I've left home, at least for now. But I have some ideas and I want to discuss them with you if I can."

"Let's go inside. Tommaso will be home soon and we can all sit down together for a meal while you tell us about these ideas of yours." Sure enough, her husband came in the door soon afterwards and he too was both surprised and delighted to see Antonio again. After they chatted about this and that, Concetta told her husband that Antonio had something more specific he wanted to a talk about.

"What is it that you have on your mind, Antonio? We're all ears."

"Well, two things mainly. The first, as I said to Concetta, it was time to get out on my own and that's why you see me here before you now. Obviously, I need somewhere to live as I get started and I'm hoping you may be able to help me with some suggestions. I want to stay in Bovino. I just need a small corner big enough to put a pillow under my head to start.

Maybe you know somebody who might have a spare room? It may take a few weeks of exchanging work for rent at first, but payment will be made in real money as soon as I have it in my hands." Tommaso and Concetta looked across the table at each other then back at him.

"I see questions in your eyes. Let me explain a little about how this all came about. To me, I think my father really has been like a different person from some years ago. When I was small, my memories of life in Bovino among the olive groves were good ones. And every time we visited Bovino the atmosphere seemed to lighten up—there were more smiles and laughter, the mood was upbeat and positive compared to what it felt like Bagnoli. They don't talk about it much, but I think it was the change that did it, when they went from here, from all things olive, to keeping a shop. I think my father just wasn't cut out to work indoors in a store all his life, and the frustration and resentment built-up over time made him unhappy and changed his personality. You know that's one of the two things I believe I have in common with my father: I'm not the shopkeeper type either!"

"And the second, Antonio? You said there were two things."

"I want to eventually manage our part of the olive operations here, as miniscule as they are at the moment, like my father manages the store. Even though I know quite a lot about our Bovino business from visiting over the years, I know I need to learn much more. I believe I could be ready in a year or two to handle it on my own after that. Old Tobia would surely be ready to turn it over by then, maybe even sooner, if I'm ready. That's about it—big changes, I know. But what do you think?"

They took a few minutes to discuss among themselves while they let him eat then offered him a bed in corner space in their home as a temporary solution. With a little moving around of furniture the small nook could be reconverted into a cozy room, just like it was before they enlarged their house. As for the olive business, they would not interfere in that; it would ultimately have to be between Antonio and his parents to work out. But that didn't hold them back from letting him know what they thought about his ambition. Olive trees had been part of the landscape of the Puglia region and in and around Bovino itself for centuries, brought to the Italian peninsula by the ancient Greeks. But it wasn't until the 18th century that olive oil farming became an established and leading economic trade under the rule of Charles of Bourbon.

"As you well know, Antonio, olive groves and olive oil are the heart and soul of Bovino. But we must tell you it is not an easy position to be the one who is responsible. I remember that even your father Gaetano talking about the amount of labor it took to do the job right. The work is hard but demand is increasing so there are no worries of having nothing to do. And the satisfaction of seeing what comes from your own calloused hands makes it all worthwhile to us anyway. But you should know most of the ancient *trappeti* will need to be replaced as soon as possible in order to produce enough oil to be competitive. Our aging grinding and pressing mills—old friends to be sure—have stood the test of time for so long but now more modern ones are needed to keep up."

"How will the other farmers handle what would surely be a major cost to them, Tommaso?"

"Since all the mills are co-owned by the owners and the community it's not as big a problem as it might seem. Each one is shared by many producers so the investment required for a new *frantoio* would also be divided among the same group of users. Cooperatives have worked well in the past and they must work well in the future if all are to benefit."

"I sort of remember now hearing about how the oil mill is supported by a group of member growers. So what you say makes sense; nobody owns enough acres of trees, I guess, to warrant the use of a mill and olive press full time all by themself!"

He should have expected it. After sending word to his parents about assuming the olive affairs in Bovino he had held hope there might be a chance of a favorable reply though. The answer was short and to the point: "Antonio, leaving the household as you did shows that you are not ready to take responsibility. Let us know where to send your other belongings. Your Father." Tommaso and Concetta just shook their heads when he read out loud the unyielding contents of the letter. What was he to do now?

"Domenico Petrini, the farmer with the large orchard near the highest point on the hill, on the right side of the road, mentioned the other day he needed more help," Tommaso came to the rescue.

"You mean on the way to the *Palazzo Ducale*?

"That's it, exactly. You have a good memory, Antonio. I think the best thing to do would be to see him first. If that doesn't work out, there will be other possibilities for such a strong and willing young man such as you. I wouldn't worry, isn't that right Concetta?" Nodding in agreement, she drew close to Antonio and wrapped him in a warm embrace. "We know you are a good boy—things will work out and soon, you'll see."

Their idea for obtaining work turned out to be a good one after Antonio had approached a stocky man standing on a ladder with his head nearly buried in overhead branches. Domenico Petrini of course knew the Paulone family from the time before they had moved back to Bagnoli. And he also even foggily remembered Antonio and his siblings running around, watching them as they grew bigger, from their frequent return visits over the years. The four children of his own family—two daughters and two sons—were roughly of the same generation as Antonio and his brothers and sisters. They ranged in age from fifteen to the eldest, a married daughter of twenty-two.

Allowing himself a only a quick assessment as they exchanged old times, Domenico decided he liked the look and sound of this young man, and without taking any more time to think it over longer, gave him a job working on his farm. This was unlike him for he usually took his time and stayed away from spur-of-the-moment decisions. But a gut feeling told him there was something special about him; he liked his spirit of independence in striking out on his own and his willingness for getting his hands dirty. And as Antonio said he would be also looking for a place to live, Domenico went even further in saying there would be room for him in the loft over the tool and storage shed. That is if he didn't mind the simple rustic living quarters after being accustomed to town living in Bagnoli!

No need to take time to think it over; he accepted both offers presented to him on the spot. He would move to the Petrini's in the next few days if that suited everybody concerned. Antonio Paulone couldn't believe his lucky stars in following Tommaso and Concetta's suggestion to see

Domenico and in the kindness demonstrated by his new employer.
　　He was on his way to a new beginning!

RISORGIMENTO

Bagnoli Irpino, Campania, Italy, March 1871

When the news broke on the 17th of March 1861 that the proclamation of the new Kingdom of Italy had been given Aniello Conte was neither surprised nor particularly interested. Sporadic insurrections and revolutions in the independent Italian states had been heading in that direction for as long as he could remember during the preceding decades. These conflicts had set the stage for the amalgamation of a semi-unified group of entities into a thin and elongated stretch of land. A hodgepodge consisting of more than ten separate states, large and tiny, existing in early 19th century was now one. Primarily fulfilling duel objectives of ridding the presence of foreign powers and aiming towards economic and political consolidation, these Italian states had mostly seen their earlier revolutionary efforts doomed to failure.

But that was to change in forthcoming years. Still, the Southern provinces had withheld participation in the newly formed Kingdom of Italy until the very last moment, prudently watching the movement towards nationhood unfold in states in the North. Preferring to maintain their separate Kingdom of the Two Sicilies, it was only through the use of military force led by the republican Giuseppe Garibaldi and Victor Emmanuel, the man who would shortly become king of a unified Italy, did the greater part of the Mezzogiorno reluctantly give up independence in 1861.

Was it any wonder Aniello Conte had felt the way he did? He was no different than the majority of other southern Italians. And when he thought further about it, his ancestors Onorio, Angiolo, Nicola and Vito—shepherds, shopkeepers and manual workers—would probably have been in agreement with him. What benefit would southern Italy receive by joining the North to form a single country? Campania may now have become an official part of a new kingdom, but in reality southern Italy was still like a different country. It was looked upon as backwards, provincially-minded, engulfed in poverty, crime ridden and illiterate, from its wealthier and more enlightened neighbors from Rome northwards. Some of it was true of course, especially the perception of poverty, which was for many part and parcel of their daily existence.

Aniello Conte and his best friend, Lorenzo Lenzi, took it for granted the disparity between the two halves of Italy could not and would not change soon, but scoffed at the stereotype of a southern primitive subculture dwelling in the past. They may not be living as comfortably as the more prosperous northerners from a thousand years of non-unification, but southern agriculture fed northern stomachs and southern minds were just as keen as those of their more well-heeled counterparts. That's not to say they did not have their own prejudices in believing the same economic and social dichotomy to be valid when applied to perceived differences between themselves and their own southern compatriots in

Sicily. Lumping the two distinct geographical areas together as the previous kingdom had done had never been entirely acceptable. But a true *risorgimento*? Hardly! Unification in many respects would be just a hollow slogan for as long as they could foresee.

Even though there were no sentimental reasons they could think of to recall the event now ten years later, even if it was on the exact day of the year that the declaration occurred, it could still be a good excuse for Aniello and Lorenzo to share a bottle of their favorite red wine made from local Aglianico grapes at the Bar d'Oro, the bar on the main square. Not that they needed one! At least a glass or two of this excellent wine would be one thing that hadn't changed since bygone times, and that was a real blessing to all of them.

"*Salute*! I guess we'll be hearing all the gossip today about how our single country has made everything so much better," Aneillo Conte said sarcastically with a fake expression and an attempt at a pitiful tone in his voice. That the two of them had always shared a negative opinion of their brethren to the north, like many other of southerners, was no secret. Besides, how could they have called it unified when the most important city, Rome, and the Papal States, not to mention Venice, had remained outside of the newly crowned country when the document had been signed? Of course these places had been brought into the fold over the intervening years but not without some resistance. And it was a well-known fact Victor Emmanuel, the so-called king of Italy, never really wanted the South to be part of the kingdom that is until he was forced to include it by the potent military arm of General Giuseppi Garibaldi.

"It's true. What a shame it was at the time to have waited

so long for good news to happen. I don't know what we would have done with ourselves if it hadn't since we are all one big happy family now," Lorenzo's comments reaching the same level of derisiveness as his companion's.

"You and I and the rest of us know it hasn't and won't make an iota of difference. We'll still be called Italy's poor country cousins and ignored just like before only now as second class citizens." Characterized as uncivilized and uncouth by the Piedmontese and their other northerly cohorts southern Italians did continue to be subjected to the same sense of superiority, snobbishness and entitlement from northerners as before. The single exception as always was Naples. Northern attention was focused on the city as an easy target for exploitation of its considerable riches to line its own pockets. The former capital of the Kingdom of the Two Sicilies was one of the few places in the region where poverty did not reign supreme.

But before they continued their parody of the "big change", Aniello's older brother, who had seen the pair of them sitting together, had crossed the street to say hello.

"How are you two loafers doing? You know, there's still plenty of good light to do the things that need doing," Alfonso Conte kidded.

"Sit down Alfonso and join us in a libation; a glass for my brother, please. Our work for today is done and we are pretending to celebrate our country's first decade of existence. And the sun will rise and fields will still be there tomorrow!"Alfonso pulled up a chair but before seating himself completely he stopped midway and stared over the heads of the two young men sitting across the table from him, his attention caught by something happening a few steps away. Both Aniello and Lorenzo turned around to see what it was, or in this case who it was, that had become the object of so great an interest. They should have guessed; it was naturally one of the local beauties: Maria Teresa Conte, one of many cousins of the brothers bearing their own surname.

"I can't stay too long, our parents are expecting me back before it gets too late to check on a crack in the back wall."

"Now that you're here, brother, give Lorenzo and I an idea of what you think of our new Italy now that a few years have gone by." It was hard to keep Alfonso engaged because his eyes kept roving over and over again between words towards the slim figure of so much feminine charm in his eyes while she continued talking to a female companion as they proceeded further down the street. And when they disappeared altogether arm-in-arm around the corner, he stood up to leave too.

"Sit down, Alfonso. You just got here and we want to hear what you have to say about our nation on this important day." Having been convinced that they really did want his opinion, he sat back down. About a half hour later he did finally depart. It turned out to be bad timing since five minutes later the young lady of interest walked by their table apparently having reversed her course for some reason. Dark brown hair swaying below her shoulders with just the right amount of waviness, small straight nose, lips a shade on the thinner side and sturdy legs supporting a posture emphasizing confidence in each stride she took; they could easily see why Alfonso Conte had been so distracted. It was too bad she was a cousin, and too bad that she may possibly already have a serious suitor. That annoying Vito Nicastro had confided in a friend of Lorenzo's that he had an interest in the lovely Maria

Teresa. The friend had in turn mentioned it to Lorenzo and now Aniello knew too. But was she interested in Vito as well? And how serious was Vito really? The latter was viewed as someone whose eyes roved from shapely form to shapely form without constraint. It could be part of the follies of youth, but the reputation of a man of no particular constancy might be hard to shake in the future. Who knew, perhaps it would become Vito's life story. In any event, it was not the time or place to spoil Alfonso's dreams, especially if doing so might be unnecessary.

Before Alfonso had left the table he had added few comments of his own supporting the contempt shown by the others for the likelihood of any tangible improvement in the economic and social realities dividing the two halves of the peninsula. If anything, Alfonso was even more adamant in his condemnation of the political leadership of northerners. To him, they had no understanding of the traditional social system that had kept the small southern farmers depressed and impoverished in medieval feudal style long after the end of the Middle Ages and into their own 19th century. And the saddest part of it all was there seemed to be nothing in the new government's agenda that sought to remedy the situation upon which they could pin their hopes and dreams. Pitting peasant against elite so firmly entrenched in the country would continue despite a symbolic joining of hands with the two sides of Rome. The big landowners would continue just as they were: big landowners. Some form of land redistribution was not even mentioned. And there were no specific plans to transfer any of the advanced agricultural techniques and inroads into industrialization from the North to the South either. In Alfonso Conte's opinion, it would remain status quo as it always had.

What were the advantages of unification then? Two regions would still stay like two different countries unless sometime in future the old social order crumpled. But there was certainly no present belief equalization would be happening any day soon as far as the three of them could tell. Indeed, as far as their own Italian hemisphere was concerned, even after feudalism had been abolished by Bourbon rulers during the first decade of their own 19th century, things had not really shown much improvement for the small mountain towns. Land ownership had just shifted from the old kingdom into the hands of aristocratic estate owners. The rural villagers had been left to fend for themselves with no opportunities of moving closer to becoming a more economically stable middle class—unless they were to migrate to the North to join the bourgeois communities there.

When he thought about it over the long term, the new kingdom was just another iteration of their southerly land conquered and ruled by a host of outsiders. It would take fingers on both hands to name them off. As far back as the 8th century BC the first Greek immigrants arrived on Italian soil, continuing their colonization for centuries to come. At least the Greeks became thoroughly Latinized before the onslaught of Byzantines during the Middle Ages followed by Romans, Germanic tribes and then Normans in the 1100s. It didn't stop then; incursions from the Arabic empire, and then more recently from other European countries, including the French warring with Spanish Bourbons in the 1700s for southern Italian hegemony, and ultimately the Austrian empire. An assortment of languages, changing laws, varying tax burdens and exploitation of resources, including human capital, all of this had left an imprint on southern culture. But somehow the *italiani del sud* had retained most of its distinct character—along with impoverished living conditions and a life expectancy of below thirty years, unfortunately!

Subservience during the long feudalistic centuries had been perhaps the hardest to endure. But survive they did. The abandoned *Castello Cavaniglia*—a medieval Norman-built castle perched on a hill overlooking the entry to Bagnoli—was a rock-solid testament of a feudal overlordship that had, thankfully, disappeared. Perhaps the longevity of their town had much to do with its geographical isolation in the foothills of a mountain range too. Isolation was truly a double-edged sword, providing the natural protection of distance in one direction, but resulting in economic and political underdevelopment in the other. But whatever way you sliced it, the same families that had first settled this piece of Italian countryside had stayed. The same group of surnames when combined with a couple of dozen traditional first names was tangible evidence ancient family bloodlines continued to exist. And the role of strong religious faith, supporting them spiritually through ashes raining down from volcanic eruptions, earthquakes both major and minor, cholera epidemics and the other deadly diseases afflicting their small populace with regularity, should not be underestimated. There was just something about the town they called home that had managed to keep the majority of them there.

***

His brain still rattling from the conversation with his brother and Lorenzo at the café, he was at the same time bothered by thoughts of Maria Teresa Conte. Far from being naïve about the existence of a possible competitor for her attentions, Alfonso Conte had also been made aware from another source about Vito's interest in her. He had also known about Vito's past forays with young village girls. Not much was kept secret in Bagnoli, as was the case when one of Vito's previous meetings had led to his scampering away from an outraged father who had spotted the two of them alone in a too secluded alleyway. Fortunately for them they had been separated by a couple of feet at the time or things could have gone from ranting to much worse. How could Vito expect to get away with pursuing girls in that kind of manner? Neither he nor his romantic quest had reached the age of independence from parental households. Still, even at this early stage Alfonso was worried over Vito's rivalry for her affections. He would definitely keep his eyes open and ears peeled about any relationship changes his rival may have made with regard to Maria Teresa

Smells of mushrooms simmering in tomato sauce and oregano meant the evening meal would be coming shortly when Alfonso arrived home. But before these enticing odors reached that point, his mother reminded him his father would be home soon and the chickens needed feeding before he arrived. The sight and sound of the flock clucking as a group in waiting to share a meal reminded Alfonso of his recent conversation at the café and how Italy should have done the same. Instead, the country had failed to bring north and south together with the promise of a better life for all. If only a real plan had been put into action it would have drawn southerners into a true single entity, just like the hungry birds gathered at his feet. Sure, there were those hens who were a bit bolder or quicker—or even more intimidating than the others—but in the end they all got along and had enough to eat to squawk another day.

Ten years had come and gone and still nothing to show for it. If anything, the disparity had only worsened. Where was the government reform needed? Why had the tax burden increased instead of lessened? How many civil wars in around Naples and in Sicily opposing a fake unity would it take before the North awakened to address the "southern situation"? Removal of agricultural protection measures and free trade policies that had provided a modicum of economic balance for a while had just added to the misery in the long run. Rome seemed to have forsaken them, helping to spur brigandage from struggling farmers who were starving. And then there was corruption from those seeking an angle to get ahead in the cities too. It was only six years ago, back in 1865, that the government sent troops to reestablish the principals of law and vanquish much of the criminality. More than one hundred thousand soldiers had been mobilized, which had led to the execution of a huge number of so-called peasants, in order to accomplish these objectives

But enough of those unpleasant thoughts for now he decided in turning his head to the side to spit in one last gesture. It was better to dream about Maria Teresa and how he could prevent the objectives of Vito Nicastro from interfering with his own potential relationship with her. If she came to understand his past penchant for switching attentions from one female to the next, she would surely reject any of his overtures towards herself. But how could he increase his own chances without it seeming like petty jealousy if he should be the one to forewarn her? Maybe it was best to let things follow their own course; just trust her to make the right choices. Yes, that's what he would do—just drop it for a while.

"What are you doing, Alfonso? Dreaming your life away again, I suppose. Those chicken better have been fed. Your father has been here for ten minutes and we're all waiting for your royal presence at the table."

"But I'm almost here now, mother." No further thoughts were given that evening on the sore topic of national unity—or chickens!

BAD AIR

Bovino and Foggia, Puglia, Italy, August-October 1873

    Beads of sweat dotted every inch of Antonio Paulone's forehead. Their number so great they had melded into rivulets streaming down like waterfalls from his scalp alongside his nose, into the corners of his eyes and ultimately onto his pillow now heavily dampened and in need of changing. As soon as he wiped away one ocean of perspiration it materialized again as if by magic. He felt as if he was drowning in a torrent of his own sweaty soup! What had possessed him to leave his pregnant wife and the cooler climes of a village on the fringe of the Daunia hills to traverse the *Tavoliere delle Puglie* in mid-summer? He knew better than that; his wife, the former Maria Michela Petrini—one of the daughters of Domenico Petrini at whose farm he first stayed in Bovino—knew better than that; every townsperson knew better than that. To exit the heights of Bovino and submit himself to the furnace of the immense plain highlighted by the city of Foggia at an altitude of only two hundred and fifty feet at time of soaring heat was pure madness. No question it felt all too much like that at the moment and he was mad with himself.

But the allure of a special variety of olive tree had been more than Antonio Paulone could resist; visions of plump and juicy olives that would mean a more prosperous future had blinded him to good sense. He wouldn't be gone long, he hoped, before he would be back in Bovino and breathing the cool air of home again. He should be able to withstand whatever Mother Nature could throw at him for a few days at any rate. Indeed, over half the distance of some twenty-three miles had been walked in a single day. Tomorrow he would see firsthand the offerings of the tree merchant; then he planned to run a few other errands to take advantage of his rare visit to the big city. On the third day he would try to leave in the late afternoon and stay overnight again somewhere on his way back. Once on higher ground again the rest of the journey home would go by quickly since the heat would be less, the air fresher and breathing easier.

For now, Antonio Paulone walked from one shady spot to the next, pausing each time to avoid as best he could any prolonged exposure to the sun. With the strength of the rays flexing their muscles in late afternoon even more mightily than during the morning hours, he had already realized leaving to return home at a similar time would be very unwise. He revised his plans accordingly to accommodate a journey back that would be mostly uphill and much slower going than the descent into city. But if he could tolerate the heat for a little longer today, perhaps he would find a little relief as the sun lowered in the sky.

As soon as he arrived in Foggia, Antonio made his way directly to his cousin's place on the Via Calvario, just down the street from the Church of Crosses. His knock on the door was greeted by a warm welcome in more ways than one from

Vittoria, his cousin's wife.

"Antonio, it is Antonio Paulone, isn't it? Come in, come in. What a nice surprise to see you again. It's been so long and so unexpected I almost didn't recognize who it was at first. I think the last time we were all together it may have been at a wedding in Bovino. But you look exhausted and must be famished too. Sit down, please; sit down here at the table and have something to drink. A plate will be ready for you in just a few minutes."

"Your memory is good, Vittoria; it was at the wedding. But first let me apologize for visiting you without any kind of notice. An opportunity for doing some business in Foggia only came about a few days ago so there was no time to write and get to you beforehand. I didn't want to miss out on coming to Foggia since it could possibly help our olive production at home. So here I am pestering you with my sudden presence."

"Nonsense, Antonio. You know you are always welcome here. Whatever your reasons, my husband and I are always glad to see you. Of course I hope you will stay with us. Nunzio should be home soon." As she spoke delicious food appeared as if out of thin air. How could she have prepared it so quickly? "This is just something to tide you over until we have our evening meal soon. Mangia, Antonio, mangia. Put some meat on those slender bones of yours. You have grown much too thin."

Eating did not cease when Nunzio entered the door as the main meal was served within a half an hour. And Vittoria made sure Antonio would not leave the table if he was still the least bit hungry, adding more to his plate whenever she saw a corner empty. In spite of protests that he was full an encouraging "just a little more" was repeated so often he didn't know if he had ever eaten so much. It was with a great deal of unsteadiness, almost as if he was drunk, that he finally did manage to rise from the table. Later, when it came time for bed, he was still too overstuffed to fall asleep. Yet sleep did eventually come, fitfully, with the window wide open to catch any hint of a passing breeze. Rising early the next morning and still a bit woozy from the evening before, Antonio Paulone excused himself from even the light offerings of a typical Italian breakfast, pleading the need to beat temperatures already mounting and to maximize the time of the only full day he had in Foggia. He was already mentally preparing to diplomatically resist any pressure of overindulging a second time when he returned to stay the second night at his cousin's place. He would need to be at his best when he left for Bovino the next day to make the long trip back home.

Finding the special olive tree exhibition—a variety said to have originated in Greece and first planted in the northern Apulia town of Corato within the city of Bari confines—an hour later went without problem even though it was on the far side of Foggia from where he was staying. There were two larger Coratina trees, perhaps two or three years old, to demonstrate what the saplings that were being sold would be like when they matured. Olive oil bottles containing the golden results after pressing were also on display. Naturally, a tasting of the Coratina olives themselves was a must and an essential part of any good sales strategy. Antonio, like many others who sampled, found the ripe black and green olives to be both juicy as well as high in fatty acid content. He felt immediately if these saplings eventually produced olives such as these, there would be significant increase in his oil output without any sacrifice of quality. Indeed, the quality would likely be improved as well as far as he could tell. Sampling the oil itself, first a few drops au naturel on his tongue then afterwards with bites of freshly baked bread dipped into a dish of the clear liquid confirmed his opinion.

Potential buyers gathered around to listen to the salesman explain that the popularity of the Coratina olive was spreading quickly in the region with many oil producers also blending it with other oil varieties to serve multiple purposes. By the time it was his turn to engage the attention of the dealer Antonio was convinced he needed these trees. The usual negotiation process on a price for fifty saplings to be delivered to Bovino was cut shorter than normal as there were a number of other interested buyers ready to make a purchase. The interest being so keen only a slightly lower price than the opening one was settled upon and that deal was only possible because of the quantity bought. But Antonio Paulone left feeling satisfied with what was accomplished. Spending so much of what little resources they had on more trees than he had intended would be stretching their household budget for a good while. But it had been justified to support a soon to be growing family with Maria Michela due to give birth soon. Their olive oil business needed to be put on a more stable footing; it needed to expand along with the Paulones, and would be worth any temporary sacrifices he felt. He hoped his wife would see it that way too!

He told his cousins of his success soon after he got back to Via Calvario. It had been another sweltering day and he was mentally drained. The ordeal of making the decision to invest in their future, unaccustomed as he was to a large urban environment, had worn him down. But before the evening meal, he was wise enough to make a point of telling his hosts he had eaten late, just before returning because he had been too busy with business to do so earlier. When Antonio Paulone retired for the evening it was even muggier than the night before so he slept with an open window again on top of the bed without any covering. Thankfully, his sleep was sounder for the most part than the previous night having managed to escape overeating heaping portions. It was interrupted, though, a few times by an annoying whining around his head and in his ears. His attempts at swatting away the nuisance apparently finally ended in success when the noise stopped for the rest of the night. When he told Vittoria the next morning of his battle with mosquitoes, she immediately smacked her forehead. She had forgotten to tell him when windows were left open at night mosquito nets were needed to keep them at bay.

"Don't apologize, Vittoria, it was my fault. I was just too lazy to get up and close the window. I hope you and Nunzio were not also bothered by my negligence."

"I should have remembered about needing nets this time of the year although we do have spices growing in the garden that help to keep them away. Especially Basil and Rosemary are supposed to do the trick." She was still rubbing her forehead as she went out the door and returned with a few leaves and sprigs of the two plants to show him.

Other than giving into the urge to scratch himself where the mosquitoes had left their calling card—only five bites in all—Antonio wound up his stay with his cousins, breakfasting this time with the two of them. On his second and final morning in Foggia he had several shopping errands to run before he would be ready to begin his trek home. His main focus would be on the outdoor marketplaces and the homemade pasta shops that were around every corner. He would forgo the temptation to buy mussels and cod specialties; they would never survive the temperatures on the trip. Instead he would concentrate on the vast variety of different spices—lightweight to carry over a distance—and a few special vegetables, such as the *Cipolla Bianca di Margherita*, the small white onions so good in *tiella* in adding flavor to the potatoes. It was their stick to the ribs dish that sustained them during the coldest winters. But these onions were an absolute favorite of his wife in cooking several other dishes as well.

Of course he must look for something for Maria Michela, and for the baby that would be soon on its way. A set of handcrafted wooden bowls in three sizes nested together would be compact enough to carry and was bought at a fair price. By the time he was finished getting a few other items, including food for later while he walked, and had eaten his fill with local specialties from the stands, his knapsack lay heavy on his shoulders. His stomach would not complain for hours. Now he just needed to fill his canteen from one of the fountains and then slowly make his way to the edge of the city while he digested. Soon he would be striking up a faster gait to cover as many miles as he could towards Bovino before nightfall. On this mid-summer day there would be many hours until the last glimmers of light left the sky and the stars began to twinkle in the dark Apulian heavens.

Antonio slackened his pace again after a few hours, not wanting to push himself too hard going uphill when the sun was still the overhead enemy. Reaching the same fenced field he had skirted on his way to Foggia, he decided to climb over the locked gate to cross the field this time as a shortcut. The farmer wouldn't mind as long as no damage was caused. The small herd of black cattle not far away he hoped would also accept the company of a brief intruder. But as soon as he took half dozen steps the herd began to approach him. Maybe with their unfriendly glaring eyes they were drawing nearer because they were only curious about a stranger? After taking a few more steps while watching them carefully, the herd closed ranks, no longer just curious but menacing. They definitely meant business. It was then that Antonio noticed the several small calves among them. That decided it, mothers with their calves, the moment had come to reverse course, to retreat before it was too late.

He had heard stories of cows coming together to butt and stomp an unwanted guest but had never himself seen it before. Their victims had been left with injuries such as broken ribs, smashed pelvises, concussions and even a few had died. Now he was experiencing the possibility of cow trampling firsthand. In a few bounds he climbed back over the gate and tumbled down on the other side of the fence. Then the unhappy herd that had followed on his heels nonchalantly turned their backs to him and sauntered away as if nothing out of the ordinary had happened. They had instantly returned to the normally placid beasts he had come to expect. Glancing back one last time, a lesson had been learned. It may take longer, but the next time he came upon a group of cattle with youngsters—or a bull in a field should he have the misfortune to encounter one—he would forgo any thoughts of saving time.

Now he needed to get going again. Antonio Paulone lengthened each stride and his legs also moved more rapidly. About two-thirds of the way home at dusk he found a good place alongside the road to call it quits for what had been a long day. Legs weary and hunger giving notice, he finished all but a few morsels of his provisions, saving them for morning. He spread a light wrap over himself and found little trouble in slipping off to sleep on a bed of straw left over from the harvest. At first morning's light he had to rub himself to shake off the effects of the more chilly air of an upper elevation. The stiffness in his legs and back disappeared as the remaining miles to home quickly fell away. Antonio was back in Bovino just at noon with the ringing of church bells to greet him.

Seeing the roundness of his pregnant wife again made him even more aware of how close they were to the big day. An absence of only three and a half days had been enough to see things with refreshed eyes. He must be increasingly aware of doing more of the work inside and outside the abode. Maria Michela praised his decision to purchase more olive trees when Antonio told her about the bargain he had struck in Foggia. But from the furrows springing to life across her forehead and the worried narrowing of her eyes, it was clear their cost was of concern without voicing her misgivings. She knew what it would mean to a family already pushed to its limits. How would they manage to feed another mouth and clothe another body pinned on the hope of more olives one day in the future? It would not be easy but then again it never was in the world of farming.

Two months later the olive saplings finally arrived. It had been hoped the delivery would have been sooner but with sales booming they had to wait his turn. It was a pity Antonio did not have the thrill of receiving them himself; he had taken to his bed, suffering from fever, chills, pains and a slew of other complaints for some days already. It was the first time in his life he had felt so sick. Maria Michela hoped he would just get over it as he had with other illnesses but called for the doctor after his condition continued after ten days. During his more lucid moments Antonio had insisted he was on the mend and almost better and that a doctor was unnecessary. Then he would relapse into drenching fever and a muddled mind. It was a good that she did finally have the doctor come since he appeared to grow weaker during the hours before his arrival. She worried she had waited too long in listening to Antonio's pleas that no medical help was necessary instead of relying on her own judgment.

His diagnosis was swift and thought to be certain: **Mal' aria**! During his physicians training in Naples he had seen many cases of the disease of bad air and Antonio's case met all of the signs of malaria, especially the repeated sweating, trembling and the pains centered in his abdomen. With slow repetition the doctor was able to elicit from his patient enough details to determine if the sickness fit recent circumstances.

"I know it's hard to form words when you are so ill much less answer questions, Antonio, but have you visited anywhere else recently?" Teeth chattering and almost inaudible, he tried to give an answer but whatever he said was unintelligible so Maria Michela answered for him.

"He was in Foggia but he seemed fine when he came home. That's what he was trying to say I think. But it's been way too long since this all started a couple of weeks later," she explained wringing her hands as she spoke.

"That's what I suspected. This type of sickness usually begins in cities, particularly at this time of year when the air is heavy and heat at its extreme. I've studied the history of malaria in our area, and even long ago it was most prevalent during the summer months. There was a marshland in ancient times a little north of Foggia called Arpi and it was there the disease was first detected in our area. And it was pervasive enough to be taken seriously and written about as far back as the last millennium. The thick sickly steamy air emanating from these humid marshes apparently was the main factor in causing its spread. There are very few cases I've come across here in Bovino though. The climate is better at our altitude than below, never stagnant like a swamp, and the winds blow more frequently and are stronger."

"Malaria, I've never heard of this word. Was it a sickness called something else before?"

"Not that I know of," the doctor scratched his chin and thought for a moment before he replied, "but it must have had other names because of its long history. But the word malaria itself, which it is what it's known by in most places, is Italian in origin as the name suggests. And current research to learn more about how to effectively treat it has been led by our own country," he proudly added.

"What can we do right now, at this moment, doctor? He's so ill. Isn't there anything you could do to relieve his suffering today?"

"There is one drug that can help, a treatment made from the bark of a tree, believe it or not. It's the cinchona tree to be exact. I have some of this bark but not with me of course. But I think I still have some in powder form also. If I don't, it will take me perhaps an hour or two to grind some of the bark. It's called quinine and it's been used to treat malaria for a long time. But I should go now. I will hurry back as soon as I can. Have Antonio drink as much water as he can. Plenty of liquid is essential in replacing all that he's losing through perspiration. If he becomes dehydrated, it's even more dangerous. And try to keep him cool when he's feverish and warm when he has chills, obviously."

And with those final words the doctor was out the door and on his way. In less than an hour he returned with the wonder drug in his bag and a first dose was administered immediately.

"It could take three or four weeks of treatment before he returns to health. However, there should be improvement from the worst symptoms he's experiencing now after the first few days. Be sure to continue to give him the same dose around the same time daily. But never give him more of the medicine than what I've prescribed or there could be negative effects. I've seen what happens when a patient has been given too much and the effects can be very troublesome."

Maria Michela managed to think of thanking the doctor even though the kind of disease and its remedy by this strange quinine medicine made from bark had left her wondering if it would actually work.

"Try not to fret too much. It just takes time. I will be back tomorrow to check on him."

After he left she held Antonio's hand for a good hour. Thank goodness the expected birth of their child was a month away at least.

LA TARANTELLA

Bagnoli Irpino, Italy, November 1873-February 1874

Even though it hadn't happened as soon as they would have liked, the big day was now in sight. Alfonso Conte had hardly let a day go by without thinking about her after first seeing Maria Teresa Conte, one of many cousins in Bagnoli, on that fateful day so long ago now. There must have been some magic floating in the air that late afternoon when he sat with his younger brother Aniello and friend at a café. Whatever it was, she had stolen his attention away when passing near them. She had disappeared from his view in a minute or two but by then he had made a vow to himself there would come a time when she would never disappear from his life again. She had been chatting and walking arm-in-arm with a female companion without even once casting a glance in the direction of their table. Unaware of his existence as it seemed, it had been a one-sided pledge on his part. But even then he was sure the day would come when she would feel the same way too.

If someone had questioned Aniello about his brother's resolve in making such a pact with himself, he would have been quick to say Alfonso should never be doubted when he was serious. It was said Alfonso had skipped a generation, that he looked like and had the same feisty character as his grandfather Angiolo, the intrepid shepherd who fought off wolves in protecting his sheep. Whatever Alfonso set his mind to do he went about achieving with determination. It would certainly be no different with a girl who had captured his fancy and definitely not with one such as Maria Teresa! It may have been an exaggeration, but that was the perception of Alfonso held in their household.

Maria Teresa Conte, on the other hand, played her cards closer to her chest when it came to most things, and that applied to romance as well. At home with her family she went about her role as the eldest daughter in an unassuming but correct manner. Her attitude was one of helping out whenever she could without needing to be asked and she was a like a second mother to her younger siblings. Her legs moved like the wind and she had the carrying capacity of a burro when it came to transporting the shopping from marketplace to front door. Politeness and cooperation were part of her nature, yet it should not be taken for granted her resolve was any less than Alfonso's when pursuing something—or someone—to the fullest extent if she chose to do so.

At the time Alfonso Conte had studied her movements from a distance while at the café, Maria Teresa had no idea that he or anyone was watching her. But that's not to say she hadn't noticed Alfonso at other times. She had thought him to be a very pleasant and good-looking cousin when family get-togethers had taken place, infrequent as they had been of late. When she had heard him speak, however, she thought there was a touch of cockiness in the way his words were spoken and accompanying gesticulations. Not necessarily a bad thing, though, if channeled in the right direction. Confidence was something needed in order to make your way in this life, Maria Teresa believed, and she did her best to always keep that belief tucked away in her own mind.

Apart from family gatherings there were not many other chances for the two of them to come together at the same place for any length of time. But the single most likely place for an encounter, the place where most Bagnolesi congregated as sure as the sunrise like the Bible says, was at church service on a Sunday. But in their case a big problem existed. The chance for their paths ever crossing at church was practically nil because Alfonso attended the "newer" 15th century Catholic church, La Chiesa di San Domenico, on the east side of Bagnoli whereas Maria Teresa and her family went to the closer church to where they lived on the western side, the Collegiata di Santa Maria Assunta, which was even older having originating in the 13th century. These two places of worship were less than a quarter of a mile apart, but the distance in a small town like Bagnoli was like miles of separation when church bells began ringing to call the congregation to their pews. As for meeting at school—in the classroom or on the playground—it was no longer in the realm of possibility since they had both already finished the required minimum years of education.

One other common gathering place which stood a chance for meeting someone was the weekly market held in the principal piazza on Wednesday mornings. Because the purchase of basic items at general stores and bakeries had slackened due to inflationary prices and poor harvest years, farmers' markets were visited less frequently these days. Demonstrations over the mounting cost-of-living and strikes for better wages and against increasing taxes impacted daily lives throughout urban Italy. Why should folks living in the Neapolitan provinces pay for governmental mistakes and corruption? But they had. And unrest might be heading for a new eruption on an even greater scale in the near future. Could revolution be around the corner once again? That the impatient Alfonso would find himself in proximity to Maria Teresa by happenstance soon was unlikely given the circumstances. A plan must be contrived to make it happen; and for that he needed his brother's help.

"Aniello, stop with the firewood for a moment, will you," Alfonso directed in pulling his brother aside from his chores of stocking the stove basket and then nearly pinning him against the wall. Using coal instead of wood was making minor inroads, but the villages with plentiful surrounding timber growth such as Bagnoli were not eager to exchange their abundance of natural resources for more costly fuel brought in from elsewhere and supplied by an unreliable train service. "Listen to me. I've had no luck in randomly meeting the girl I've been wishing to get to know better for a long time. You must remember Maria Teresa Conte, the one we saw who's a cousin of ours. I can't wait any longer she's bound to be scooped up by another fellow if I do. So I need you to do something for me. I need someone to keep a lookout for her whereabouts, not just for hour or two but until she's spotted somewhere for sure. There must be enough time to let me know wherever she is so I can get there too before she leaves. Not near her home, though, because there would be too many prying eyes and big ears around there!"

"Are you really talking about watching for her all day? If that's the case, you know it comes at a price, a very big price,

Alfonso."

"I thought it would. There's not much money to spare but how about if I do some of your chores for a week. How does that sound?"

"Make that a month—and all of my chores—and I'm your man."

"It's a deal then. How about this Saturday, when we're both free from other work for the most part?" Then there was a quick handshake that sealed the agreement.

Actually, Aniello was rather pleased with himself in having been entrusted with this assignment. It was a rare day that his brother let him become involved in any aspect of his personal life. The shop selling a thousand varieties of pasta and a few other things proved to be the one where she was spotted. It was one of the three or four places Aniello had thought of to keep an eye on especially as it was on a Saturday when a dish of pasta was an easy menu choice. Sprinting the short distance back home, he shouted for Alfonso to come right away.

"She's there at the store buying pasta. There was a line in front of her so she should be there a few minutes, I think. Anyway, let's get going now; if she's not still inside she will at least still be somewhere near the shop and not at home." Alfonso threw on his coat and ran as fast as he could with Aniello trailing a few steps behind. He saw her instantly still waiting to be served. Then her turn came and the order was completed. Watching her movements through the window, he saw her approach the door with a loaded basket. He stepped forward as if to enter while intentionally brushing against her. It was perfectly timed and even better than he expected. The basket knocked loose from her grip fell on the steps spilling the pasta along with a few other items she had bought. An outpouring of *Mi scusi* left his mouth, of course, as he bent down to help her collect the items.

"It's all right Alfonso," she shot back while looking him squarely in the eyes as they both knelt down, "it's so nice to see my cousin whatever the circumstances. And no apologies are necessary." As they stood up Maria Teresa Conte continued, "So much time has passed since all of us have been together. We don't want to become strangers to each other. I think it's a sign of the times we live in. So many things to worry about, nobody seems good at keeping family traditions alive."

He had thought she had been barely aware of his existence much but now she had actually addressed him using his own name. And with what ease she had struck up a conversation; his confidence was boosted immensely.

"You remember me a little then, Maria Teresa? I certainly remember you very well; even from the time when we were kids during our school days, although you were three years ahead of me. It's so nice to see you now again despite my clumsiness. Please forgive me."

"Of course I remember you; and there's nothing to forgive. You seemed like the shy one at our family reunions. You always stayed in the background with a faraway look about you as if you were deep in thought."

"That was definitely an illusion. I probably was a bit shy, like you say, but certainly there were no deep thoughts going on in this head. Nowadays my friends would say timid, Alfonso, no way? Not the Alfonso we know. I guess it has disappeared and has been replaced by someone who's maybe a little too outgoing on occasions. In fact, I'll show you how much I've changed by asking if I can help carry your packages home as sort of a penance for causing this little accident."

"Well, accidents are just that, accidents; and there's no need to make amends. Nevertheless, I could use some help if you don't mind stopping at two more shops on the way. I still need some bread and beans."

"My pleasure. I was hoping not to let you go on without assisting in some way. I'm ready if you are."

During the half hour it took to finish shopping and walk home, the stream of conversation flowed smoothly about a little of this and a little of that. At her doorstep they parted in saying they wished a family reunion would be arranged soon so they could see each other again and continue their conversation. He held his head high floating on air as he made his way back home. He hadn't said as much, but there was no way he was going to wait for a reunion before seeing her again. Why had he been such a fool in waiting for so long when she had been so easy to talk to and friendly? She could have been snapped up by any number of young men he knew by now. How fortunate for him she hadn't seemed to be.

November slipped away as silently as a leave spinning through the crisp autumn air. At the beginning of December Alfonso and Maria heard the news they had wished to hear; a family Christmas reunion would be held in spite of dismal economic news bombarding them every day. They could not let disdain for the government snatch all the joy out of the Christmas season. Each new government seemed to reinforce the reputation for making things worse instead of better for the common man. But senior family members would do their utmost to steer the evening in any direction but a negative one. The evening would be for reuniting *la famiglia*, celebrating the season and sharing laughter together. Everything would be done to make sure the message reached all concerned well before the event was to take place.

Alfonso and Maria Teresa had been able to meet twice more and now had come together for a third *appuntamento* a week before the family festivities were to take place. If the third time was the charm, it should be enough to cement the relationship. And so it was. Alfonso declared his love and proposed, all within the space of a few propitious minutes. Accepted with tears streaking her cheeks, Maria Teresa was sure her father would give his consent. Of course Alfonso also understood the importance of gaining the approval of her parents. The follies of youth no longer belonged to the current Alfonso version. If anything, he was too serious and driven at times. Tears dabbed away by Alfonso's soft handkerchief at the ready, they returned to earth and then immediately started to discuss what their next step should be now that they considered themselves to be betrothed.

"When do you think I should talk to your father? With the family all coming together in a few days, probably sooner rather than later is best since Christmas celebrations are already well underway."

"It's the Immaculate Conception in two days and after that the party on the 8th of December. Then it's one thing after another so we should not delay and do it right away—tomorrow, or maybe even this evening, it you could be ready," Maria Teresa suggested

"Why wait even another day. And I am ready as I will ever be. I just hope he doesn't throw me out the door when I tell him the part about being already engaged. Just kidding, sort of. I'll need a glass or two of red wine and some deep breaths to keep my knees from wobbling just like those branches of the row of beech trees near the cemetery do on a windy day."

Putting her arm through his, she reassured him that her father was not the type to overreact. "He won't bite your head off because I will talk to mama before you see him. There will be ample time to fill him in advance so any surprises will be over and done before it's your turn. Besides, I've already mentioned you to them several times in past weeks and they must have an idea by now there could be something going on between us."

It was probably a good thing Alfonso did not have much time to prepare his words to deliver to her father. Even waiting a day two would have been too long to let the pressure build. His nerves would have been a wreck. This way, with only an hour or so to wait, his anxiety would not have the time to mount until he became tongue-tied with fear. Still, when the hour of reckoning did come and he entered her parents' home more than his hands were wet with perspiration. He was initially met by them both but her mother soon excused herself to go to the kitchen. Left alone with a man whose stony face at first betrayed no notion he was aware of Alfonso's purpose, the words somehow spilled out of Alfonso's mouth, perhaps not in the order intended. Indeed, he wasn't even quite sure of exactly what he was saying. But after they were spoken the impenetrable countenance slipped away and then his wife was called back into the room. Alfonso found himself engulfed in the arms of Gabriele Conte with both sides of his face peppered with a barrage of kisses. And then her father pumped his hand over and over again until his arm almost fell off.

Maria Teresa's strategy had worked!

All that was left for Alfonso to do now was to make Maria Teresa an official proposal, which he did later that same evening. It was a formality not necessary to either of them at this point, but everything must be done the proper way to avoid any later regrets or recriminations. Furthermore, the woman of his dreams, his wife to be, deserved it! Next, a wedding date must be discussed, not only between them but with both sets of parents involved as well. At first the young couple argued for a Sunday in mid-January—southern weddings almost always took place on a Sunday. Their parents thought that date would be too soon. With Christmas festivities barely over, there would be insufficient time to properly arrange things with the church and the dressmaker, for example, and guests needed to make plans to attend too.

Since the affianced couple were adamant about being sticklers for adhering to traditions—even when some in the community were forsaking them—there would need to be adequate provision for preparation of all the marriage accoutrements. The production of fabric, involving dyeing and spinning, would be represented in part of her dress as it was a legacy of southern Italy's occupation by the Kingdom of Aragon between the 11th and 15th centuries, which culminated at the end of the 1400s with the founding of Spain. And silk would be an essential ingredient to the ancient tradition of her *Pezza Bagnolese*. Some attracted to more modern ideas would consider this to be too old-fashioned but not Maria Teresa. Sericulture would be ever-present in their plans to add to the beauty of their special day and silkworms would play their part without question in her bridal trousseau just as they did for her mother and the mothers before her.

Sunday, the 15th of February, halfway through the second month of 1874, was ultimately the wedding day settled upon, but not without overcoming many opinions to get there. And it would take place in the more senior church of the bride-to-be, the Chiesa di Santa Maria Assunta on the hill. The intricately carved wooden choir, the 17th century Il Coro Ligneo, would serve as the background for friends who would be lending their voices in song to the ceremony. But before the nuptials took place, the pre-Christmas long-awaited day of the family reunion was held at Maria Teresa Conte's home. Of course it was the perfect occasion for not only announcing the forthcoming marriage but also for extending wedding invitations a tutti in one go without having to contact families individually. Fathers of the bride and groom had put their heads together beforehand to work out how they would proceed.

During the short break between dining courses, Gabriele Conte and his counterpart Angiolo Conte, fathers-in-law to be, both rose from their chairs next to each other at the same time.

"While we are all together here in one place, Angiolo and I want to share something we are very excited to report."

"We have been made very happy fathers, Gabriele and I, because two of our wonderful children have found each other. For me, what makes my family so elated is that our son Alfonso is to be wed to the beautiful and intelligent girl sitting right here in this room," he nodded at her and then turned again towards his brother-in-arms to continue.

"Thank you, Angiolo. I also want to say that it gives us a great deal of pleasure to have the honor of telling you Maria Teresa and Alfonso are to be married. We hope all of you and many other friends not present here today will be able to share in their ceremony in mid-February.

"I echo the words of my good friend. You know how time flies, so the fifteenth of that month will soon be upon us. These two young people will be delighted to see all of your familiar faces there—or else! he quipped with mock-seriousness. Isn't that right, Angiola?"

"Or else!" he repeated. "Now let's all raise a glass to the upcoming marriage of these two lucky ones who will now stand up to receive our wish for much happiness." And, with a good deal of prodding, they did rise with some embarrassment, unaccustomed as they were to being the center of attention.

With so much to do, December to February did seem to move abnormally fast for the intended ones and their coterie of helpers. But when their day arrived, the magnificent old church was resplendent with flowers and other decorations. And the young priest stood erect and ready to perform the ceremony, albeit looking a bit pale. He gave the impression of nervousness as much or more than the bride and groom themselves. Just prior to the wedding, again in keeping with Italian traditions, several bouquets of flowers were presented to the bride from the groom. And of course, the *Qualcosa di blu* custom was honored by the bride, whereby a lovely blue flower was taken to be worn in her hair from one of the bunches. And as they crossed the threshold in leaving the holy place of worship they were sprinkled with a shower of rose petals. The traditional sugar-coated, almond flavored confetti would later be served alongside plates at the wedding dinner.

Another special ritual was left to the evening before the day's festivities were complete for the two traditionalists: *La Tarantell*a! This dance that was a metaphor for life: the dancers holding hands spinning clockwise in circle then suddenly reversing direction, things going one way for a while than heading crazily in another direction, all the while with ever increasing speed. It was a circle stopping then starting round again in the other direction, over and over again. They were laughing as they swayed one way than the other, some supported by others as they nearly collapsed; but this was how it should be as the years pass to make it all worthwhile in the end.

CAMPANIA

Bagnoli Irpino, Southern Italy Part I, Summer 1964

Travelling with one's own mother isn't often the easiest thing to do for a twenty-two year old young woman born and raised in the United States; nor is it for her mother when it comes down to it. But that's what Marie's daughter did in the first half of the 1960s. The destination: a visit to the small town of Bagnoli Irpino where Marie Conte had been born to Michelino and Antonia Conte in the South of Italy. It would be the first and last time Marie was to go back to her place of birth but not for her daughter. The story goes something like this. The two of them went to rent a car in Naples. After the agent asked them why they wanted to go to a town forty years behind the times, they decided to take a train to Avellino instead. On the train from Naples Marie had started to talk in Italian to two teenage boys from Bagnoli. She told them who they were. All four of them left the train in Montella, the nearest station to their destination but still over a mile walk to reach the town. It was dark and there were no buses or taxis given their late evening arrival.

The boys offered to carry their suitcases while they all walked together the final distance from the bottom of a long hill. As they were about to enter the town their guides shouted out to two young girls talking to each other under a streetlight wearing what looked like bathrobes, that they were with Maria Conte who was returning from America to visit her old home. As soon as they heard this news, one of the girls ran like the wind up the steps to a big house close by and her father came out the door. He looked very much like the grandfather of Marie's daughter as it was his brother. Invited in, he immediately got out the anisette and they were offered both a drink and their host's own bedroom for sleeping.

These relatives were obviously not poor as they had a chestnut export business and their older daughter lived in a house next door. Word spread like wildfire about their arrival the next day. After a thirty-six year absence, the return of the Maria Conte—only eleven when she had left for America—had caused quite a stir. It was a lot for the almost fifty year old woman and her daughter to absorb. What was it with the passing of old generations and the creation of new ones that had aroused locals to such a state of frenzy? How were they even able to even recognize Marie, if they really did, after what intervening years had wrought in achieving adulthood and child rearing?

Presently, the reason came to her as to why she had left an indelible mark on the town—a legacy so memorable it had broken through the marks of time. After more than one of the town's citizens reminded her of the images they still had of her as a bold and forthright child—especially when it came to defending her older but milder brother—Marie began to understand. Not a milquetoast exactly but definitely gentler in nature than Maria, Antonio sometimes found himself subjected to abuse by the town's bullies, the kind that seem to be loitering on a corner or at the end of an alleyway. In a small town everyone knew who they were but that didn't seem to faze them. Antonio had managed to ignore most of their verbal attacks but sometimes it became physical even though he tried to avoid conflict. More than once a miscreant came out the worse for it after Maria had caught him in the act of bothering her brother. And, if she found out after the fact he had been mistreated earlier, she made sure offenders were paid back for the errors in their ways. But things changed as Antonio grew older and bigger. The tables were turned when Maria wearing her new shoes was intentionally shoved into a puddle by a boy on the way to school. Antonio was quick to step in and shoved him back. But when the bully did not back down and moved towards him instead, he received a quick punch in the nose knocking him to the ground with blood trickling down his face.

Not only was her protectionist character and physical prowess once the talk of the town, but her vocal volume served as a deterrent to mischief as well; it had not been uncommon to hear her powerful lungs permeating the whole neighborhood! It's uncertain whether her fellow citizens considered her fearsome persona a good thing or a bad thing when she lived in Bagnoli but it was obviously a memorable thing! And it served its purpose well, for both her brother and sister survived in a town where poverty together with ignorance sometimes led to a rough-and-tumble element. It could be seen as analogous on a very small-scale to the *scugnizzi*, the young Italian urchins roaming the streets of Naples during the Second World War. Some of these same urban-hardened scalawags even ended up as immigrant school children in post-war America where they found it difficult to adapt.

Marie had stood-out from the crowd and she had not been forgotten. Speaking in Italian, she was naturally a bit rusty at first but soon gained momentum, conversations flowed with family and old friends to the chagrin of her daughter. Hardly knowing a word of the language, Marie's daughter had no idea about what was talked about and felt left out and isolated. On her own part of the time, she tried to compensate for her lack of Italian by making an effort to speak to those who might understand a little English even if they were not able to really speak it. She befriended one of the more educated young men, a cousin of course—on a career path to becoming an architect in the future—who spoke a few words of English.

A few words were apparently enough for a closer interest to blossom over the next few days. When Michele took her hand in his while walking up a hill one evening there could be no doubt that it had. It had not gone unnoticed for it had been witnessed by more than one of the town folk. Word quickly radiated to the older ladies sitting on benches busily crocheting—a craft practiced in the town forever—and men that had sent other tongues wagging as well. Wedding bells were soon ringing in their heads with Michele and Maria's daughter walking down the aisle before long. Although it was the 1960s, 1963 to be exact, and strict proper mores were not what they were a hundred years ago when a chaperon was mandatory for two young people interested in each other, there was still a perception that holding hands meant something more than a casual friendship. And it was not just in rural towns folks felt that way. One wondered if it was, indeed a sanctioned arrangement between the newcomer and a local boy to have gone this far.

Regardless of whatever opinions were rippling through Bagnoli society, the handholding which took place was actually a good thing for Marie's daughter. In this monolingual Italian enclave, someone was finally paying attention to her in his own way despite verbal communication between them at a minimum level. It was a pity Marie had not taught her daughter at least some basics of her native language so she could have understood, interacted more, and been part of each day's planning along with the others. If not for Michele, it would have been hours of boredom. Of course, part of what was said among the older adults was explained later, especially the more animated discussions that were puzzling. When they were finally alone together at bedtime, and after they had left Bagnoli altogether, there was time to answer her daughter's questions.

Marie's daughter had been left to rely on other sensory experiences in order to develop a picture of the place to put it in context while they were still in Bagnoli. Why were there strategically stationed observers all around town? They seemed to have their eyes and ears trained on any ordinary or extraordinary activities. Intentionally conspicuous watchdogs, nearly all men, they were armed with notebooks and recorded everything they saw. Who were they and what were they up to in an out-of-the-way village in 1963? It took asking several people before Marie had an answer for her daughter. Since the end of the Second World War the Communist Party had been one of the big three political parties in Italy. But during the entire twenty year post-war period, until 1965, it had not played a prominent role in Italian government. At first the focus had been on factory workers and the like in the North, but recognizing the need for greater support, the party's aims had been expanded to the working class in general, including the great number of rural laborers in the South.

Not only were they on the lookout for new party members in towns like Bagnoli, where selective crops and livestock predominated, Communists were ready to deliver propaganda to any and all to support their cause. Especially targeted were those who demonstrated an interest in change, which happened to fall to some of the least well-off in the community. The townspeople seemed to tolerate their presence—maybe there was nothing legally they could do about it—but an undercurrent of unease existed. There was a fundamental conflict between Roman Catholicism, the principal tenets of communism and big capitalism in the North. Promises of distributing wealth of the country in a more equitable manner were tempting but other factors caused hesitation. Were they really ready for another revolution?

One of the main reasons for making the trip back to Marie's birthplace was to visit the grave of her mother who had died a month after Marie's fourth birthday. She had been present and retained vivid memories of when her mother had first fallen ill and passed away shortly thereafter. At the top of her list was the desire to see her mother's burial place once more. After nearly forty years away, there was curiosity to see what had changed and what had remained the same from her memories before she departed for America in 1926. To feel familiar mountain air touching her skin again, to inhale smells and see scenery so different from her time in Pennsylvania, New York and California, to immerse herself in the culture of her childhood once more, to give her daughter a glimpse into a different world that was once all she knew, all of these things played a role in her return as well.

When the day came for them to visit her mother's gravesite they hoped to be able to find it on their own without a great deal of trouble. But the relatively small cemetery was crowded and complicated enough that a guide was needed. Mother and daughter followed the footsteps of a cemetery worker up and down a hillside strewn with narrow paths, some of which were faced by multi-story concrete vaults on either side. Each vault grouped the remains of many individuals in separate containers similar to a bank's safe deposit boxes, often with a photo of the deceased on the end. But there were also elaborate individual and family gravestones interspersed with tombs to navigate before eventually making their way to the one sought. Finally the guide halted and pointed to the site where he said Antonia Conte rested a few feet below where they were standing: a tombstone in the shape of a pyramid! What was the meaning of that, they wondered? They got no answer to this question. It just was what it was as far as the guide's personal knowledge.

Their stay in Bagnoli Irpino came to an end in the same fractious way it had started. One of the gifts presented to their hosts in thanking them for their hospitality was an assortment of high quality fabric for making clothing they had brought with them from America. Instead of graceful acceptance, unfortunately something was said during the drive down the hill to the Montella train station that had caused a heated exchange to take place—in Italian of course. When her daughter asked what all the commotion was about later on the train, Marie was still dealing with her anger when she explained. A gratuitous remark regarding their parting gift was made by one of her father's wealthy relatives to the effect that Marie must think they were still living in post-war early days, when the need for everything was so desperate in Italy. Textiles to replace worn out and threat bare clothing had been coveted at the time. They were no longer poor mountain folk dependent on donations of homemade garments. It was an insult; the war had ended long ago and so had the delivery of care packages in Bagnoli!

***

Bagnoli Irpino, Southern Italy Part II, Summer 2012

Fast forward forty-eight years: the moment had come for Marie's daughter to take a second sojourn to Bagnoli this time with two family members in tow. It was now her turn to introduce her husband and daughter to the place she had visited so many years ago. They travelled by rental car rather than the train Marie and her daughter had taken in the mid-1960s, and they expected it to be a quick trip from where they had been staying in Naples. It wasn't long before the terrain began to change after leaving the coast behind and immediately heading inland due east. The type of landscape was so unfamiliar as to be completely unrecognizable to Marie's husband who had thought he had a fairly good sense of the country's topography from former travels, which had been mostly confined to Rome northwards. There had been one exception when he was twenty; a journey by car from the port of Brindisi on the coast of the Adriatic Sea northwestwards had exposed him to a small slice of the South.

After a half hour of driving the scenery had begun to change again as the altitude increased with each passing mile. Unlike the rolling, verdant hills of Umbria and Tuscany, or the flatlands of Milan, Bologna, Siena, the terrain was ruggedly mountainous. Deep ravines and steep slopes only gave way infrequently to feats of road engineering highlighted by lengthy spans of highway supported by long columns rising out of canyon floors. Elevated highways bridged precipitous gaps between rocky mountainsides, and impassable terrain meant miles of driving between highway exits. In fact, when the correct exit had been passed by mistake, thirty minutes of extra driving time was added to the journey. Taking the next exit and reversing course would have taken even longer if the highway hadn't been in such perfect condition; it was like it had been freshly paved the day before. And this road was not even one of the storied *autostradas*, the Italian toll expressways that usually met the highest standards.

Avellino, the capital of Avellino province and the most sizeable city in the vicinity of Bagnoli, was bypassed for the present even though its importance to the region was acknowledged. The city of Avellino offered a variety of commerce and it was the seat of civil registration for all of the smaller communities within its purview. But since the main objective lay just ahead, it was decided to postpone stopping until later and to continue driving along the highway bordering the main part of the city. When the town of Montella was reached—the last place of any size on the map between itself and Bagnoli Irpino—it was a sign our destination was only a few minutes more of upward climb away. The three of us would be on our own this time around. Marie Conte had passed away the year before so we would have to rely on her daughter's earlier memories to steer us to old haunts from when her mother was a child.

Several storefronts on which the Conte name was still

emblazoned were soon passed by. It was reassuring that there were plenty of relatives still carrying on the family line although it also came as a relief to be free to roam the town without recognition or obligation. A two-story building close to the heart of the town held special meaning. Even though the address of 37 Via Ospedale, Marie's birthplace and home before emigrating, had lost some of its luster it once had in becoming the town's city hall after she left for America, it still held a place of prominence as the present-day town library. An incongruously small sign attached to the massive double wood doors quietly announced the *Biblioteca Comunale "S. Pescatore"*. An old building of quality it had served multiple purposes throughout its lifespan but it was obvious by the bold lettering still remaining that its use as a city hall was the most important. Each oversized letter in cobalt blue individually anchored to part of the wall high above the enormous wooden doors when taken together spelled out the word "*Municipio*". Yet, it wasn't hard to imagine the room where Marie had been born long before the residence had changed functions. Looking upwards from the street at the second floor window, Marie, the headstrong girl, could easily be pictured surveying the neighborhood she once called her own.

This old building, however, was not finished as a piece of historical memory. Below the city hall sign were several engraved and embedded plaques naming dignitaries both local and national. A bust of Michelino Lenzi, the Bagnoli born painter of renown who also served as mayor of the town, took center position in-between the top of the doors and the blue lettering. The town square actually held one of Lenzi's works, a bronze sculpture of *putto*, a boy standing inside a huge old baptismal font removed from the San Domenico church of

Bagnoli. We passed through the Piazza Leonardo di Capua several times during our two day stay, remarking on how at certain hours of day there was barely a person to be seen much less occupy any of the many benches ringing the baptismal fountain and the square itself.

Afternoons were a different story; when mid-day mealtime was over there was not an empty place to be found on the same benches, and there were plenty of people standing around and talking too. It was "the place" for gathering, for sharing news and gossip or for just relaxing and enjoying the mountain air and sunshine in an inviting spot. But it was during one of the quiet times of day that Marie's daughter furtively returned a small portion of her mother's ashes to the garden greenery that formed a good part of the square's interior. It was a gesture in sharing her grandmother's early demise with her mothers, and celebrating how vital her Bagnoli roots on the edge of the Parco Regionale Monti Picentini had been to the rest of her life in America.

A decision was made to drive a few miles up the road to the hamlet of Laceno with hopes of having better luck there after efforts to secure a hotel room in town were fruitless. With the wilderness for a backyard and at an altitude of three thousand six hundred feet—a steep, curvy and short rise of fifteen hundred feet from Bagnoli below—accommodation was found without difficulty. A stroll around the now non-existent Lago Laceno was essential for duplicating the time Marie and her daughter had spent in the same place years before. The lake had actually had water in it back in 1963 but had since dried up to a shallow basin, an occurrence attributed to the change in geology following the massive Irpinia earthquake of 1980. At least ski slopes still opened during winters when there was sufficient snowfall on the surrounding mountains that cupped the lake area like a bowl.

Call it coincidence or strength in numbers, but when conversing with the young woman at the hotel reception desk the next day it was learned she had married someone bearing the Conte surname! What's more she was born in Switzerland, the country where many of the Bagnoli men had found work as *taglialegna* in Ticino, the southernmost canton bordering northern Italy. Migrant woodcutters were much needed by their Swiss neighbors following the conclusion of the Second World War. Moreover, Switzerland was the place in which the three American visitors shared a common interest and where they had lived and worked for many years.

Twinkling lights illuminating a quite popular restaurant drew us in after driving back down the road at dusk to search for a restaurant to have dinner in Bagnoli. The menu was also enticing after we had been seated at our outdoor table on a warm summer evening: truffle ravioli, the famed *Tartufo di Bagnoli*, was one of the highlights. The black truffle, along with the *castagna*, or Montella chestnut, and Pecorino Bagnolese goat cheese were the three specialty foods produced locally for which the town had gained notoriety. The return trip back up the small windy road to our hotel in Laceno, in pitch black, after lingering over desert became a white knuckle experience that definitely would not be repeated at nighttime.

The town's cemetery was first on the agenda the next morning, the same cemetery Marie and her daughter had visited to see the grave of Marie's mother in 1963. Expecting to be able to find Antonia Conte's grave site again without help because of the marker's distinctive pyramid shape—her daughter's memory of its approximate location still clear from the past—we wandered up and down the hillside for at least a half hour before a cemetery worker turned up. We were able to understand just enough Italian words and hand gestures to gather that the same huge earthquake that had drained Lake Laceno had caused much destruction throughout the region and the cemetery had not been spared. Many burial vaults and grave markers had been toppled and decimated, including the one for Antonia Conte. He then gestured for us to follow him to what was a very large and more recent structure in the cemetery. Attached to its wall was a plaque with large lettering:

I VOSTRI NOMI SONO SCRITTI NEL CIELO....
GESÙ
Luca 10:20

YOUR NAMES ARE WRITTEN IN HEAVEN...
JESUS
Luke 10:20

On the evening of the 23rd of November 1980 at 7.34 pm local time the earth shook violently for less than a minute but long enough with multiple aftershocks to become a major disaster for towns in Campania. The province of Avellino, as well as in some of the poorest and most rural parts of Basilicata and Puglia regions, suffered particularly heavy damage. Many were killed or left homeless in weather that had already turned cold. When the Bagnoli cemetery cleanup was done afterwards there was no way to accurately restore what had been lost. Monuments had crumpled into dust or were so fragmented and intermixed that reassembly was impossible. So a structure was built to house remnants of remains and tombstones in order to collectively pay recognition to the deceased whose graves could never again be identified individually.

After such a short stay it was a somber ending but our visit to Bagnoli Irpino was over. A stop at Pompei awaited us the next day, fittingly somber as well, before heading back to the Naples airport.

FRANCESCANTONIO

Bovino, Puglia, Italy, November 1873-September 1894

It ended up a positive delay when the olive trees ordered in Foggia by Antonio Paulone failed to appear in Bovino for over two months after his return. He had come down with malaria and, while the worst of the suffering was over by then, it would be another two weeks before he felt strong enough to even look over his purchase. The young trees, still frail and needing more care than their older and hardier counterparts, had been watered frequently to survive the driest time of the year. The merchant and Maria Michela Paulone had seen to that. His wife was just as conscious as Antonio of the importance the new varietal could have for their future. But the risk of such an investment on sparse resources was a constant worry. Maria never questioned her husband's judgment in purchasing such a quantity in a single transaction to his face. Antonio would never have made the deal if he hadn't bargained for a price that was fair. Springtime was always the best season to plant saplings but autumn could also be a good time of the year. It would have to be. At least they had more time then to take root in their pots over the summer; hopefully they would be strong enough to meet the harshness of winter just around the corner.

And when spring did arrive the following year only two of the young trees had not survived the winter. Two lost trees were a reasonable outcome in light of Antonio's less successful battle with recurring bouts of malaria. On three more occasions over the next seven months since returning from Foggia, the debilitating disease had resurfaced with fever, shivers and bodily weakness gripping him again. Each time he resumed taking quinine to shorten the attack with the hope of carrying on at least a minimal level. Psychologically, the reoccurrences had been almost as taxing; it seemed as if he was going to be cursed with these repeated spells of ill health for the rest of his life.

Antonio Paulone had been thankful for being healthy enough to play his part in taking care of a newborn when their baby was born. That she had the assistance of the best midwife in Bovino during the delivery had been non-negotiable. Yet, when in 1874 the day did come last May, when the intense labor pains worried him as much as her, and when the midwife finally told him he had son, Antonio's knees shook and his head spun. All of a sudden he had started to doubt his own capabilities of being the kind of father he should be. How was he to handle this delicate bundle weighing less than two or three litres of olive oil with hands hardened from planting, pruning and all manner of other orchard work? Finally, after going back and forth, they had managed to decide on a name for their bambino that pleased them both.

At first Antonio had pushed hard for his own first name, a tradition for past generations of his ancestors. But Maria Michela was equally firm about the name she preferred: Francesco. A brother by the same name had died when he was only sixteen and it would be in honor of his memory. A minor battle soon began. In the end a compromise was struck in a combination of the two names, Francesco plus Antonio: **Francescantonio**! Her husband, showing good sense, had ceded to her wishes in letting her choice fill the first half of the rather large mouthful; it sounded better than the reverse anyway. But what he hadn't fathomed until later was that another one of Maria Michela's brothers was also named Antonio, so she hadn't conceded that much after all. Smugly, she had walked around their home doubly pleased with the outcome. In the longer run, though, it was their son who later decided what he should be called.

Francescantonio was not raised by his parents alone although he was the only child born to the couple. Maria Michela had been married once before, and that marriage had produced three children. Her first husband, Mariano Ianora, had died suddenly under harsh circumstances after he had been caught outdoors in a late winter storm deep in the countryside. He had lost his sense of direction in what were whiteout conditions and had fallen down a small cliff into an icy creek. His body was recovered the following day. That he had not lived long enough to see the birth of his third child a month later magnified the tragedy. Maria Luigia, the youngest daughter from her previous marriage, was ten years older than Francescantonio. Two other half siblings—all three children living with their grandparents next door—were even older at the time of Franscantonio's birth: Maria Gaetana, thirteen and Gaetano , twelve.

His half siblings doted on Francescantonio like they were additional parents rather than competing with him. All of this extra attention on the young boy had its pluses and minuses.

For Antonio and Maria Michela Paulone, it meant more time could be devoted to olives since they were able to enlist their aid in watching over Francescantonio when they were both busy in the fields or at the marketplace. But it also meant that it was difficult to control the entitlement a spoiled child often incurs. A tendency to try to get his own way, to never admitting being wrong and to always trying to have the last word had become quite pronounced even by the time he was in his fifth year. Maria Michela and Antonio had an intense discussion one night about what could be done to change the behavior after their son had gone to bed. They decided to make every effort to be more aware of when it was happening and immediately remind him of the proper treatment of people, good manners and sharing with others. Secondly, they would talk with his stepsisters and stepbrother to discourage any self-indulgence at the expense of others. Lastly, they would try to nip in the bud any mischievous activities he was inclined to get up to.

    A turning point occurred when Antonio had prearranged to meet his wife in town one day. Walking towards his wife and child from behind and out of their view, he saw Francescantonio tugging on his mother's dress. By the time Antonio was at their sides, the tyke, now nearly four, had dropped halfway to the floor in the midst of a full-blown temper tantrum. Caught in the air midstream by the strong hands of his father, he was given a firm swat on the rear end. It was behavior Francescantonio had always gotten away with in the past with his mother, but the shock of his father showing up unexpectedly had ended the outburst as fast as shutting off a water tap.

    Maria Michela had told her husband a few times that

when their little man was tired and wanted his own way, he might cause an embarrassing scene wherever they might be. Antonio had not given her words much heed because when Francescantonio was with him alone this type of antics had not been displayed. At any rate, the idea that his father may show up at any time had cured the child of further tantrum incidents. However, changing the pattern of other mannerisms was slower-going for the next couple of years. By the time he was seven, Franco, or Antonio, the version preferred by his father, seemed to have developed a better control of his emotions, showed a greater respect for others and loved animals. Indeed, there might also have been something in the fact of having a lengthy first name that had contributed to a surfeit of self-importance, a sense of being a bit too big for his britches. The use of shorter, common names by his parents may well have aided in bringing him back down to earth. But now, after achieving the ripe old age of eight, another page was about to be turned.

"May I clear the table now, please?" he asked after the evening meal one evening instead of the usual rushing away after eating without a word. "I have some schoolwork I need to finish." His parents' quick looks towards each other were joined by jaws hanging slightly ajar.

"Of course you can, Franco, since you're all done."

When the clearing was completed, his parents stayed seated instead of straightening up the kitchen. This had become a special occasion for a private conversation.

"Do you think he is up to something," his father began, "I'm not sure that was really our son or an imposter that looks like him."

"I know what you mean. Let's check on him in a few

minutes—to make sure he's okay. As far as the schoolwork goes, maybe he overheard us talking last night about our local school."

Education in Bovino was the hot topic for discussion all around town these days. There was a renewed push to turn around the staggering percentage of the population that remained illiterate. At one point not long ago it had seemed like illiteracy would become a thing of the past in all parts of the country. When compulsory education had come into force just prior to Italian unification in 1861 eight out of ten could not read or write. By 1882 the illiteracy rate was not much improved and now, more than twenty years later, the Italian population was not even close to approaching fifty percent who possessed both reading and writing skills.

The situation on the mainland, as opposed to Sicily, was worse in southern Italy and worst of all in some of the remote provincial towns. Maria Michela and Antonio were determined to keep their son from contributing to this problem, the same never-ending one they had been a part of in their time. They were convinced Francescantonio was achieving a basic level of literacy when he demonstrated his proficiency in reading out loud to them. And when they saw his pen moving with alacrity across paper and later spoke directly to his teacher about his writing skills, they were confident the scourge of illiteracy for him and for future generations of Paulones had been vanquished for good.

And they were not wrong. With their encouragement and regular contact with schools—teachers were unable to avoid Maria Michela and Antonio's prompting to keep Francescantonio on a steady track of achievement— inadequate learning was in retreat. But there were other challenges to face, challenges an education could help overcome and some that it couldn't.

***

"What's happened to your sister? Maria Gaetana and the wagon should have been back hours ago. I don't know what's gotten into her. Your half sister seems to be living in her own world most of the time these days, head in the clouds always dreaming about her upcoming wedding even though it's still weeks away." Maria Michela was not exactly complaining to Franco, her son having shortened his name and now in his eighth year. Even though ten years had gone by since she had married Antonio, she could still remember the giddy feelings she had when it had been nearly her turn to walk down the aisle. How she forgot to do her chores, how her stomach had failed to tell her when it was mealtime, how she had almost taken the wrong direction home from the market, it was easy to become flustered when your future is about to open wide before your eyes. But rather than complaining, Maria Michela was just talking her worries aloud for she understood it was dizzying period in the life for a young woman about to make a huge transition. Nevertheless, she would give her daughter a piece of her mind for being so long overdue just to bring her back down to earth, to plant her feet on the ground and restore a semblance of reality; these were her thoughts when her attention was drawn to a clatter of wheels and raised voices.

"What's going on here?" she exclaimed as she poked her head out the door and saw not one but two wagons in front of her place. One she recognized as belonging to her family, the other, the one with someone lying in the back partially covered with a cloth, she was unsure about.

Not for long.

"There's been an accident!" one of the men shouted out to her. "I'm Mattia, the one your daughter came to see for supplies. She's badly hurt her arm. I hope it's not even worse than it looks. She was weak enough to want to lie down. Not to unnecessarily frighten you, but that's why we brought her home like this in the wagon."

Rushing over to Maria Gaetana's side with Franco trailing in her footsteps, she blurted out to the men: "Do you think we can bring her into the house? I should ask her first. Are you able to make it Maria Gaetana if we help you up? Can you hear me? We will get the doctor as soon as we can." Moving ever so gently together, they were slowly able to take her indoors and into bed. It didn't take a doctor's diagnosis for them to see the arm was badly broken, for a small portion of bone could be seen to be protruding through the skin once the makeshift bandana bandage had been unwrapped. Blood had stained a patch of her dress, but the bleeding appeared to have stopped.

"Would one of you men go get my husband from the orchard please and the other fetch the doctor, please." Later, when she reflected on the moment, she wondered how she had remained calm, to be able to think clearly with no panic with her daughter suffering from the nasty wound. The one thing she had not considered, though, was that Franco who had been listening to every word she spoke had not said a single one himself!

"Stoke the fire, Franco. And could you also heat some water. We must clean the wound as best we can." Uncertain of when the doctor might appear, Maria Michela tried to do all she could in the meantime. Her husband came in the door just as she was dabbing away some of the dirt and clotted blood. He had news to tell them. The doctor had gone to the neighboring village of Panni, about eight miles away, to attend to another patient he had learned from one of the men who had gone to find him. It would be a while but he would be asked to come as soon as he could when he was back. Indeed, it was a few hours by the time the doctor had set the arm and wrapped it in a proper bandage stabilizing it with a splint. By that time more than a half a day had gone by.

"We must keep a close watch on her. When a bone breaks through the skin like that there could be problems. Normally, an internal fracture will take care of itself once aligned, and heal fine with time. But her case is more serious, more complicated. I will check back tomorrow in any event," the physician assured her. And keeping to his word, check in on his patient he did. Immediately he could knew she had a fever after feeling her forehead. To see how much her temperature was above normal, he pulled from his bag a strange looking instrument about six inches in length. They may live in the southern provinces, but this doctor had equipped himself with the latest medical tool—a modern, accurate thermometer! After about five minutes, the reading on the new device confirmed a dangerously high number. The following day the evidence of an infection became more pronounced as could be seen in the expanding red skin color around the wound. And within two more days Maria Gaetana, the daughter at the doorstep of beginning a new chapter in her life, was no more—gangrene and sepsis had swept away dreams, dreams so close to becoming fulfilled but now gone forever.

THE TIES THAT BIND ~ ABIDING FATE

***

No one spoke of it much during the years afterwards, but Franco Paulone never completely got over witnessing the trauma of his half sister's death. Even though only ten at the time when she died in 1894 he didn't need to be reminded in words with the passing of each succeeding year; a silent pall fell over their home on the days surrounding the anniversary of her death date. Candles were lit and his parents and half-siblings lingered in the church to reach out to her spirit, their silence as evocative as any speeches could be. Now sixteen and classroom education over, Franco was better educated than most southern Italian children whose parents chose to send them to school for a short time or not at all. His interest in knowledge of any kind, formal or otherwise, had persisted even though formal schooling had finished two years ago. So when all the chores had been marked off one by one—the last concluded under the branches of olive trees—he took whatever time that remained in the day to poke his nose in a book or put a pen in his hand.

He was meticulous in making entries in the journal he kept even during routine days that might otherwise appear to be mundane. It didn't need to be a special event or an unexpected visitor or a trip to the market to garner a notation. It was just as often thoughts swirling through his head that stirred the pen into action. Notions he developed about historical works he had read, or writings of adventures occurring in other lands, even a few of them in English, sent his imagination spinning as well. This was the language he had been trying to learn for some years with the help of a teacher at school who spoke a little English herself, thick

Italian accent included. The young and attractive Signorina Ciccarone, recruited from Naples, had become attached to Franco and his eagerness to learn while he was her student at school. But now she had volunteered to assist him in continuing his educational journey whenever she could. It was not often in their town a pupil with a promising intellect had the self-motivation to extend his years of study beyond the school yard into adulthood. Many of the books he read had been borrowed from the Signorina, and her keen sense of what suited his tastes was reflected in the volumes she pulled from her personal shelves that almost always hit the mark.

Keeping his thoughts to himself was not hard for Franco Paulone. He knew he was a little different from others in his age group in Bovino. A few times he had shared different ideas it had not gone well. Teasing was commonplace among some of his peers, especially the ones where jealousy was involved. When he mentioned it to Signorina Ciccarone, she was the one who counseled him to be careful of what he might say, and if anything came up which had to do with learning English, it should be kept between the two of them. She would do the same as well. But a day came when all of the good advice was put to the test. While on the way home one afternoon he was cornered by three older boys near the *duomo*. They must have felt empowered by male herd mentality for they verbally taunted him. That much he could endure while trying to ignore it as best he could. But then they began to physically push him around, each one taking a turn at having a go.

"If you're so clever you should be able to make a lot of money someday. So why not share what you have on you with less fortunate folks like us? You won't really need it anyway."

Backed against a wall, two of them held him while the third roughly stripped him of the few coins he possessed. Then the three of them wrestled him to the ground, landing a few kicks to the body while he lay there. With phony laughter, one of them quipped, "If you mention what happened to anyone you can expect more of the same the next time we see you, *sapientone*."

Perhaps the undeserved reputation as a wise guy, know-it-all spread around the town by the likes of the ones that had assaulted him was part of the reason why he spent less time in town and more in the olive orchard helping his parents these days. The idiots continued to be a problem for a while, but as time passed by they eventually faded away too. Out of habit, nonetheless, he still avoided the more isolated parts of town, ever more so after dark. The sun continued to rise and set the next five years as usual and during these days many issues occupied his mind. The seemingly fragile state of the Italian nation was the one most often that grabbed his attention.

If you read the newspaper, as Franco could with his level of literacy, you could easily become disenchanted with Italian government, politics, and current affairs in general. Not that it was so unusual to feel that way no matter where you lived. But there did seem to be an endless number of questionable decisions and policies. And bank scandals, widespread corruption, war-mongering colonial expansionism in East Africa, strikes, riots and uprisings were happening so often it was like they were commonplace. Government import duties to protect Italian industries had turned sour when met with retaliatory tariffs. Entire sectors collapsed: steel, wine, silk, cattle—and most significant to his family's interests, the **olive oil** trade—all had dried up when markets were cut-off.

Disillusioned by the state of affairs in the country and influenced by the huge numbers of southern emigrants leaving to go to North and South America for better prospects, it was not surprising that Francesco had practically made up his mind by 1894 to do the same as soon as he could. He had turned twenty and it was time to do something radical to change his circumstances. Aside from his family, the one person who he would miss the most was his teacher. His special relationship with her as his mentor for language learning as well as in sharing her wisdom on coping with the difficulties of youth meant a lot to him. As she had taken to him, he had also taken to her despite the barrier of more than a dozen years that separated them from each other. But whatever fantasies he had flirted with in the past were at an end because six months ago she had married a Bovinese. It had been bound to happen sooner or later—no longer Signorina, she had become Signora. Still, it was hard to swallow that his dreams had been dashed so definitively. There could be no doubt about it now. It was time for Francesantonio Paulone to move on.

NAPOLI

Naples and Pompeii, Southern Italy Part III, Summer 2012

Naples was meant to be a brief warm-up to what life was like in southern Italy. A brief visit so the three of us to get our feet wet in an Italian culture so different from the North before making our way to our ultimate destination—Bagnoli Irpino. A city of such historical and strategic importance to the southern provinces merits its own recounting as limited as our time would be in Naples. Climbing into a car rented at Naples international airport soon after we landed, we headed directly into the heart of the city to find our pre-booked hotel located not far from the famous Neapolitan shoreline. With some apprehensions retained from a short stop in the city many years before—but more on that later—new first impressions of an imposing city of some three million inhabitants began to take shape. The city spread across and down a curving hillside mirroring the curvature of the Bay of Naples itself. Although the grandiose scale of Naples together with its celebrated coastal neighbors would be nothing like tiny Bagnoli, maybe a short and sweet immersion in urban culture would help a little to prepare us for our arrival in its country cousin to the East. And before long we were immersed much more than we ever intended.

Somehow the traffic-congested city center was navigated in reaching a roadway near the harbor's edge. We were unable to identify the exact street that supposedly led directly to the hotel in the quarter of town where it should have been, or catch a glimpse of the large distinctive building seen in pictures. At that point it was decided it would be easier to park the car and scout out this quieter part of town on foot. Once the hotel was spotted, the plan was to make our way back to the car memorizing one-way, two-way and dead-end streets, right and left turns required and any other obstacles on the way. Any wrong turn or uninformed decision might slow our arrival at the hotel parking garage and end up in a busier part of town.

However, searching for a place to park the car and begin our reconnaissance had its own problems. Several ill-advised efforts were made driving down small streets, which only brought us to even smaller ones, some with crowds of shoppers blocking passage. We hoped locals startled by the presence of a car in their midst would be forgiving of the trespasses of another lost tourist. The stress caused in trying to extricate ourselves from narrow streets, streets where only a Vespa or maybe a Fiat Bambino would attempt to negotiate, somehow prevented us from hearing epithets that must surely have been hurled our way. These urban Italians had probably viewed us as not having an enough sense to pound sand into a rat hole.

This wasn't our first encounter with up-close life in Naples. On an earlier trip through Europe many years ago, well before our daughter existed, a sample of the seedier sides of the city had inadvertently happened. Naples had not been chosen as a must see destination in the late 1960s, rather it was simply where we were let off after hitchhiking all day. We began by roaming through backstreets littered with trash and buildings missing sections of plaster and begging for a new coat of paint with the objective of reaching the youth hostel listed in the guide we carried. It was quite apparent we had landed in a poorer section of town somewhere on the periphery. The unplanned for introduction to Naples was a lot like what we thought it might be when we had decided to skip it in our planning. Even a few children still playing outdoors on concrete and asphalt—no green anywhere in sight—in the twilight looked to be as ragamuffin as the unkempt, grassless and hostile environment itself. These scrappy urchins probably had street smarts that matched their living conditions, a situation unlike anywhere else we had seen in Italy.

Our travel plan at that time had been to visit as many of the main attractions as we could in Europe. But by chance a young and recently married couple doing a European tour on a very limited budget in the late 1960's had ended up in an unwelcoming corner of Naples! If this is what the rest of the city was like, it was time to make a hasty retreat towards the exit door. Still, there was the lingering thought that the rest of Naples might be a shining light and only bad luck brought us to the worst part of the city. Perhaps the sordid tales we had heard about from fellow travellers were only storytelling embellishments, to be taken with a grain of salt, as we had found to be the case when visiting other places.

Repetitive reporting, for instance, that the French were unfriendly and rude was untrue based on our own experiences. Earlier in our travels, while hitchhiking on a busy road in the south of France late in the afternoon nearly at dusk, a motorcycle officer wearing full motorcycle padding pulled over and stopped to talk to us. At first we thought we were going to be in trouble for standing where we were on the road, but instead he was concerned with our safety since the daylight was quickly fading. We explained that we were going to a youth hostel in Carcassonne, the next town ahead. He then proceeded to walk to the side of the road, blew his whistle loudly and waved down the first car passing that looked to have room for two more people. The driver, a single man, must have thought he had committed an infraction of some sort because he appeared visibly shaken at first. In lieu of a ticket he was given instructions to take us to Carcassonne. Many thanks were heaped on the officer as we entered the vehicle. He responded with a salute and he parting words: *À votre service*!

A single night in a Neapolitan hostel was all that was necessary before deciding we had gone as far south as we needed to go. The next morning, we turned back in a northerly direction, giving up seeing what Naples had to offer. But in the intervening years we regretted we hadn't given the city a fair chance during our first visit. Now the opportunity to rectify that oversight was in front of us again. And it was assisted by the motivation from a very eager daughter determined to explore the sprawling metropolis as much as possible in the two days we had there.

Neither my wife nor I were disappointed with what we saw and did this time around. Narrow alleyways where everyday life could be seen on either side gave the city character. Webs of wires crisscrossed small slices of open sky between old multi-story buildings on both sides of the streets. The corridors so slender it seemed you could reach out the window and shake hands with your neighbor. Motor scooters zipped around hither and thither; shopkeepers in white aprons stood in front of their doors ready and waiting for the next customer to come by; and laundry hanging on clotheslines above and below tiny Romeo and Juliette balconies sought a shaft of sun and a breeze to dry. Essentially useless, these balconies projected out from a third or fourth floor and appeared only to serve as decorative enhancements. They lacked even enough space to place a chair for watching the lively commotion below. Painted in traditional warm, earthy colors of yellows, sienna, pinks and whites along with a wide assortment of beiges typical of southern Italy, these residential apartments mostly from the 19th century confirmed the city's reputation as both vibrant and colorful.

Equally impressive were the broad streets serving as the city's major arteries to get from one side to the other, a stark contrast to the eyes when emerging from dark and narrow passageways. Sundry vehicles wound their way around corners and through multiple street intersections, many of which were so congested as to require extra attention to avoid collision. The central train station was another example of the city's contrasts: small shops versus buildings of scale. But the size of the Piazza Garibaldi, the vast space allotted to the Stazione Napoli Centrale prominently positioned at one end of a square, had to be an anomaly when compared to the rest of Naples. And it almost was for only occasionally in our meanderings did we see anything approaching such grandeur again.

Naples' seaport came closest to mimicking the piazza and train station's proportions. It stretched out in a narrow band of more than a half a mile and harbored several large cruise ships at the Stazione Marittima when we passed by. Unperturbed bathers also found make-do spots next door to the massive ships to sunbathe and cool off in the sea. Concrete blocks sandwiched between eight or nine sizable piers that jutted out into the bay substituted for sandy beaches. Not to be outdone, two castles of formidable dimensions safeguarded the shore with walls built strong enough to thwart potential invaders. The Castel dell'Ovo, just a few feet offshore on a small island, was brutally block-like in design and devoid of any kind of adornment. It appeared more like a fort or prison and was accessed by a short bridge from the mainland. The view from the castle top included the Sorrentine Peninsula to the South, where perched on cliffs, the much-heralded town of Sorrento overlooked the coast. Running on a tight schedule, Sorrento was skipped, as were the island of Capri and its famous Blue Grotto, perhaps to be seen at future date on a third trip.

The second structure, the medieval Castel Nuovo, only a few hundred yards inland a quarter of mile away from the Castel dell'Ovo and near the city's shore as well, resembled much more of what a traditional castle should look like. Five massive towers brought to life the more romantic and fairytale picture that we have come to expect when the idea of a castle is conjured up. When viewed from the front, the height and diameter of three of the towers overwhelmed the rest of the castle.

Earlier it had been decided against spending much of our time indoors, in cooler museums, galleries or churches. Even if they provided respite from the temperature, the limitation of only two days in Naples meant something had to be sacrificed. Eventually we took a break from our walking tour of the city after the heat had taken its toll and hunger took over. Our daughter led us to a pizzeria she had meticulously researched beforehand touted in the literature as best among the top places in the city to sample an authentic Neapolitan pie. It appeared that many other tourists had read the same glowing review as she had by the length of the line gathered in the piazza in front of the building. Or could its popularity possibly be because the patiently waiting crowd was composed of natives familiar with the many pizza offerings and knew this was the place to go? Whichever, we elected to join the takeout queue to make our way very slowly to the order and pick-up window since there was no chance of finding a seat in the pizzeria's small indoor restaurant.

With the risk of giving a smattering of offence, we were sadly disappointed in tasting what was the American equivalent of a less than mini-sized pizza even after our appetites had grown in the long wait. The three of us were disappointed in the paucity of small dabs of presumably mozzarella cheese—little white islands with a sea of open space between them; disappointed that most of the bed of transparently thin tomato sauce remained vacant of anything; disappointed in the limpid appearance that made it look like some of the worst cardboardish American pies; disappointed in a size that would require at least two pizzas to satisfy a normal appetite and three by the time we got ours; disappointed that it was not hot; and very disappointed in the lack of spices and taste. We were aware Neapolitans proudly flaunt their pizza's basic and simple recipe, different from other places in Italy, and very different from the dough thickness varieties of American pizza often loaded with an array of toppings. But this pizza was just not good by any measure in our humble opinion. Dismayed, we left this quarter of town shaking our heads and still hungry having been unable to swallow the entirety of even the small portions of a traditional failure.

Returning to our tour of the varied life of Naples—gritty in some descriptions—we arrived at the Piazza Plebiscito. Another large and public square, not only noteworthy for its vastness but also of historical importance as the place where the vote was taken allowing Naples to become part of the Kingdom of Italy unification in 1860. Crescent-shaped, it housed the Royal Palace and the San Francesco di Paolo Church, the latter a picture of whiteness. The two structures wrapped around about a third of the square and formed a partial delimitation. But the square's sheer expansiveness, second only in size from what we encountered in the train station's Piazza Garibaldi, stood out above all. Strolling through the small streets and passages again, the colorfully stocked shops that were once cellars in old buildings drew our attention. Oversized doors stacked with products opened to an interior where, like the doors, every inch of wall space contained more goods. An assortment of pasta varieties hung on hooks from iron bars attached above the entrances. Each cave-like shop fully stocked with jars of Italian delicacies, bottles of local alcoholic beverages, packages of tortellini and other specialties invited the customer to enter. To differentiate between the multitude of products jammed into the dimly lit cool and cramped basements and those displayed in the cascade of goods at the entrance was a challenge. In particular *Mozzarella di Bufala* was highlighted at each store visited, presumably to make sure that no one store had a competitive advantage over another in offering this Neapolitan specialty.

Suddenly a wondrous great glass-domed building stood

before us. The Via Giuseppe Verdi had been stumbled upon in attempting to find a broader avenue again as a change of pace from the lack of full daylight in narrow passageways. For a minute we thought we were at the Musée d'Orsay, the famed Beaux-Arts museum housed in a restored train station in Paris. Reminiscent of that legendary museum on the left bank of the Seine, the *Galleria Umberto I* was, if anything, even more resplendent. The vastness of its interior was made even greater because of its near emptiness; both shops and shoppers had disappeared in this once popular venue. This unique and enchanting Art Nouveau building was like sanctuary of coolness and tranquility from the outside world, a world that could only be rejoined by walking through the same arched doorway again.

When our second day in Naples proper came to an end it did so with reluctance instead of having left as quickly as our feet could take us some forty years previously. Still, even for this visit we knew much had been missed and there were many other wonders just minutes away if only there had been more time. We still hoped that perfect Neapolitan pizza was there and waiting to be discovered somewhere within the city limits. But a planned visit to Pompeii was waiting the next morning. So, taking the slower coastal option as opposed to the faster *autostrada* toll route—the distance was still only a short seventeen miles down the coast—we were back on the road again. All during the short drive around the south side of the Gulf of Naples the intimidating Mount Vesuvius loomed before us from different angles. The ancient city of Pompeii rested at its foot, volcano and ruins inextricably bound together for eternity. The Pompeii expanse immediately opened up before us after a short walk from main parking lot making it difficult to decide which direction to start.

Remains of mosaics on floors and walls stood out among the highly excavated and restored ruins of this once wealthy and thriving city. But even more eye-catching and curiosity-provoking were the erotic graffiti on walls, and the body casts of humans and animals in the exact positions in which they had met their demise. The shapes left by bodies that had been submerged in mud and ash were captured and preserved in plaster of Paris injected into the hollows in early 19th century excavations. Like with many natural catastrophes such as fires and floods, a number of individuals living in the shadow of the volcano had refused to leave despite warnings and orders to do so. They had stayed in their homes rather than escape after the Mount Vesuvius eruption began on an August day in AD 79. It may have been because they wanted to safeguard their possessions—it was a wealthy Roman town after all—or they had thought the worst was over so why leave then. The second day of the eruption brought an abrupt end to the lives of those who had decided to remain, although the majority had made the wise decision to depart. The casts of inhabitants lying in the prone position suggested they could have met their end in believing they felt safe enough to get some sleep.

But what was striking, beyond the sophisticated art, body casts and salacious pictorials, were the physical tracings of consistency and longevity. Ruts worn into road beds made of massive lava stones by the wheels of carts and carriages over the centuries were tangible evidence of a long history. Standard axel width must have been rigidly enforced since the rut dimensions from side-to-side did not deviate from street-to-street. Parallel water channels along both edges kept cambered roadways clear by capturing rain water runoff. And huge stone blocks between wheel ruts and gutters every hundred feet or so provided stepping stones to assure level and safe street crossing. Both were real examples of Roman road-building ingenuity. But for visitors, the shimmering heat waves from hot-to-the-touch stone sidewalks were a reminder of the hazards of touring ruins on a mid-summer's day in Italy. If the normal outdoor August temperature then was anything like what it was now in July, it must have already been blazing hot, only to be increased nearly fivefold during two days of volcanic eruption that engulfed Pompeii. Hot enough to bake bread without using an oven!

ONWARD

Puglia, Southern Italy, February-March 1898

Two family lines, the Contes of Campania and the Paulones of Puglia, had managed to survive life's trials and tribulations over the centuries in an ever-changing southern Italian environment. Their close trans-Apennine geographical proximity and the connection shared between adjoining provinces of Avellino and Foggia had been demonstrated by the fact that Franco's father Antonio Paulone had been born in Bagnoli Irpino and had migrated to Bovino as a young adult. One of their physical traits that had remained consistently characteristic over time among many of the townspeople in Bagnoli was the presence of blue eye color. The Etruscan civilization that came to the area of Campania as early as 750 BC may have been the origin of this inherited pattern if some of the citizens of Bagnoli were to be believed. Other local lore attributed blue-eyed ancestors and children to Greek colonization of the region in 7th and 8th centuries. This was hard to accept because invading blue-eyed Greeks would have been a minority in Bagnoli since most Greek immigrants had settled in Adriatic coastal areas.

For by far the largest number of citizens the legacy of

blue eyes was attributed to the subsequent Norman conquest of the South that had left a reminder of their presence long after their rule from the final year of the 10th century until 1139 AD was over. Ruins of the monolithic Norman castle Franco Conte gazed at nearly every day with his own blue eyes as he walked by attested to the fact that Bagnoli had not escaped the Norman's sphere of influence, so it was possible. There could be no denying the power and importance of these ambitious conquerors, migrants from faraway northern France who had themselves intermingled with even more northerly marauders, the blue-eyed Vikings, long before they ventured southwards to Italy. Whatever the origin, the Conte lineage often shared the blue eye trait with many other families in Bagnoli, which flew in the face of the typical brown-eyed images of Italians.

On the other side of the Apennine Mountains, in the eastern coastal settlements extending inland from the *Golfo di Manfredonia*, part of the Adriatic Sea, the Normans would surely have left their calling card as well to a portion of the population living in Apulia. But it seemed that endowment had bypassed most of Paulone families in Bovino, if it had truly been there in the first place. Brown and hazel eyes had nearly always been predominant for generations. Gaetano Paulone, born in Bagnoli, was not part of the blue-eyed contingent and neither was his son Antonio. Gaetano's wife, Teresa, also born in Bagnoli, shared the same dark color as their Bovino born and bred grandson, Franco. Apart from the Paulone family, nevertheless, blue eyes still occupied a strong second place overall among citizens of the Apulian hill town.

So it was now, having survived the heartbreak of a first lost crush and deciding he would soon leave Bovino to seek the greener pastures of America that Franco Paulone took the time to reflect on his life in southern Italy. With his contemplative eyes of brown he was about to say his goodbyes for good. He did not do so alone, however, for he was joined by three friends who were all on a hike together above the town. They would, after departing the town center—the site where Hannibal was said to have made his base before engaging in battle during one of the Punic wars in 217 BC—pass their own Norman relic. Similar in its setting to the one in Bagnoli, a castle strategically overlooked and guarded the entrance to the town.

"It would be hard to deny the beauty of the rolling hills and greenery of our Daunia on this splendid morning would it not my friends?" he practically sang out. It was difficult to know which one of Franco's companions was the first to signal agreement either by nodding or muttering replies under their breaths.

Vincenzo, Marco and Giovanni, either separately or in twos or threes, had all traipsed the surrounding countryside with Franco since they were boys. He was happy once more to have the small group together again on his twenty-first birthday even though warm dress was needed to fend off the chill of an early morning frost and clear January sky. Mountain-raised and hardened, they were used to it. Passing time with them would be bittersweet, though, because it could very well be the last before he would go. Aside from leaving good friends, it hadn't been a difficult decision to make in some ways. What was left for him in Bovino anyway? He had been only eight when his father passed away fifteen years ago. His mother had then assumed the role of the owner and manager of the olive business in partnership with Alessandro, her brother-in-law. His wife, Rachele, had died when she was sixty-one, an even a younger age than her own Antonio. The collaboration between the two in-laws had been working out well for many years until three years ago.

Maria Michela and Alessandro had started to work in the orchards when they noticed that something was wrong with a few of the olive trees. Olives, wilted and brown with rot, instead of green as they should have been, were dropping off from a few of the trees well before they had a chance to fully ripen. It seemed to have happened overnight and to just a small number of the trees so it was viewed as a limited tree problem. But when the number of affected trees escalated to about a quarter of the grove and unripe olives fell off branches with the gentlest of breezes in the next days, worry turned into grave concern for their livelihoods should the entire crop come to ruin. With the help of community elders, they learned the cause was the return of the age old blight they had only heard tales about. The tiny, seemingly inconsequential, Mediterranean fruit fly had once again become much more than a nuisance to be simply swatted away!

They realized they should have taken the time and made the effort long before to closely inspect the olives on the trees and compare them to the fruit on the ground to look for telltale signs of this infestation. If they had, they would have noticed the small tunneling trails and lumps on their skins left by the flies. And there was also the presence of maggots, another sign of disease. Why hadn't they paid more attention to reports of fruit fly damage in other parts of Apulia in the late 1880's into the decade of the 1890's? To their credit, once they had recognized the causes and the danger they rapidly moved into action. The remaining healthy crop was harvested within days with the help of a crew of day laborers. But it was clear, picking olives not totally at their peak, undersized and lacking maximum oil content, would mean the loss of future oil production. But it was better than nothing at all. And after learning that this pestilence was seasonal and it greatly depended on the amount of old fruit and decomposing debris left on the orchard floor, it behooved them to also clear the ground with expedition. So, with Franco's help and a small army of hired hands, they did their best to discourage this small but lethal predator. The succeeding year wasn't much better, however, jeopardizing their business altogether.

He hoped to be able to persuade his aged mother it was time to move on from growing olives, the business which had been started two generations before by his grandfather Gaetano Paulone. The time was definitely right for Franco to make a change, who in his heart of hearts was not really interested in anything to do with olives even if the grove had been thriving. It had been like that for quite awhile with him. So when Vincenzo made a last attempt to change his mind about leaving Bovino on hopes for an improving economic situation, and the unlikelihood of a third year of insect invasion, Franco was quick to respond with his own thoughts:

"Nothing ever seems to change for the better for long around here. When there is a little daylight, something like the Mediterranean fruit fly comes along and brings us right back into the darkness. Any real shift in economic conditions for the good happens in the north of this country, just like it always has. Maybe a little bit trickles down to us later, that's so they can say "look how the South is benefitting too". I think a lot of the Northerners still believe we speak a different language and are hopelessly inept Neanderthals."

"There's already a lot of talk of changes in education, with schools focusing on teaching standard universal Italian in the classrooms instead of regional dialects as they now do," Vincenzo added in defense, "and many realize crime here in the South will be reduced when poverty has become less too." None of Franco's good friends wanted him to leave of course. "Then why do you continue to hear about so many people emigrating, or at least thinking about leaving our country? And what about those of us who already work in another country part of the year just to be able to send a little money home to feed their families?"

"You're forgetting about all of the news we have heard only recently, Franco. Some taxes have actually gone down, thanks to our own politicians in office, and there are new road projects and other development plans for irrigation and schools that will help us draw closer to the North. We can't overlook the positive things and dwell only on the negative, can we?"

"And there's the fact that more and more of our Southern Italians are able to read and write nowadays. Some things, like literacy, are improving you'd have to admit, Franco," chimed in Marco in supporting their attempt to dissuade Franco from taking a rash and unnecessary step in their estimation. And you've heard, like I have, that Campania is economically much better off than the other southern provinces and way ahead of Sicily."

"I know you all feel more positive about prospects here than I do, and I really appreciate knowing you want me to stay. But for me, whatever small steps are being made are just that, small. Way too much so and too late for my liking. Nothing happens fast enough around here. I don't want to see the years pass by growing old and hunched over while still waiting for the big changes that have been needed and talked about forever."

Back and forth the four friends chatted along the away, time passing so quickly they had reached their first stopping point before they knew it. The *Santuario Madre del Figlio di Dio* offered a sun-warmed wall to lean their backs against while sheltering from any sneaky winter breezes which wormed their way through sweaters. And resting for a few minutes they could enjoy the food they had brought with them to tide them over. The sanctuary was only a mile and a half from the center of Bovino but a world away in what it was like to be there. Before they had sat down, they had paused at the holy well for a sip of water and felt the peace that permeated throughout the splendid complex. They looked on all sides and straight above at a sky so big that it couldn't help but announce the spirituality of the place. This was as close to what it must be like to be in heaven one of them said.

Vincenzo stood up to face the small party and began to address his friends. "Do you know the story of how the church came to be built on this site? Don't worry, it isn't a long one, but I'll shorten it even more because we should be on our way. Anyway, a woodcutter named Niccolò back in the 1200s was visited by a woman in white, seemingly an apparition of the Holy Virgin, who asked him to go to a nearby spring and fill a bucket with water for her. In return for helping her, Niccolò had her promise to load his donkey with wood. He asked who she was when he spoke to her as she toiled and she replied she was of the Mother of the Son of God. And she had come to defend Puglia, and especially the town of Bovino, from further conflict. The area had recently been taken over by the French

King Charles d'Anjou, who had installed himself as Duke of Puglia. Before she disappeared, she requested that Niccolò build a church on the very spot to be named *Santa Maria di Valleverde*."

"So that's how the church supposedly got its name; I wondered about that."

"Hold on Franco, I'm not quite finished. Niccolò procrastinated and in the end failed to comply with the Holy Virgin's wishes. He woke up one morning to find himself crippled, his face misshapen and in severe pain. He only was healed from his physical woes after finally deciding go to the Bishop with her proposal. Not willing to leave it to chance, she entered again into his dreams one night and specified the exact location in which the church was then built."

"Good tale, Vincenzo, and lesson in there somewhere, I suppose," he sarcastically joked.

"It is interesting and it makes you think. I mean who really did choose this location for the church? Get up everyone. Let's get going before any of us drift off into the land of dreams ourselves!

Then they did set off again and any serenity from their all too brief stay at the sanctuary evaporated when Marco changed the conversation in asking if any of them were worried about the events that had taken place in Africa again. He was referring to the news about the Italian military's latest foray to the nearby continent. From tranquility of tale telling to the battles of a colonial war, this dramatic shift in discussion revolved around the Italian army's invasion to seize part of the Ethiopian territory. The army's defeat by Ethiopian forces, which had been underpinned by France and Russia, was an unmitigated disaster for the government. Political reverberations of the military's failure to secure any of the foreign territory they had so confidently planned to annex in 1896, and widespread government corruption in conjunction with other painful issues, culminated with the resignation of the first prime minister from the South.

The country left one period of turmoil only to enter into a new time of unrest after Francesco Crispi terminated his term in office. Bread riots in Bari and Naples, demands made by southern socialists and unions, peasant leagues and anarchists to alleviate economic hardship, frequently met with a heavy-handed authoritarian response. The government elected to repress rather than listen and address protesting voices. There was great uncertainty among many young Italians they had not experienced before. To keep abreast of the splintering of society into radicals, socialists, syndicalism, anarchists, unions and other associations—conflicting factions often with tentacles extended even towards the peasantry of Puglia—put a strain on the average southern agricultural worker. Actions of these anti-traditional government groups and their limitations in the battle for greater civil liberties, the rise and demise of the *fasci siciliani*—the peasant league revolutionaries even further south—as well as constitutional issues had left the country's cloak of national unity in tatters. These events when taken together could be the foundation on which the country's future direction would be based, a future riddled with chaos too. And that was a frightening prospect for many, including Franco and his friends.

"It's not only due to the crazy decisions of our alleged unified Italian government, but it's the economic situation that leave folks like us unable to work our way out of the struggle to make ends meet. Maybe the trade unions can help improve wages and working conditions of those in the North, but they do nothing for our families here in the South," Franco lamented as if the weight of the world had been placed on his own personal shoulders. "Our pitiful wages can be seen in our exhausted muscles, our bent backs and empty stomachs."

"You must admit, Franco, even here, almost at the end of the earth, there's talk of how we as the legitimate working class can fight for our own betterment. We can join together to put a stop to outrageous socialist reform policies of corrupt Socialist Party leaders."

Vincenzo's words were worthy however they practically fell on deaf ears as far as Franco was concerned. Yes, there was talk of revolutionary methods for changing the social order but it seemed to him it was just talk, with things mostly carried on the same anyway. Where was the shining light in the so-called class struggle? Why were breadlines still as long as ever, and bread running out before half of the hungry had a chance to set foot inside the door? He was fed up with the empty shelves and the waiting. If real change came to pass, change that actually improved the plight of the underclass instead of filling the pockets of the wealthy, it would be akin to a present-day marvel. But Franco Paulone would, at any rate, have to hear about it from his new home in America. Of course he would be among those Italian immigrants jumping up and down and cheering loudly for his fellow countrymen left behind in Italy. He prayed that although they could not hear or see him, they would be able in some way sense his support in winds blowing eastward towards the land of his youth.

Breaking away from Bovino had not been easy in another way, though. Mentally he had been more than ready to make a change, but circumstances again took control of best intentions. His mother's partner, Alessandro, had appeared to enter into a rapid decline. The doctor had attributed no single cause to her brother-in-law's failing only surmising that it could be partially due to bodily weariness from tending to the olive orchards for so many years. The thought of how his mother would cope with running things on her own now impacted Franco's impending emigration plans and he could tell she needed him at least until she decided what to do. It was true, her early enthusiasm for her son's ambition of achieving a better life had at some point given way to a selfish desire that he would stay a little longer, although she had never entirely admitted it to herself or said as much to him.

Eventually she had taken to heart there would be no one left to inherit the old dream of a self-sufficient family through the oil of the fruit which had supported their lives for so many years and given them so much contentment. In any event there had been no way he could leave in February as planned until Alessandro had either regained his health, which from the impression left by the doctor's could only be by a miracle, or had succumbed to his illness. Whichever way it turned out, she had needed his help both physically and spiritually for the time being. But his decline did indeed taken a rapid course, even faster than either the doctor, his mother or Franco had thought would happen, and he had passed on to a better place by the end of the month. When all was said and done Franco's departure for the new world had only been delayed for a short time. And in less than a week after the funeral was over, Franco was in Naples and ready to board the Karamania for a scheduled March arrival in New York.

That city was still basking in the limelight of celebrating

the consolidation of the five separate counties of Brooklyn, Queens, Staten Island, Manhattan and the Bronx into Greater New York City in January 1898. The newly formed metropolis presented no problem to Franco in finding his way to a relative's abode on Mulberry Street in the heart of the Italian quarter. As soon as he became familiar with his surroundings he would look for his own inexpensive room somewhere among his fellow countrymen in Little Italy.

INTERLUDE

Bovino, Puglia, Italy, June 1898-1899

In early summer, the same group of friends minus one, returning from the same sojourn they had taken with Franco Paulone during the previous winter, was talking about him again. They recalled the words he had used to try to convince them his decision to leave the shores of Italy had been the right one. Three now instead of the four when Franco had been with them, they had just passed through one of the many portals of the village and down a flight of stone stairs flanked by houses also made of the natural material found in the local river bed. From the bottom of the stairway they could see a large number of townspeople milling around the town center, with even more approaching from all sides. The young men looked at one another in puzzlement. What was going on here? This was not the usual time of day for gathering outdoors, when relaxing around the square and swapping stories and making gossipy remarks about this or that person or family was the thing to do. And it was not late enough in the day for strolling or sitting on benches. No, the abnormal commotion must be due to something else altogether. The long-legged Giovanni strode ahead of his companions to find out. "Why does it look like everyone and their brother seems to be in the middle of town at this hour?" he inquired after stopping the first person he saw.

"Haven't you heard the news by now? It's the Prime Minister. Rudini is out—again! Here we are in 1898, only two years in office and his government's been overthrown for a second time. The first time he only lasted a single year before he was ousted as leader back in 1891 and 1892 if you remember. So I guess he's shown improvement and at least he ended the war with Ethiopia."

"Unbelievable, unbelievable!" blurted out the stunned Giovanni after he had rushed back to Marco and Vincenzo to tell them what had caused such a stir.

They were all amazed that it could have happened so suddenly again. There was a perception if someone who had been dismissed once was resurrected from the political graveyard to become head man again, he would have learned how to govern and would be around for the longer term. Apparently a misconception in his case! They could hear Franco's words ringing in their ears as if he was still there among them: "Just more of the same; didn't I tell you so?" he would have immediately spat out. The wise one would probably have agreed with them that the riots in Naples must have been the final straw. "Another of our would-be Sicilian brothers brought down to earth, twice, apparently having learned nothing from his first time in office. A man incapable of making the right choices by taking sides rather than helping the common people," Franco would have added if he had been present.

Franco would not have been surprised over learning the news of the latest disruption, but even if he were it wouldn't have lasted long because this was Italy, a country where lasting stability was impossible to achieve. How could anyone expect to get anything done with governments popping up like garden weeds only to be yanked out every year or two replaced with new ones? Yet, for the moment, the three friends were so stunned they had trouble finding words—except for Marco, the one who couldn't help himself from always stating his thoughts out loud. "One day the Fascists are in and the Socialists are out and the next it's the opposite. It's a merry-go-round, a circus of political buffoons. If it wasn't so hard on the average man, a series of leaders possessing personality flaws, creating bizarre policies and making bad decisions would be laughable—a real comedy of errors, as an old man in England once wrote. Italian conservatives, liberals, radicals, no matter what they called themselves, it has been a mess and remains a mess. I mistakenly believed there might be some hope with Rudinì, but this puppet is just like the rest of them and he's let us down too."

Antonio Starabba, marchese di Rudinì, a prominent Sicilian and revolutionary supporter of Garibaldi, began his ascension to the top of Italian leadership after becoming the mayor of Palermo. He had several traits that had made him appealing to Franco Paulone and his friends and many others hailing from the southern provinces: first, he was from the South; number two, he had showed strength in reducing brigandage that had been plaguing Sicily for so long, a problem that had beset Puglia as well earlier in the century; thirdly, he had demonstrated an even-handed approach in disbanding the Fasci in Sicily; and lastly he had made sure social measures were passed regarding workmen's compensation and voluntary funds for disability and old age pensions. He looked like someone who really cared about the conditions of the working class. Positives were countervailed, however, by his ineptitude in handling colonialism, party politics and foreign policy and a host of lesser affairs. Rising prices and upheavals in major urban centers, including bloodshed in Milan where over eighty were massacred by the military in food rioting, were the nails in the coffin that spelled his downfall. It was a perfect example of history repeating itself from only a few years before when Crispi had been in charge. The news of another failed government would have been the coup de grâce when added to the other reasons Franco had put forward in justifying his decision to immigrate to America before he had left the country. If he had been with them there would have been no further arguments from his compatriots now that they realized his decision had been justified.

Although it was too soon to be sure, rumors were already flying his successor might be another military man, a certain General Luigi Pelloux. A couple of June days later it was indeed confirmed. Pelloux, the man who came from about as far north in Italy as you could go, now held the reins of government in his hands. To the majority of southern Italians his name was not well known. Pelloux had lived the first three years of his life in the tiny town of Roche-sur-Foron within the Kingdom of Sardinia. His birthplace would become part of France's Haute Savoie region following French annexation of Savoy in 1860. The changeover had occurred prior to Luigi Pelloux's fourth birthday. His parents' decision to retain Italian citizenship instead of electing to become French had devolved upon their son as well. He had been ordained practically from birth to become a career military man and graduated from a Turin academy, rising through the ranks after distinguishing himself by fighting in several battles. Shifting to politics he served as Minister of War in the cabinets of three different governments, including the abruptly ended one of Rudini. He also had been elevated to senator along the way. It was King Umberto I himself who had handpicked Pelloux to form a new government, the former soldier assuming dual roles of both prime minister and minister of the interior.

This all looked good on paper, but when the young men met together anywhere in Bovino, their skepticism remained firm: it was not a question of "if" but "when", in regard to Pelloux's chances of longevity in office. Franco Paulone's distrust of the system had completely taken over his friends' view of political life as well. Downfall of governments didn't stop with Crispi and Rudini; the impermanence of Italian leadership seemed to be endemic. With few exceptions, from the beginning of Italian unification in 1861, the problem of short-lived regimes continued, almost as if it had been intentionally built into the system. Taking the past three decades alone, how many premiers had there been? There were thirteen during 1870s, '80s and '90s—all of them male of course—one every two and a quarter years on average.

"And then there was Giolitti, again from the northwestern part of Italy between Genoa and Nice, who was selected to be head man in May 1891 and resigned in November 1892. In office a year and a half and brought down mainly by bank corruption that had been already rife in government when he became prime minister, paradoxically, and by the strikes in Sicily," Vincenzo commented in impressing his comrades with his knowledge of history, almost as if he was a walking encyclopedia. "The 1880s were better but not the '70s. The decade started out positively with Giovanni Lanza serving for four years until 1873 but then went downhill from there. Minghetti, a Bolognese, was next before his ties to the revolutionary movement sent him packing after three years. Afterwards, there was Agostino Depretis, for two years before briefly leaving then returning to leadership twice more. The exception, Depretis actually served the longest; when you added the number of years of his three terms together it came to ten in all!"

"Wasn't there another prime minister who was stabbed while in office?"

"There was indeed. Your memory is also good, Marco. Benedetto Cairoli had the misfortune during his first year in office of receiving a wound while trying to protect King Umberto I from an assassination attempt in Naples. Because of the injury he sustained, he was relieved from office after only a few months. Like Depretis, he returned soon thereafter to form a second ministry, though."

"Why do you think Italian governments turn over so quickly? This seems so different from other countries, like England or the United States, whose leaders have more years in a row to get things done their way."

"I don't know for sure, but my theory is that it has a lot to do with having both a king and a premier at the same time. I know England also has the same set-up, but Italian kings seem to have much more power in steering the direction the country, power that often conflicts with the prime ministers. And maybe so many men with military backgrounds had a big influence in making decisions, which are not always in the best interests of civilians and the country as a whole."

"That sounds at least partially right, Vincenzo. It all ends up in a mistrust of leadership that relies on a carousel of new faces to keep looking for answers to solve the inevitable problems that constantly arise and probably always will. If you were someone like our old pal Franco Paulone who had enough of it all, you're probably better off going to America."

What was the outcome of poor government and turmoil on the citizens of small towns like Bovino and Bagnoli Irpino and southern Italians in general? One phrase could sum it up for those who had immigrated: *L'Isola Delle Lagrime*. New York's Ellis Island was the first place for Franco Paulone's fellow countrymen to sample American soil after leaving Italy in their wake. Trading a history harkening back to before Roman times for life in a country created a hundred years ago; trading olive groves and shepherding for steel mills and fledgling skyscrapers; trading *pasta e fagioli* for Coney Island hot dogs on buns; trading generations of family togetherness for thousands of nameless passersby. This is what the immigrant had to look forward to after stepping onto the Island of Tears.

***

Bagnoli Irpino, Campania, Italy, June 1898-1899

On the other side of the Apennine divide, the four parents of Antonia Conte and of her cousin Michelino Conte often found themselves deliberating the state of Italian affairs as well but from a different perspective. They were doing so now *en famille* as they sauntered to the town square for the annual celebrations in honor of the Immaculate Conception on a perfect June day. Aged seven and eight, Antonia and Michelino along with the other children were running ahead of the adults. They were too young to care about the quirkiness of governments but not so their parents. Alfonso and Teresa Conte, and Antonio and Maria Conte, in their separate households and sometimes when they visited each other, debated current developments from a personal standpoint. Their focus was as much on foreign relations as on domestic affairs, and they worried how recent changes in other countries might affect their daily lives. If not pan-European in scope, new arrangements, at least by the largest countries in Europe, could soon have a negative impact on their livelihoods.

For years seasonal work abroad had supplemented traditional farming at home. Sheep grazing, higher altitude crop growing, foraging for the *Tartufo Nero*—the black truffle delicacy the town was known for since ancient times—and chestnut grove cultivation were some of the Bagnoli mainstays. But migrant work opportunities as woodcutters in Switzerland were very rewarding. Irpini men, using skills honed in the rugged forests covering the hills above Bagnoli, were needed to meet the specialized labor demand from their northern neighbors. Plentiful timber harvested from the nearby forests around Bagnoli Irpino had translated into a ready-made source of lumberjacks, men who were well prepared to deal with mountainous terrain of nearby Switzerland. The pay was good, more than twice what they could earn at home, but they also made sure requirements for wood at home were satisfied before travelling northwards.

So it was for both Conte families. Nephews and cousins trekked off each summer to work in the forests of Ticino, the

Swiss canton where their native Italian tongue was spoken, albeit it with a unique cadence and some peculiarly Swiss pronunciations of common words; where the alpine weather was similar but more changeable than their own Apennine mountains; and where the sweat from their brows was aptly paid for hard work done by capable hands. But for some time now the shifting power structure between Germany, Austria, France and Russia had become alarming. New alignments would likely alter the relationship between the neutral and petit landlocked Switzerland situated in the middle of them all, excluding distant Russia, of course.

The threat of change concerning the possible lack of foreign earnings, which many Bagnolesi families depended upon to make it through the year, was real. The Conte families had shared their concerns several times recently. They knew enough about the history of the small country they leaned upon for economic support to know Switzerland had held the same political position for ages. The signing of neutrality agreements within the Treaty of Paris in 1815 seemed to be the formal beginning of its stance. But neutrality or not, how long could the Swiss keep their country intact if any one of the large belligerents surrounding them decided they were easy pickings, and could be used as a stepping stone to even more lofty prizes?

Lately, the threat from France felt a little less immediate since the French were heavily engaged in colonial pursuits, hopefully excluding their non-pugnacious neighbor, home to a sizable francophone population in the cantons of Geneva, Vaud and Neuchâtel. Together, these cities contained a greater number of French-speaking citizens than Lugano, Bellinzona and Locarno did for Italian-speakers, to name a few of the larger places familiar to migrant workers from Italy. Over to the East, Austria-Hungary had diminished its sphere of influence in relation to redrawn territorial dimensions when compared to the past. And it appeared to be mainly concerned with Russian expansion objectives, allying itself to Germany as means for protecting its own security. Russia alone, at a great distance, would probably not pose a direct threat to the Swiss that could affect Italian migrant worker arrangements.

The two Conte fathers, Alfonso and Antonio, were talking politics once again as they strolled down narrow alleys in the historic center of Bagnoli. But then the topic of conversation shifted to their immediate surroundings. The oldest section of town, the Jewish district, was called the *Giudecca*, as it had been for centuries. It was thought to have been established about 1300 to 1400 AD, during the latter part of Middle Ages.

"Do you think the Jews who lived in this quarter experienced persecution? There isn't anyone I know who identifies as even a smidgen Jewish these days in Bagnoli so there's no one left who might have had stories passed down to them to ask about it," Antonio reflected.

"I don't know about that. But it would be unusual if they hadn't. Isn't it a bit ironic, though, here we are walking behind the Church of Santa Maria Assunta, our Catholic Church, while wishing these old cobblestones could tell us about the Jewish feet that once trod upon them?" Their wives a few paces behind had caught up to them as they paused for a moment. Maria Teresa, who had overheard the question and answer, joined the conversation: "The Jews didn't magically vanish, you know. And in Italy they certainly did suffer persecution like elsewhere. From what I studied, they were among the very first to settle in Bagnoli and were an integral part of the growing community to come. That's at least one of the reasons why we still recognize this part of town as where they lived to this day. It wasn't a ghetto, however. Of course the presence of Jews in Rome went back not just centuries but millennia, to the pre-Christian era. But from what I know, Jews in the South and Sicily were expelled, like in so many other Jewish communities, but to a lesser extent. It seems our Norman overlords allowed greater freedom and were somewhat more tolerant."

"You're right. There's not a person in town who wouldn't know these small streets and the distinctive architecture of the buildings."

"During the mid-1500s to mid-1600s," she went on, "and there was an expulsion of Jews in significant numbers by the Kingdom of Naples. That's when many in our town left too. Extra taxation placed on the Jewish community was another problem. Those that remained eventually merged into the rest of our population; ethnicity and names were absorbed into Italian versions along the way. Southern Italy has always seemed to have had a small Jewish population all the same so total numbers affected were nothing on the scale of other countries."

"How do you know so much about Jewish history, Maria Teresa? Your understanding in very impressive compared to ours," Antonio remarked.

"Living near this quarter, I became very interested in learning more about its history when I was at school. I asked questions at recess while the others were running around on the playground. And I paid attention to the answers, unlike a few others I know quite well!" The party of four laughed in unison then they proceeded ahead and returned once again to concerns over working in another country. What would happen to those who went for temporary work and stayed permanently in Switzerland if foreign powers exercised their influence on Switzerland? It was finally agreed they would just have to wait and see what the impact of European strategies would be.

As soon as the families arrived at the *Piazza Lionardo DiCapua* for the traditional *Maria Santissima Immacolata* festivity Antonia left her parents to join other girls from the town. They reappeared as little angels, all in white dresses from neck to toe, topped with small sky blue head coverings like half veils. From the looks on their exposed faces, they seemed composed and ready to take part in the serious religious occasion venerating the Virgin Mary by the singing of the *Canto delle verginelle di Bagnoli*, a prayer set to music. Their local rendition of the Song of the Virgins was beautifully done. Because of the conversation their parents had only minutes ago, two of the four line stanzas of the hymn stood out over the rest:

Grazie implora per Bagnuolo
Nostra patria tanto amata,
Per l'ingegno rinomata
Per pietà per viva fe'.

Pel commercio suo lontano,
Per l'industre pastorizia,
Pei lavor di nostra mano,
Per gli agricoli lavor.

> **Thank you please for Bagnuolo**
> **Our beloved homeland,**
> **For its renowned genius**
> **For its piety for its living faith.**
>
> **For its distant trade,**
> **For the pastoral industry,**
> **For work by our own hands,**
> **For agricultural work.**

These simple lines reminded them of who they were: small family farmers of sheep and other livestock; producers of fabrics using traditional dying and spinning practices; women crocheting in front of their houses sitting on armless wooden chairs; cultivators of silkworms raised to produce silk fabric; traders of chestnuts, pecorino and truffles beyond their walls; foreign workers; and farmers of small scale crops at a higher elevation. It didn't seem like much when you added it up, nevertheless it had kept them going for centuries and they were proud to be part of the Bagnolesi community, of what they accomplished and how they accomplished it. And it pleased them to no end to watch their children Antonia take the hand of Michelino afterwards as they all walked home together with the young Conte cousins now carrying the customs of the past and future on their small shoulders.

HARDSCRABBLE

New York City-Newark, New Jersey, April 1898-July 1905

Frank, as he was now known instead of Francescantonio, Francesco or Franco, former incarnations by which he had been addressed by family and friends in Italy before taking the plunge to immigrate to America, found 1898 life in New York city not quite as he had imagined. Just what Frank Paulone had expected upon arriving—with less than twenty dollars in his pocket and only one extra shirt and pair of pants in his suitcase—wasn't clear. In his eagerness to move forward, Frank had neither the time nor inclination to focus on what he was giving up at home in Bovino. He had just acted with the carefree abandonment of youth. But what did he have now in its place? Nothing but a dingy room in a lower Manhattan flophouse on Baxter Street! A run-down room in Little Italy was all he could afford after taking the first job he found digging ditches. The only compensation was the neighbors who spoke the same southern Italian dialect as he did.

Ditch digging was soon ditched, mercifully, when an opportunity to work in a barbershop became available. Not only was Frank's back aching from that kind of manual labor but his mind had protested even more. The drudgery of shifting dirt around was not what he anticipated doing for a living when he had set off for new horizons from across the sea. And when one day a fellow digger complained, with his face close to Frank's and using disrespectful anti-Italian slang, over a spadeful dirt from which a teaspoonful had fallen onto his new boots, Frank punched him in the nose. It cost him the job but there were plenty of other ones of the same kind waiting to be filled. Knowing a thing or two about barbering from a little practice with his uncle back home in Bovino, he had concluded this was the best path to follow to rid himself of ever wielding a pick and shovel again. There would always be a need for hair to be cut just as there was for ditches to be dug.

    Neither was living in a ghetto-like part of the city to his liking. So, as with many of his compatriots, he left New York City for the somewhat less congested urban pastures of New Jersey. A little more than a stone's throw away, it was almost as if Newark were just an arm of its larger neighbor. Distance and time from one city to the other would be quite manageable when choosing a work location. There was a large contingent of fellow Italian immigrants squeezed together in a single location in Newark as well, but he decided this time he would avoid living on one of those streets. And by the middle of 1899 he had found a small boarding house on Broome Street, in an ethnically mixed quarter of town. In fact, he would be living with a Jewish family over a mile away from Newark's own version of Little Italy. A totally different environment, but still close enough to walk to Seventh Avenue when he felt the need to mix with Italian-American culture. When he craved the best authentic Italian food to be found on either side of the Hudson River, he knew where to go.

Before he traded one state for the other, Frank Paulone had introduced himself to the owner of a barbershop in one of the busiest, prominent areas of New York City. The barbershop proprietor on Columbus Circle had then given him the start he needed working late evenings. He also took on a second job working in a factory to supplement an apprentice's income. But by the time he moved to Newark in 1899, he already had a year of constant work under his belt as a full-time barber and had put factory work behind him. He was now a full-fledged barber in every respect, experienced and capable for handling all types of hair, hot towel steamers, close shaves and other shop offerings. And best of all, he actually enjoyed it. For a short period of time he continued working at the same place in Manhattan after moving to Newark, until commuting for over an hour each way became too tedious. For a young man whose ambition was to someday have his own barbershop, he needed to forge ahead in his neck of the woods. His next goal was to become more familiar with the different parts of Newark and learn more about managing the business side of running an establishment. One thing for sure, moving to the western bank of the river did make a real difference: rents and food were cheaper and good opportunities were greater in New Jersey.

He also hoped a new environment would give a fresh start in helping to combat the loneliness he so often felt in Manhattan. It was not easy to be a stranger in such a large city like New York. Alone in that situation, of course he was not. But try as he might he had been unable to make meaningful friendships much less explore companionship with anyone of the fairer sex. And he still felt as if he was living on the borderline between passable existence and impending destitution when confronted with cost of living expenses in the city that never sleeps. At times all of this hit him like a punch in the gut and homesickness on a grand scale set in. But at other times he felt as if he was making progress and his earlier enthusiasm was restored. Fortunate the family he lived with seemed to grasp the mentality of a young man on his own, and Frank Paulone was most appreciative when they invited him to share at their table on Jewish holidays.

Because of their acceptance of an outsider and the kindness shown to him, he took it upon himself to learn a few words and phrases in Hebrew—in Yiddish to be more exact. Next-door acquaintances were always much surprised, quite impressed and very delighted when they found that Frank Paulone could "talk a little Jewish" after hearing a few words come out of his mouth. He had a good laugh when one of them said "We'll be seeing you soon at the *shul*, our synagogue, on the Sabbath!" And he was invited to attend the bar mitzvah of the son of his Newark family. In spite of his knack for learning dribs and drabs of a very foreign language, funnily enough he never lost his Italian accent when speaking English.

Finding new employment in a Newark barbershop was not difficult for Frank given the experience he already had in cutting hair. With a new job in the new city of his choice, he turned his attention to other areas, the most important of which, and most elusive so far, was meeting someone with whom to spend his free time, someone who might even be interested in a longer-term relationship. Could the right person exist in this rapidly growing city? And if she did, might she also become a suitable marriage partner in a place where most people strolled by without taking notice of one another?

Perhaps, because of his choice to live apart from those sharing his heritage, and because of his openness in accepting the ways of a different culture, Frank Paulone's matrimonial ambitions were meant to lie in a different direction.

Yet, he was aware of at least some of his shortcomings that could affect a relationship: he had a temper and a stubborn streak and was overly strict with himself at times. These traits would, of course, need to be subdued in developing a long-lasting bond with the right woman. To control them, not just temporarily mask them, became his goal going forward. He was soon to understand that this was far harder to do in reality. What could have been the beginning of budding romance with a girl named Lucy ended abruptly in a small café one evening after a supercilious waiter gave the impression of intentionally ignoring them. When the waiter was about to pass by them for the third time without deigning to cast a glance their way, Frank stuck out his arm to halt his progress. "Are we for some reason invisible to you? How about thinking of serving all of your customers? Isn't that what you've been paid to do? I have a good mind to speak to your boss," he remonstrated in a voice loud and angry enough to be heard by those at the other tables whose eyes then bore down upon the couple.

"I think I'd like to leave now," Lucy whispered to him as she rose from her seat after a few minutes. As soon as they were out the door, she followed-up by saying she was tired and wanted to go back to her home. His outburst for something so trivial was too much but she didn't dare to verbalize her thoughts. But if he couldn't handle an everyday occurrence in dining out without becoming excessively upset, then how would he handle more personal situations?

On another outing with a female Frank again was unable

to stop himself from overreacting. This time he and a new lady friend named Ellen had made it through a bite to eat without any drama. But after strolling though the recently opened West Side Park several blocks away and on their way back to their own neighborhood, Frank started to lead her around a corner. Ellen paused, "Let's go straight for another block or two before turning. The old streetlights on Rose Street are so beautiful at this time of the evening."

"But I always go down this street. It's the shortest and fastest way back," he answered as he began again to lead in his preferred direction. Ellen hesitated for another moment, but since he kept on walking she caught up to him. But all it took was this little gesture for never wishing to see him again. If someone whom you are just getting to know is obstinate over such a minor request, then that person can just follow his own path without her. Apparently, Frank still had a lot to learn when it came to women!

His failure to sustain relationships with women became a pattern of behavior over time. He knew he wasn't a bad person but he also knew he had problems with listening, compromise and number of other issues. Maybe it was going to be his lot to remain a bachelor permanently since his personality flaws were not conducive for matchmaking with these city ladies. And maybe his ways were just too set and old-fashioned to change. If that was the case, then so be it. And it was at that point that he became reconciled to a bachelor's life. He would no longer put himself in situations where he might meet with rejection. Working, eating his meals, shopping, taking care of the laundry, sleeping, the basics would have to suffice. A boring existence for many, but at least there would be no more awkwardness to endure. Swearing off normal activities too, there would be no more dances at clubs, no more striking up conversations after church service, no more strolling in the parks with an eye to the opposite sex. He would confine his socializing conversations to his barbershop customers. They at least listened and followed his directions when he told them to tilt their heads forward or to the side, or when he gave them hand mirror for a closer look. And the best thing, they came back again and again!

With the popularity of the safety bicycle increasing during the 1890s and into the early 1900s, Frank Paulone was among those who could not resist its allure. Both men and some women seemed to be zooming all over town. Frank could be at work in less than fifteen minutes when he rode his bike during the warmer part of the year. It was while cycling to work one day that he broke his own rules. He had turned his head to the side upon hearing another rider pull up to a halt alongside of him, both of them stopping because of a number of horse drawn vehicles crossing ahead. The baggy bloomers she wore down past her knees and long stockings covered her legs completely leaving only her feet looking as they normally would. On her head was perched a wide-brimmed hat pinned down in some manner so as not to fly off as she pedaled off. And below the hat was a face that returned Franks glance with a smile on it. They rode off at the same time. Two days later he thought he saw the same girl again. Not that many girls rode bicycles yet and he was sure it was her. This time it was Frank who rode up and stopped by her side at the intersection.

"I like the bicycle you're riding, and you look like you're getting good use out of it too. Aren't you the one I saw a couple of days ago riding on this same street?"

"I take this route often. But I think I recognize you as

well. A fellow bicycle enthusiast I see." With only time to exchange those few words, they pedaled off again. But when they met for a third time the following week, it felt like the moment to take advantage of the coincidence. Frank suggested if she had time, they might pull over to the side and properly introduce themselves. She did. The two things that stood out about her right off the bat as they walked together pushing their bicycles on the sidewalk were, first she was very pretty, and second she was very young, around eighteen or nineteen at most in his estimation. It crossed his mind that she must see him as belonging to a different, older generation. And with his thirtieth birthday approaching, they must be a good ten years apart.

Whatever the age discrepancy might be, there would certainly be no mention of it at first. Instead, conversation seemed to flow naturally, ending in an agreement to meet again at a local coffee shop—a fad which had become quite the thing to do—on Saturday morning. By then he was sure she did not have a drop of Italian blood in her. It was of no matter. He was accustomed to relating to all and sundry at the barbershop and there was his own living arrangement too. It pleased him that she spoke in precise English and had mannerisms very different from those from which he was accustomed to growing up. She had said her name was Lydia when they had first introduced themselves to each other. But at the coffee shop she had told him Liddie was the name she actually preferred and what most of her friends called her. As for her impressions of him, she could also tell by his thick accent—not by his appearance alone, for he was slim and tall with thick dark, wavy hair flowing over his forehead, fitting a profile in keeping with a number of Mediterranean ethnicities—that he was Italian.

"Were you born and raised in Newark, Liddie?"

"I was. Right here in good old Newark. My father was also born and raised here in New Jersey, however I have roots in nearby states as well. My mother was from New York. Not the city. She was from a small a small village called Willow, near the town of Woodstock on the fringe of the Catskill Mountains."

"For some reason I think I've heard of Woodstock."

"Since we still have family living there, I've visited a few times. It's sort of famous you know, because of the artists who stayed there while painting the surrounding countryside, the Hudson River Valley that is. These artists are part of the Hudson River School. Also, some of the more well to do city people have second homes there."

"You certainly don't have a typical Newark way of speaking. I guess it must be a bit of New York State mixed in that was from your mother."

"Well, I've been told it is sort of New England and upstate New York. My maternal ancestors were originally from Maine."

"Whatever the origins, I like how you pronounce your words. It must be a bit odd to you, though, because I still speak with a southern Italian accent even though I've been in America all of ten years now."

"Not at all. It suits your personality and I like yours too. Really, your voice is part of who you are. It's one of the reasons it's fun talking to you." As they spoke her body had inched a tad closer to his in the booth.

"For a while I felt a little ashamed of my accent. Eventually I stopped thinking about how it would be to not have it anymore since I couldn't lose it even if I wanted to. It's so much a part of me and I guess that's the way it's meant to be. I just don't have the gift or ear or whatever it takes for adopting the way other people speak when it comes to speaking in English. But I know of other Italians who you wouldn't be able to tell the difference from native English speakers. You'd have to go by all of the hand talking to get an inkling of their origins!"

"Just don't change yours, Frank. To me, it's special."

He didn't know exactly when it happened, but Frank realized one day that he hadn't thought much about Bovino or Italy in general lately. And he no longer had the hollow feeling that sometimes hit him when he came home from work and was alone for the rest of the evening. Even at the barbershop customers saw a shift from what was a cynical outlook on issues affecting most people to flashes of humor and laughter, the lighter side of life. The day he recognized this change in himself was the day he decided he needed to make sure it would stay that way. The reason for his greater contentment was obvious: he was head over heels in love with Liddie Fleming! Now if only she felt the same way. It seemed that she did but how could he know for sure? Because of her age, she hadn't turned nineteen yet, and lack of experience, their time together could easily be just an early adventure of many more to come in her mind. She may not at all be ready for a serious relationship, the kind possibly leading to marriage. There was only one way to find out, he would have ask her directly the next time they were alone together.

The pair of them stopped for a moment while strolling along the riverbank above to look into the depths of the Passaic River where it flows through downtown Newark.

"The river looks so calm now, Frank, it's hard to imagine two years ago it overflowed and flooded so many places. No one who lived here can forget how it raged right through the middle of Newark. And that wasn't the first time. The big flood of 1902 and even bigger one in 1903 were also really something to behold, I'm told. I don't remember them myself since I was too young. But for the recent one it seems like only yesterday when branches and logs and even parts of buildings and all sorts of other things went floating by like an express train. The newspapers said poorly constructed dwellings of the less fortunate were really hit hard."

"But look at the river now, so placid it's really like a big murky lake, so stagnant and giving off the most unpleasant odors on some days or on others moving so lazily to be imperceptible to the eye," Frank remarked.

"It's a pity that's the impression you get living in the city during this time of the year. But if you've ever been to any of the small towns upstream, not even that far away from Newark, you'd have a whole different image of it. The Passaic is really a thing of beauty when you see it winding through the countryside and before it reaches these factories near us where it changes for the worse," Liddie added, obviously letting herself be carried away by her local attachment.

Patiently waiting his chance then inhaling and exhaling a deep breath, it was now Frank's turn to do what he had promised himself to do: "But enough talking about our river for now. I've been thinking a lot about you and I and the future lately. You know how much I like being together with you. I'm hoping you feel the same way even though it's taken me so long to get around to saying it." She laid her arm on top of his as if to stop him. "Let me finish Liddie or I'll never get it out. I've been wondering what you would think about making it more permanent. I mean in marriage of course; that's what I'm trying to say but making such a bad job of it." He took out a handkerchief to mop a forehead beaded with perspiration with hands that were clammy.

"Are you sure about that? Do you really want to marry a New Jersey girl?" she giggled coyly. Saying nothing, he just nodded. But the thought she still might say no swept through his brain like a wildfire so he waited for her lips to form the words he wanted to hear.

Looking into his eyes, they came: "If you're ready, I'm ready. You know I love you, Frank, and for a long time now."

Gratified, he guided her over to a nearby bench to sit down. "Should I then talk to your father…soon then?"

"I don't know if that's the best thing to do. We shouldn't think of setting a date yet because I'm not sure how they'll react. Tell you what, I'll test the waters first by letting them know more about you and you must meet them too before we take the next step. You know, I'm the baby of the family and they have ideas of their own of what my future should be."

Lydia Fleming's understanding of her parents was all too precise, unhappily. They were explicit from the outset in not sharing their daughter's cross-cultural choice for a mate. Not only were they not thrilled when she stopped beating around the bush and told them that she and Frank were already thinking of a date, they were dumbfounded the idea had even crossed her mind. Why had she put them in a position to try to persuade her not marry a poor Italian immigrant whose future probably looked dim? When she countered their arguments by asking them to meet Frank to give themselves a chance to see what kind of person he really was like, they flatly refused. It was out of the question. They didn't want him in their house much less talking about a wedding with their daughter. A husband at her age would be ridiculous and a travesty at any rate. That fact alone should be enough to put an end to any more nonsense about a marriage.

It wasn't.

Her parents had misjudged with whom they were dealing; they should have known better. Lydia Fleming was a chip off the old block, as stubborn in her beliefs as her parents were in theirs. The couple patiently waited for two years while making repeated pleas to change their parents' minds before finally accepting they would never gain approval even if her age was no longer a factor. Frank and Lydia went forward and married anyway. It had seemed pointless to postpone it any longer when both of his parents were no longer living and hers holding firm in refusing to attend the ceremony.

Moreover, having shared a one bedroom flat for the past year, another reason had made an appearance, one that often kept them awake at night. The cart had come before the horse! A few friends had sufficed at the wedding along with Lydia's brother. Lewis, who at the risk of alienating his parents as his sister had done, had been steadfast in supporting his sister throughout her pre-marital days. After their marriage and the presence of a grandson Lydia's parents continued to hold fast to their disapproval and even took it to the next level. Further contact with their daughter and her husband was entirely over. Banished from her childhood home, Lydia and Frank were left on their own to face the challenges that lie ahead. Like pariahs, they were shunned by the only living parents between them; it was clear Lydia's father was the driving force. His choice for an occupation as a tough-minded police officer fit well with his rigid nature, a nature which had manifested itself in a stern and home life. They tried not to let it dampen their happiness, but the outcasts were living under the shadow of a dark cloud.

MEZZOGIORNO

Bagnoli Irpino, Campania and Southern Italy, 1900-1909

No longer known as the Kingdom of the Two Sicilies, or Magna Graecia even further back in time, the Mezzogiorno at the turn of the 20th century may not have been in shambles but was pretty close to it. Benefits derived from carving out an Italian nation some forty years before from a group of disparate states had failed to materialize, according to many southerners. Southern Italy, the land of the strong "midday sun", was sorely in need of new approach to satisfy its inhabitants. And it was never more apparent when additional restrictions of civil liberties by a succession of prime ministers drifted into the small inland towns of Campania and Puglia.

But passing new laws to suppress unionism and take away other freedoms soon backfired and led to the defeat of the incumbent government in the election of 1900. The outcome was a major reversal in permitting a new form of radical syndicalism, spearheaded this time by socialist groups that were allowed to move forward with little restraint. While few of the townspeople in Bagnoli and Bovino were able to participate in the election—the right to vote was reserved for the male middle class and above, and not the so-called peasantry—the numbers from other backwater places when added together with the rest of the country was sufficient to induce a wave of hopeful change after years of repressive authoritarian rule.

Then, only a month later, came the shocking news that Italian King Umberto had been assassinated. Just when the future was looking brighter with a new government in place would his murder create renewed strife and another reversal of freedoms for the common man? Fortunately, that was not the case. The movement towards a more liberal Italy brought forward by the recently elected prime minister was actually supported by the new king as well. Victor Emanuel III, the son of Umberto, was a man who also advocated for a return to a constitutional style of governing and greater freedoms instead of the opposite.

Fresh support for trade union activity, educational investment, better wages, tax reduction for agricultural goods, improved infrastructure in terms of roads and irrigation and a revival of cooperatives, all of these changes, although still more evident in the North, reverberated through parts of the South as well. Even greater availability of quinine to treat malaria for all parts of country was part of the new direction! But along with these social reforms that a more liberal leadership brought forth to address the concerns of a disgruntled populace came growing pressure to comply with tenants espoused by Socialists, Marxists, revolutionary syndicalism, and worker ownership groups even in the southern Italian countryside. There was an expectation that even rural bumpkins must realize it was in their own self-interest to join the economic swing towards organized labor, for instance. And if they didn't, well then there was always the use of good old-fashioned persuasion tactics.

Ten year old Michelino Conte saw two men approach his father one evening in front of their home in Bagnoli Irpino, men whom he had never seen before, and he immediately sensed something unusual was taking place. The startled look on Antonio Conte's face confirmed his son's suspicions. Michelino watched his father intently as an interchange between the three men continued for at least ten minutes. Neither a hint of a smile nor a whisper of a guffaw came from these men with serious sounding voices but the typical hand gestures were much more animated than usual, indicating an exchange running at a high emotional level. The only thing he clearly picked up as the pair of visitors walked away was that one of them said they would be back again to see his father in a few days. Antonio paced back in forth in front of their garden wall for a few minutes then entered his home again.

As soon as he passed through the door Maria saw that something was wrong with her husband, as if he had been laboring hard all day long and was sore all over, which she knew wasn't the case.

"Come here, Antonio, and sit down. You look like one of our goats kicked you in that sore knee of yours. What's the matter?" Michelino had followed right behind his father and his ears perked up in thinking something important was about to be said.

"You won't believe it. Those two men I was just talking to are from one of those pushy trade unions. They want me and others in town to try and bring the farmers together to join their cause."

"What! Those city radicals are bothering poor villagers in the countryside now with their crazy ideas? Maria exclaimed with fire in her eyes. "What are they thinking? Why can't they just leave us be, Antonio?"

"That's the problem. They think rural folk like us don't know what's going on in the cities and the rest of the country. And they look at dull farmers as easy marks for being convinced by the promises these unionists make for a better life ahead if we join with them. But what they really want is to let their leaders control our work and money by benefitting from the sweat off our brows. They think we've been going about our lives with blinders and just waiting for their superior guidance to show us the right way forward."

"They really have some nerve coming here. I hope you told them to take their socialist ideas elsewhere. Let them try using their kind of persuasiveness in the North where these notions originated in the first place. There are enough poor people there too, so see how far that gets them. How dare they try to shove their ideas down our throats!" Michelino Conte had never seen his mother quite so upset before.

"Calm down, Maria. It's not that we should be totally against all trade union organization here; it will probably have to reach some level of acceptance someday. But their ideas are too extreme for our small town when they start talking about the oppression of capitalism, production units and the power of strikes before even knowing anything about us. We're not as naïve and slow-witted as they think we are. What's happening in Italy, France and other countries is not only news made for them to hear. It's on the tongues of so-called unsophisticated folks like us as well. We've survived for centuries without their wisdom and we will survive for centuries more if need be."

The two syndicalists did return to Bagnoli as promised,

convinced that persistence would pay dividends once there were a greater number of the townspeople prepared to accept their notion of labor relations; Antonio and others needed to spread the word. They were, however, soon to be disappointed. Antonio had indeed talked to others while not holding back his own personal views. The reaction was much alike in rejecting any type of radical organization. It wasn't long before the unionists resorted to a more threatening manner to get what they wanted once they had learned of the community's negative response. There could be very disadvantageous consequences for local shops and farmers, and even for shepherds roving the hills, should they refuse to listen carefully to their fair proposal. The use of bullying tactics got nowhere with townspeople who were prepared to act with one voice to dismiss changes too militant for them to accept. It was true that most of the villagers were engaged in similar agricultural work, but they were diversified enough in location and crops to not be lumped together under the umbrella of a single trade union, especially one with revolutionary tendencies.

The two men did not leave graciously; menacingly, they warned others would be coming to "better educate" them in the benefits of joining hands together. However, these contemptible remarks failed to shift attitudes. In the end it was their future livelihood that was at stake no matter how paltry it seemed to know-it-all city dwellers. And they were determined that trade union thuggery would get nowhere with them. At any rate families in the town were so intertwined through marriage they had already formed their own village-like union of sorts!

Yet, the encounter with urban unionists had a lasting

effect in the minds of Bagnoli men and women; it was not a movement that would vanish of itself in time. For two years they heard nothing more and there were no further visits. Then, in 1903, the Conte family and others underwent renewed pressure to yield to the new wave of unionization that had reached the rural parts of the South. When they heard from kin in Puglia that many there were becoming members of the *Federterra*, they knew the writing was on the wall. The *braccianti* in Bovino now seemed keen on becoming part of the Federation of Agricultural Labourers, not only a handful of day laborers but in droves. Clearly, northern Italian organizations had managed to successfully infiltrate their southeastern neighbors as well.

Like in Bagnoli, there had been resistance to organizing in Bovino at first. But unionist presence had long had a foothold in the stretch of coastal towns between Bari and Brindisi and even inland in Foggia as well. It was inevitable there would be a push deeper into rural areas. And this process was sped up and brought home after two "accidents" hit businesses in Bovino following an unsuccessful bid by union representatives to make their point. Even the most independent thinking citizens became worried, fearful, there would be a third or a fourth business attacked if they chose to continue to buck the rising union tide. Where could they look for support if they did? They were not from Foggia and the closest coastal cities already deeply mired in unionization themselves.

For Maria Michela Paulone, with neither a son nor husband for support, it was time to submit. Francesantonio had left their household to make a new life in America almost ten years ago and her husband had died another ten years before that; she had managed to stay strong, carrying on alone. But she never missed them more than when the small Paulone shop—selling olive oil, jars of olives, herbs and spices, condiments, table linen and other items—in town became the second "accident" in autumn of 1905. Windows smashed and shelves and display stands toppled over, there would be much clean-up work to be done to become operational again. She would roll up her sleeves and do it by herself if necessary even though it would be felt in every one of seventy year old bones. But helping hands soon arrived, sweeping and mopping floors, removing broken glass jars and their wasted contents, repairing damaged shelving and restocking. It wasn't long before the shop was open again for business without first replacing a missing front window.

Maria Michela and her fellow citizens had enough. They were ready to appease the labor movement in order to restore peace to their town. Violence had delivered the message loud and clear. It was true that Socialist backed unions were more common and widespread in Puglia anyway. But in considering partnerships at communal meetings citizens had tended to look at Catholic associations before anything else. Catholic associations that had taken a strong hold in the North were becoming more prevalent in the South of late as well. The Catholic movement, unlike the Federterra's ties with the Socialist party emphasizing collective ownership, was a more acceptable agreement, suited to the very religious villages bordering the Apennine range. Nevertheless, given the recent events, listening more constructively and perhaps accepting unionization in some form might satisfy demands for compliance enough to avoid additional troubling incidents. And some form of unionization at this juncture might actually be a catalyst for changing things economically to slow leakage of the local population. Immigration to the Americas from both northern and southern Italy, the non-return of some of the migrants who went for seasonal work in Switzerland, France and Germany and internal migration to Italian industrial cities had never ceased depleting the local work force. Too many sons, like her Franco, had abandoned their homeland, gone forever.

***

Word soon reached Bagnoli from Bovino that their town had acceded to partial unionization. It was time. Day laborers, the largest constituency in Bagnoli, quickly met and agitated to do the same and were followed shortly by tenant farmers and small land owners. Shop proprietors were still more reluctant to join organized labor, failing to see what advantages it could bring to their business profits other than buying protection from intimidation. Hopefully, having only agricultural workers join their ranks would be enough to satisfy union zealotry.

At least that's what two bosom buddies thought when they talked about the big change. Raffaele and Angelo, born a month apart in 1875, bore the same surname of Conte. Although they were not first cousins and related by more distant ancestors, each one came from a long-established branch of the Conte family. Sharing a common name and age had resulted in a deep friendship which grew even more so when they had sat next each other as classmates in school. But as strong as their friendship was it wasn't enough to keep them from intense competiveness when it came to sports or anything else. At times winning took precedence, and even now as adults of nearly thirty, the one-upmanship mentality continued unabated. Angelo Conte, the son of Alfonso and Maria Teresa, had only yesterday placed another wager with the son of Antonio and Maria. It didn't take much of an excuse to make a bet, and this time it was over the prospect of a future marriage between Angelo's sister, Antonia, and Raffaele's brother, Michelino, siblings both younger than themselves.

Angelo was betting that as soon as Antonia and Michelino reached the age of majority they would marry. From his sister's behavior towards Michelino and vice versa, it was easy to tell the two teenagers were struggling even to wait until they were old enough. Raffaele Conte, on the other hand, had his reasons why he didn't think this to be likely. He had placed his money on believing they would postpone marriage for at least a year or two and marry in their early twenties. He felt confident he would win on this occasion but wasn't about to reveal what his reasons were to anybody.

Only a few days ago he had teased his brother about how much he seemed "in love" with Antonia. Michelino had immediately taken exception to any meddling in his personal life. He didn't deny that Antonia was a good "friend" but that's where it stood at the moment. Moreover, if Raffaele were to start saying anything about Antonia and him there would be a severe price to pay. Albeit the older than Michelino, Raffaele knew better than to question Michelino's words when it came to the threat of retribution. Michelino, the serious one of eight children, would not hold back if interfered with. He was not completely devoid of a sense of humor, but he would certainly not endure any nonsense from Raffaele.

Setting aside for now their little wager on marriage prediction, the two friends were more concerned about doing whatever it would take to keep their families out of the clutches of forced union participation. A poster on the community board outside the mayor's office announced another meeting on unions in the evening after work the following day. Their two fathers owned and managed shops in Bagnoli and they were worried whatever the outcome. Raffaele had rallied all of his brothers and sisters to attend, Irene for sure since she was the most fervent in leading their cause. Angelo's five sisters would be a powerful female force although some of them were already married with family priorities.

"We must give up everything else to be there. If we don't, a decision will be made without our voices being heard," Irene urged Raffaele that evening. Her words delivered more as a command—not unlike bossiness—rather than a suggestion were unneeded for she was preaching to the choir. Family members were primed and ready to give their opinion and lend whatever assistance they could when a decision was made.

"Don't fret, Irene, we all will be there. There will not be any Contes that would miss having their say this time around. We'll all meet at the square at seven o'clock and go as one group to the hall."

Whether or not family presence en masse would have influenced town councilors enough to sway any decisions on what course to take became moot at around five-twenty early the next morning. In the afternoon of the December 28th 1908, only three days after the festivities of Christmas had mostly shifted to business, news of a massive earthquake further south had reached Bagnoli. This was no small tremor, the kind that regularly happened in southern Italy, although it seemed that way to those in Bagnoli who had only felt a slight shaking. Reporting told of a very powerful quake centered in the Straits of Messina, the sea between Sicily and the southernmost mainland region of Calabria. Destruction had been on a large scale and a tidal wave—or tsunami as the Japanese had recently labeled it—had quickly ensued. Thousands of lives were reported to be in jeopardy in the coastal cities of Messina in Sicily and Reggio in Calabria. Their own inland community some two hundred and seventy-five miles from the epicenter had been spared this time.

The town meeting was cancelled as locals and all attention focused on the aftermath which continued to be updated throughout the day and those that followed. The Contes and most of the other families in Bagnoli switched to organizing what they could do to support their southern brothers in need. Then the news became even more dire two days later: near total destruction of cities and tens of thousands dead. National and international aid was on its way but before it could be organized and distributed the citizens of Bagnoli Irpino would do as much as they could to help. Losing momentum, trade unionization, which had been on the cusp of making a breakthrough in Bagnoli, looked to have lost its urgency. Perhaps a balance of some sort could be struck in the coming year.

RESIGNATION

Bagnoli Irpino, Italy & Ohio, U.S.A., January 1907-September 1909

In 1907 Michelino Conte had voyaged to America on board the Cedric with Antoniella, a sister as adventurous as himself, and her husband Aniello Clemente. Antoniella and Aniello had made their decision and were immigrating for good while Michelino travelled with them on what could be called an exploratory mission. Only sixteen years old, this Italiano already had big ideas in his head. But there was one thing left hanging in the air that must be tackled before he left on a trip across the waters. Michelino had developed a serious but quietly kept interest in one of the local girls in their small town. Quiet because he wanted to avoid having his feelings for her talked about in Bagnoli for two reasons: first, he wasn't at all sure how she would respond when he told her he wanted it to become a serious relationship; and secondly because of the possibility that one of the other boys in town, who might already have his eye on her, would interfere with his plans by beginning to court Antonia before he did.

About to declare his intentions to her several times, he had always backed out. But the pressure had mounted with the forthcoming departure to America with his sister and her husband nearly at hand. It was really now or never. Finally, he had screwed up his courage and blurted out rather clumsily how he felt when they were taking a walk near the cemetery in the evening. He hoped she hadn't noticed the trembling from fear of rejection. But when she slipped her hand into his very moist one he knew she approved in a much calmer manner than his own. All of his anxieties melted away when she tilted her head to one side to look into his eyes with her own of the softest brown color he could imagine.

"It's about time you put into words what I could tell you had on your mind for so long, you ninny. I was beginning to think you'd never get around to it."

"It wasn't that easy, Antonia; so much depended upon your reaction. I wanted it to be only one way of course, but wasn't at all sure it would be. But now you've given me what I wished for."

"You should know now it's what I've wanted too. So let's put both of our minds at ease."

Now nothing needed to be kept quiet, much less a secret, any longer. Eyes and ears everywhere in Bagnoli could take satisfaction in not having to resort to speculation with their relationship out in the open. But many wondered why Michelino Conte would choose to leave home at a time when his sights were set on Antonia with marriage likely in a few years. They had failed to take into consideration it was exactly because he had won the promise of the girl of his dreams that he had decided to travel at this time of his life. That they were still too young to marry was a given. This had been made crystal clear when Antonia's parents put their foot down to their fifteen year old daughter even entertaining the thought of marriage before reaching her twentieth birthday. So, if they must bide their time anyhow, why not use the waiting time in taking advantage of his sister's plans to leave Italy and tag along with her and her husband.

    The Clementes would act as his guardians so that Michelino would be able to enter the country, the country in which Antonia might even agree to seeking their future together. It would be a golden opportunity to see firsthand what life was like in advance of making such a momentous decision. If he was fortunate enough, he might even get a head start by working, possibly even at a job he could return to after they married. Why not test the waters in America when the prospects at home in Bagnoli and the rest of southern Italy seemed so limited? And what did Michelino Conte, the son of a farm laborer, have to lose anyway? It was a chance to give himself a leg up in learning the lay of the land before returning to Bagnoli afterwards. And if the eager teenager was able to sample the economic security of a livable income in America before marriage, then all the more reason to give it a go. Looking at it from the perspective of an experiment in making adjustments to unfamiliar surroundings in advance, it could be very useful in the future. And, if it worked out as he thought it would, Michelino would return to Antonia, the girl who never left his thoughts, to see if she too could be convinced that living in America was the right thing to do.

    Steadfastly plowing through waters less turbulent than anticipated for a winter voyage of thirteen days, the Cedric proved to be a reliable vessel. There were only a few rough days he would gladly forget about even though they had sailed from Naples on the 30th of January and arrived at the port of New York on February 11th. All three of them passed customs inspection routines with flying colors—Michelino the only one whose status was marked down as **Non immigrant alien**. But they had little time to enjoy their first taste of American life in the famous city since within a few hours they were travelling westward and on to Ohio, their final destination. Brier Hill, a neighborhood of Youngstown where other relatives lived, would be the city in which Michelino would take up residence. As for his chaperones, after dropping Michelino off they would carry on to Niles about ten miles away. A cousin had guaranteed Aniello Clemente a job working at the Niles Fire Brick Company. He would be joining a good many others at the factory who had been recruited from Bagnoli Irpino specifically and elsewhere in the province of Avellino.

The Clemente's settled in quickly to their new home while Michelino, left to fend for himself except for weekend visits to Niles, tried to make do as best he could. His youth had proved to be a handicap more than he had expected in getting started. No matter how much effort or what angle he took to find a job, the obstacles of underage and language were there to confront him. He had picked up a smattering of English as the months passed by but not enough to fit in. Refusals of employment piled up and began to crush his ambition, which in turn brought on despondency for the first time in his life, eventually resulting in a different Michelino Conte, one who wished he had never left Italy.

Time did not stand still in 1908, and with his illusions of a quick and easy path to stable economic circumstances all but vanished, he was finally able to put together a series of short-term jobs after turning seventeen in January. Had he made progress and the promised land was finally coming true now that he had passed the one year anniversary from docking in New York? It seemed that way but work was not steady enough to make any headway fast. And it was still another two years before Michelino had sufficient finances to book passage back to Italy. He had undergone a long and drawn out wake-up call by that time and returned as a man with the wind taken out of his sails.

Although demoralized, he also was a man now, grown up and with a new appreciation for the real world. Sure as the Rock of Gibraltar he had passed going and coming back, Antonia was there waiting for him and even lovelier than when he had left. For the three years apart he had relied on letters that never came frequently enough and a few photos that occasionally came with them. None of the pictures had done justice to the person standing there before him. Only a few hours were needed before the rust of absence had been rubbed away and it was like he never had left. And it was soon apparent that, if anything, the distance and time apart had made them even more ready to share a life together.

Youngest of a large family, Antonia still lived with her parents. But she was not unprepared for what to expect at the altar when her turn came, for she had watched the marriages of two of her sisters. But there would be plenty of time before it was her time to walk down the aisle. Michelino had just returned and they would be able to get to know each other better. And neither her parents nor Michelino's were about to allow anything more than that; two young and underage people may or may not still feel the same way a couple of years later when they were actually old enough to walk down the aisle.

***

Earthquakes were a fact of life if you lived in Campania and they were never taken for granted. Even so, they were infrequent enough that the fear of their power felt new again each time one occurred. It was actually a good thing, when you thought about it, for who would want to live every minute of their lives worrying if the next one was about to hit. The scientific-minded had their reasons for the shaking of land, but it wasn't Aristotle's winds blowing within the earth theory. The early scientist was right in many things, but hadn't been aware of fault lines. In addition to scientists there were those who searched for answers in the more mystical side of the universe. On the front page of the Wednesday 8th of June 1910 edition of the New York Times newspaper the following article appeared:

> "A report received from Avellino describes the narrow escape from death at the hands of a superstitious mob of a party of American clergymen who happened to be in the province when the earthquake occurred. Some of the panic-stricken people believed that the calamity was due to the presence of the clergymen and attacked them with the avowed purpose of hanging them.
> Fortunately the police learned of the assault and rescued the ministers, afterwards escorting them to a safe distance from the village."

Death and destruction were later categorized to be moderate in the city of Avellino itself. Nevertheless, the same newspaper article also reported that in one provincial town the "wildest confusion prevailed" and many looked for solace in asking for mercy from the Almighty, a request in conformity with local religious beliefs. Bagnoli had suffered no consequences itself, yet the ten seconds of rumbling had put its citizens on edge as well. Concern became even more telling after discovering many towns in the province had fared badly. This comparatively modest quake was still a stark reminder of the massive one in 1908 only two years earlier. Its greater magnitude had led to the deaths of thousands on the southern mainland and in Sicily. But with each quake, large or small, a lesson needed to be learned: never become complacent in thinking that a catastrophe can't happen again and happen soon and right on your own doorstep!

    Citizens were also worried over the repetitive news of another family member lost to the lure of a better life elsewhere. Unable to break the lock of subsistence living, and despite close family ties, the youth of Bagnoli families—more often than not young men—were saying goodbye to their homes. Many stayed within the country, migrating to northern Italy, but an alarming number had emigrated from the shores of Italy to America and elsewhere. The numbers were actually staggering for a small country; during the ten years from 1900 to 1910 over two million had left countrywide, more than one departing for every seventeen counted in the turn of the century census. And the exodus didn't appear to be slackening, just the opposite, it was predicted to increase if anything.

    For every one of the locals leaving Bagnoli a trail of memories was left in their wake, memories that were shared by others who had identical reasons for believing life across the sea might be better than the one they were living today. Maybe it was high time to also throw caution to the wind, to board a ship and cross the seas to America. But for every individual feeling the urge for change there was another one who felt the consequences of emigration just as acutely. These were the families who saw a member disappear into the void. A few would return but the great majority would not. When Antonia Conte's younger sister had left two years before it was like a dagger in her heart. Of her six sisters and one brother, Maria Concetta was the one closest to her. It was painful to see how her parents suffered to see her leave the Conte family fold. But there had been no stopping her for she was going to join the man to whom she considered herself betrothed. No doubt Joseph Deloss was a good man and she would be happy with him; that was their only consolation. But Antonia Conte swore to herself to never let it happen again. She would do her utmost to dissuade her other siblings from taking the same leap of fate. Thankfully, her cousin and the man she had set her heart on marrying now had his feet replanted firmly on Campania soil. Michelino Conte had his little adventure overseas would be staying put.

Looming war against the Turks was another factor influencing their marital plans. The Italian government was convinced that Libya—the enormous block of land just across the Mediterranean Sea from the boot of the Italian mainland and Sicily—was much more in Italy's backyard rather than the distant Ottoman Empire. The Italian government's quest to take possession of the territory had been simmering since 1908 and even earlier. Indeed, investments in industry and property predicated on the idea Libya would one day belong to Italy had already been allocated. Various parties and even, albeit reluctantly, the Italian Prime Minister himself had expressed an interest in staging an invasion to seize part of the territory under the pretense of mineral and water resources acquisition. More practically, though, the reasons involved a desire to show progress after years of speculation and discussions about this land across the water. It would be viewed as a sign of weakness if the government let it slip through their fingers again.

 The threat that an invasion could become a reality was keeping local males on edge in Bagnoli, as it did with the rest of the country too. An armed force must be assembled to attain such an objective. Would Michelino be called up to serve the cause? The likelihood that it might happen and soon would definitely play a critical role in any decision about Michelino and Antonia's future. One thing that was certain wresting control from the Ottomans of such a large chunk of land on another continent would not be the easy undertaking Prime Minister Giolitti and his cronies promised in their lust for Italian colonization. It never was when the land belonged to the local population and their future was at stake. Maybe it was time for this once peace-loving, now war-mongering leader—who really had set his sights on annexing the smaller northwestern sector of Tripolitania and the much larger Cyrenaica eastern half of Libya—to be relieved of his authority; ten years of uneven rule was more than enough!

BREAKDOWN

Newark, New Jersey, June 1903-1910

Her maiden name of Fleming was now a thing of the past and nearly unmentionable because of its negative connotation to her estranged parents. Newlyweds, Frank and Lydia Paulone had moved to a larger apartment on the same block of Frank's old Broome Street flat shortly after their wedding ceremony in 1905. They had their reasons for needing another bedroom. The small size of Frank's former flat on the same street in which Lydia had joined him well over a year before had clearly become an issue. They had been living there together before they were officially wedded in order to escape her parents' objections. Back in 1903, while on their way to a local café for a Saturday evening meal, the news of a forthcoming event was mentioned by Lydia.

"Now may not be the right moment to bring this up, but then I'm not sure there's ever a good time for saying what I have to say. We've been living together for such a short time without being married yet sometimes things happen more quickly than expected. They take their own course rather than depending on the normal order society usually recognizes." She paused for a moment while Frank's eyes grew bigger and the creases on his forehead deepened. Suddenly, she was afraid to carry on if the face suddenly drenched of color and pinched with worry was indicative of what his reaction would be.

"I guess maybe I better not go on about what I was going to say since…" He stopped her in midstream.

"I'm sorry, Liddie, for interrupting you. You have something important on your mind I can see. It's just that so many thoughts are in my brain at the moment. Have you come down with something serious and something untreatable, some deadly disease? Please tell me you haven't", he pleaded "But if you are ill we'll fight it together till you are perfect again, just like you've always been to me."

"No, it's nothing like that, Frank. Don't worry yourself. But it's I who should be sorry for starting up a conversation in such a way that frightens the person I'm closest to in the world. I should have thought more about what I was going to say before I began. But no, I am quite well—rather I should say both of us are quite well as far as that goes."

It took a few seconds for what she said to sink in. And when it did he tried to talk but emotions choked back the words. Another full thirty seconds went by before regaining his composure; not long in the scheme of life but for Lydia it was like an eternity. "What are you saying, Liddie? Are you telling me what I think you are?"

"I am. Yes I am."

"Then we are on our way to…to starting a family? Already?" he stammered out.

"Who thought it would happen so soon but it has. I realize it must be a shock. It was for to me too when I visited the doctor. And I hope it doesn't overwhelm you since we haven't even said our vows yet. Do you think that matters?"

"Overwhelming it is, yes but in the best possible way. This is

God working! Beginning a family with lots of kids to come is what I've always dreamed of happening. Some will look askance at us marriage certificate or not. It's not their business anyway. But this is what I think we should do. Let's just pray things go smoothly and worry about our wedding later. Possibly we can keep the date we had already planned, but if that doesn't work we'll set a new one," his Catholic enthusiasm triumphing over any of the more conservative Protestant misgivings she might have. "And like I said a few moments ago, let's make this child number one of many more to follow."

It was as if the weight of the Statue of Liberty had been lifted off her back. It was her turn to become speechless as she wiped tiny drops of perspiration away with the back of her hand that had dotted the area above her upper lip. Then Lydia too composed herself. Her momentous news had passed the relationship test. Hearing his words of happiness was a blessing she would never forget. At the moment they played through her head like a much loved tune hummed over and over again.

A change to the original marriage date in 1904 did become necessary and it was reset for a later date. May 8th 1905, a Monday, was the new date decided upon. Foregoing Frank's Italian tradition of a Sunday wedding was disappointing to him but it was convenient. The birth of their son Daniel Paulone a year and a half earlier in the autumn of 1903 had not been an easy one. Lydia's recovery from a lengthy ordeal had stretched from weeks into months. A few more months of waiting before tying the knot didn't really matter to the friends they could count on to be in their corner whatever date was chosen. Good friends understood. What mattered to Frank was that his wife and son were both healthy, and they had found a date on which they could all come together for a small ceremony before the Justice of the Peace down on Oliver Street in Newark.

Lydia announced to her husband that she was again in a family way a little over a year after their marriage. It looked like Frank Paulone's vision of a larger family was becoming a reality with a delivery expected sometime early in 1907. And that's why they were moving. It would be impossible to squeeze a fourth person into the single bedroom flat the three of them now shared. But how to afford it on a barber's salary that was barely enough to meet their current rent was another question. Wracking their brains for answers they had come up empty so far. All that changed with a stroke of good fortune.

One of the enjoyments and advantages of his occupation was the social contact he had with his clientele. Talking to clients often went beyond the weather and into health issues, financial difficulties, employer problems, family situations, mother-in-laws and all matter of other topics; except politics and religion which were taboo. With repeat customers nearly nothing was off limits when the door opened and the chair filled. Cutting hair was a ticket to breaking down barriers. A sense of trust was important as soon as the cape and collar was fastened and the scissors started snipping. When Frank had mentioned to Luigi Santi—an old friend as well as well as a regular patron—about the cramped living predicament in his small flat, Luigi recalled what another friend had said about finding the right tenant for renting his property. A short stay family, apparently intent on destruction, had soured the friend from advertising again without careful investigation.

Luigi was almost certain the owner would welcome receiving a personal recommendation, especially if Frank and he went together for an introduction. When they did meet you could feel the tension in the air at first. Everyone was nervous but the awkwardness grew even more when there was no offer to see the inside of the apartment. Instead, the owner gave Frank the once over with a critical eye and had asked him a bevy of questions about employment, pets, late night habits, smoking, family members and rental duration intentions until he apparently felt satisfied enough, all while standing out front. It was only then that he agreed to show them the inside. It was almost twice the size of the one in which Frank's family currently lived, and of course Frank was thrilled over the prospect. He was even more thrilled when the owner offered the flat at a reasonable and manageable monthly amount. No reflection was necessary. Less than ten minutes away, and literally just down the block from where they now lived on Broome Street, the Paulones' had found a new home for their soon to be enlarged family.

Things were going well during the months preceding his wife's deliverance of a second baby. Lydia had overcome a short period of morning sickness and was back to feeling her old self again. Frank had done a masterful job in orchestrating their move to their very roomy new residence. The barbershop was doing well too. An influx of population in Newark in general had resulted in a steady increase in business. All good things save for Lydia's parents who continued to maintain their distance. The young couple just shook their heads and rolled their eyes in astonishment when it crossed their minds these days, which it seldom did. So it was with a feeling of prosperity on many levels the day they welcomed James Paulone, another boy, to their family in January 1905. A brother for Daniel would give him a playmate in the years ahead although their age difference might make him more like mentor.

The first six days had passed normally after the birth and they were getting used to a new routine again. But in the middle of the seventh night Lydia and Frank were awakened only an hour or so after going to bed by a strange sound coming from their infant's cot. Not the usual crying for a feeding but it sounded like a combination of gurgling and moaning. What they saw was a tiny body shaking all over. Lydia immediately picked him up and held him close to her body to comfort him. Then she looked up at her husband with huge question marks in her eyes.

"What is it, Liddie? What's going on?" Frank's asked in reading her mind. She just shrugged her shoulders in despair while gently rocking him and pacing back and forth. His trembling body had quieted enough after ten minutes for Lydia to collect herself and put a few coherent words together.

"Neither of us has a clue of what this means. But it's not good and we need to get the doctor here now. Whatever's caused this we can't just hope it's going to get better. We need to know more about what just happened and what we should do about it." Frank could only blink his agreement.

"I'm on my way", he whispered as he pulled a pair of trousers over his pajama bottoms, tied his shoes tightly and threw a heavy coat over his shoulders. The Paulones were not yet part of the surge in telephone installations that had begun at the turn of the century, or contacting the doctor might only have required a quick call instead of a visit from Frank on foot. Little did they know that in five years telephones would be commonplace for the several million who could afford them.

West Kinney Street was only just around the corner and Frank sprinted with all he had to reach the doctor's residence; yet he wished he could have gone even faster. With each step he grew more frustrated that he wasn't already there. "Where is it? I should be able to see there by now. It can't be much further," he kept saying to himself. Finally he arrived and pounded noisily on the doctor's door. It was opened by an alert, older gentleman, who looked as if being awoken during sleeping hours was an everyday occurrence. He listened intently to Frank's description of the symptoms while he was still catching his breath from running all the way.

"I'll get my coat then let's get going," was all he said.

It had taken less than a handful of minutes before the doctor was out the door and the two of them were making the return trip to the Paulone home.

What they encountered when they got there was not a pretty sight: Lydia still holding their child was softly weeping. As distraught as she still was she was able to tell them what had gone on since Frank had left. The violent shaking had resumed than had suddenly subsided just as quickly again. Her mind had immediately flown to the worst, but she could see their baby was still breathing. His resumption to calmness, or numbness, had been almost as scary to her as the uncontrolled trembling. The doctor asked Lydia to lie him down in his cot then proceeded to examine James. He confirmed that from all of the physical signs he could detect, the infant seemed now to be normal. But then his diagnosis of convulsions for what possibly had taken place set the parents on edge again. To ease their anxiety, he explained that convulsions were similar to seizures but not exactly identical. Albeit frightening to witness, convulsions seldom led to fatality and often they were only a one-time occurrence, especially in a newborn. The important thing to do should there be another episode was to make sure the child continued to breathe by keeping air passages unblocked, and to stay calm. Obviously, Lydia's maternal instincts had already led her to doing the right thing. After the doctor had left, Frank and Lydia hugged each other for so long it was as if they would never let go.

Words from the physician's had reassured them for the moment, and maybe permanently if it had truly been a single occurrence never to be repeated again. But memories of the helplessness they felt would stay forever in their minds. But all wishful thinking evaporated when little James Paulone went into convulsions a second time seven months later. Lydia, at home and alone with him, at least felt a little better prepared to deal with it this time. She followed the doctor's directions and checked to be sure his air passages were open then lifted him into her arms to still the trembling child with more confidence than before. But this time it seemed the shaking was even more violent and went on longer. She couldn't leave her infant and run to fetch the doctor again so she just continued to hold and talk to him, praying that the convulsions would end. They did but not in the way anyone would have wanted. Whatever the cause, the severity of this seizure had been too much and their and their son passed away. Death wasn't supposed to happen with convulsions. Hadn't the doctor almost promised that? But James was gone and their grief beyond description.

The loss of their second-born never left them but did become less present in their minds during the ensuing months. Then Lydia fell pregnant for a third time a year after their second son's death and the memories flooded back with a vengeance. The fear that it could happen all over again with the next birth played constantly in their thoughts. They told themselves it was irrational since first son Daniel had never exhibited signs of the affliction. Still it could happen again, it could. And logic was completely in shatters when a third son entered the world in March 1907. Lydia and Frank were on pins and needles all through the first months of his existence, and it was if the earth had ended when he caught his first common cold. They were only able to rest a little easier in thinking he was relatively safe after celebrating his one year birthday healthy and happy.

For the better portion of these early months their son was simply referred to as "the baby". This was not unintentional. Lydia and Frank wanted to be confident the name they had in store for him would endure this time, for it was the same name they had chosen previously. Although they never spoke of it in such a manner, it was as if the spirit of the son who had died would be become part of one who lived. In using the name of James again two souls and two memories would be embodied in one. Repeating the use of the name was not something they would mention to others and they swore to each other that it would be their secret, belonging to them and to them only. Not even would their new son, who woke up each morning to greet another day, be told of his namesake's brief existence.

***

Newark, New Jersey, June 1910-1915

Expansion of the Paulone family did not come to an end with the birth of their third son. For a while they thought it might be so. But all that changed in October of 1911 when Mildred Paulone became the new light in her father's eyes A fourth child had been fated to wait over four years before she arrived on the scene. They had hoped for a girl to put some balance in a male-dominated household and her birth had been just two weeks shy of eight years since Daniel's, their first child. Ecstatic as they were over a daughter in the family, Frank had the audacity to tell his wife that it was never too early to begin planning for the next one. Needless to say Lydia wasn't particularly thrilled with his timing. Yet she understood that his dream of a family of musicians, a quartet or even a quintet, was still held close to his heart.

    Daniel indeed had already become proficient on the violin for a boy of eight. There had been no extra need to encourage him to practice for he was quite ready to take up the instrument at the drop of a hat. In fact, his love of the violin had taken the place of the need for having a good friend to depend on it seemed. As for James, it was already planned that the flute Frank had recently purchased would be in the hands of their second son in a couple of years. As assiduous as their father was in his musical ambitions for his children, he thought it was too early to ascribe an instrument to his daughter. He would let Millie's personality develop a few years before her temperament would, perhaps, reveal what musical sound would suit her best.

    Frank Paulone was steadfast about one thing: all of his children would play musical instruments and play them well. Even though Frank played the mandolin and Lydia herself the harmonica for years, she tried to protest that he might be a little too obsessive in pushing his own notions of how music could be used to hold a family together. She only dared to mention this once after a temper that was held in check most of the time flared hot. Lydia was told in no uncertain words she was not to interfere in matters that were between a father and his children then left the room in a fit of anger.

    This was not the end of temperamental outbursts nor was it the beginning. Rather, the music episode was another incidence emblematic of how Frank dealt with challenges to his authority within the family. Each time his hackles were raised over control issues even for something trivial it seemed to accumulate and affected how he viewed his wife and children. For some time there had been a slow but steady shift from the positive outlook on life of the first years of their marriage into one where pessimism had risen to the fore. That it was a good deal to do with the death of their second son was probably true. Yet, why hadn't the negative thinking stopped when so many good things had followed? Births of James and Mildred and finally Louis Paulone in 1914, their fourth living child, should have given him plenty to be happy about again. But none of these natural gifts had lightened Frank's sterner attitude towards his family. Lydia, for example, had to bite her tongue at times to prevent provoking another temperamental incident. Sometimes she wasn't able to catch herself in time and she noticed the aftermath of an outburst had grown longer.

Why Frank had changed, when he had changed and how much he had changed were probably questions impossible to answer. But Lydia had her own ideas. When she took time to reflect upon it, signs of her husband's need to dominate in what should have been family matters for discussion had been there from the beginning. She just hadn't seen it then but now recalled how set in his ways Frank was when it came to having a large family regardless of what her wishes might be. And it was Frank who decided that it was time to move and had then rented another place without consulting her first. Why had he remained so stubborn about naming their children, ignoring her favorite choices? These signs of problems had definitely been there early on the longer she thought about it. Not so evident though, and even more important, was what could be done about it to lessen the impact on family members. How do you cope with a husband who has grown more autocratic, one who insists on being right and who acts alone and tolerates no deviation from his decisions? And the worst, how to you compensate for a father who has difficulty in relating to his children? Lydia possessed enough self-awareness to know she was far from perfect. If she had handled her part of the relationship differently there might have been fewer reasons for Frank to become like he was. There were instances when she prolonged disagreements way past the time they should have ended because she was unable to stop herself. In the long run it only made matters worse when she did.

Frank's penchant for controlling things could also be viewed as a positive when it came to the household budget. His knack for making and saving money was testament to his care for the welfare of his family. Close oversight of the budget resulted in regular monthly deposits to the bank and a healthy savings account. However, the wisdom he had shown in saving money was not matched by his choice of where the money was saved; the bank he had personally chosen failed. Accumulated over three years and gone in an instant, it was devastating. No government guarantees, no family relief organization, no other means of rescue, they were compelled to start from scratch again.

Bit by bit over the next five years they built their savings account again. Lydia was as diligent as Frank in carefully watching what was spent in case they should have unexpected expenses. The earlier bank troubles were behind them, and lessons learned were all but forgotten. Forgotten, that is, until stories of bank closures throughout the country began to trickle in again. Small banks, particularly rural banks in agricultural areas, were hit the hardest. The metropolitan area of New Jersey where Frank and Lydia lived appeared to be safe from the renewed banking scourge. How wrong they were when in 1923 all of their savings had disappeared for a second time! Frank could read in his wife's eyes the mistrust she now had for his judgment. How could he have allowed this to happen to them twice? However much she tried, Lydia could no longer keep her feelings to herself.

It was his, her husband's, Frank Paulone's unforgivable choice that had put her family at risk—again!

"Is there any place we can rely on for our money besides putting it under our mattress? I mean I don't know what this country is coming to, honestly I don't," she cried while wringing her hands, unable to contain herself with yet another catastrophe.

Frank slowly turned around and stared at her with a look both crestfallen and accusatory. Not saying a word, he turned around again and abruptly walked out the door. Lydia Paulone had just received a rebuff for something that was certainly not her fault and not inconsequential to their survival. She collected herself and poured herself a cup of coffee from the pot still warm on the stove. Too anxious to sit down, she walked back and forth until pacing the floor could do no more to steady her nerves. How could they go on living like this? Strong and self-confident enough to escape her own heavy-handed father at a young age it was as if she had then married a father figure without realizing it. Had she really fallen back into the same old trap she had left behind?

WINNERS AND LOSERS

Bagnoli Irpino, Campania, February 1910-May 1914

Michelino and Antonia's marriage plans did not come about as soon as Angelo had thought they might. Other events had interceded and the cousins had to bide their time before the bet would be settled and the winner and loser revealed. But one thing remained fixed in their minds: matrimony between their siblings was inevitable, whether it be weeks, months or years in the future. Friends since they were four, the Conte cousins were not too bothered by delay, long or short as it might be; they were accustomed to things unraveling at a snail's pace in their part of the world. Still, Angelo was beginning to feel the pressure as birthdays approached once again as to whether he would be able to conquer his rival. His brother Michelino would be turning twenty in another year and Antonia was two years away from leaving her teenage years behind. There had not been even the slightest whisper of forthcoming nuptials. Usually there was never a dearth of town gossip about matters both significant and inconsequential, but the catastrophic earthquake had stolen the spotlight from a marriage that Angelo and Raffaele believed to be set in stone.

Beset by these and more minor events, wedding plans had

stalled, slipping off to the side for the present for Michelino and Antonia, the two principals concerned. But the mood in the country then lightened considerably, shifting to a more favorable climate, at least for a brief while, during the final spring months of 1911 just before the onset of the summer season. The celebration of the 50th anniversary of Italian unification was at hand and there would be a huge gathering of Italians in Rome. For those who could not join in the capital city's festivities, events on a more modest scale were also planned throughout the country. At the same time the Prime Minister had put forward legislation to broadly extend his version of universal suffrage, shrewdly seizing the advantage of the spirit of the occasion to bolster his claim to popularity. If the bill managed to pass muster, most males, including those whose economic circumstances were at or below the poverty line, would be enfranchised by the following year in time for elections due to take place in 1911.

On a warm May afternoon after Sunday's noontime meal Michelino and Antonia met on their favorite place town. The piazza was jammed with others hoping for respite from the stuffy indoors, but Michelino spread out on the bench to make sure there was only enough room for the two of them so they could be alone.

"Well, it looks like you at least will be able to cast your vote in the next election. The extension of voting rights has been talked about for such a long time so it's a major improvement. But of course only for men! I hope it's just a first step and women will soon be allowed to vote too."

"I wouldn't count on it Antonia, knowing how long it's taken to get this far."

"You know, I heard Enzo saying at his shop the other day that in America there are several states in which all woman and men had already been given full voting rights. And not only the eastern states but clear across the country; California could even join them later this year. However, as men are the only ones who will be casting ballots on whether or not women will be allowed to vote there are no guarantees it will actually happen. California could remain an all boys' only club if they choose not to play fair." It was just then a familiar voice reached their ears, grabbing their attention. Antonia's brother, Angelo, the one hoping for a marriage between his sister and Michelino sooner rather than later, was leaning over the back of the bench.

"What were you two lovebirds talking about—your marriage plans perhaps? You looked deep in conversation as I was walking up. I hope it was about finally setting a date and getting on with it. And after you've been officially united, you can then talk seriously anywhere and anytime of the day you want."

Antonia gave him a withering look as if to say not again. "Nothing like that, not that it's any of your business anyway Angelo, even if you are my big brother and think sometimes you are our father instead. It was about women being able to vote if you must know; how men are advancing here in our country without the briefest mention of women from anyone in this government. It's like we don't count and should just keep our mouths shut. And that's the way it has been and always will be unless women join forces for change. As it stands now, we're non-existent when it comes to politics in their nearsighted eyes."

Her conservative brother of course couldn't resist in adding his own sentiments. "Why should they want to complicate things? What good would come in letting females vote when they are too busy cooking in the kitchen, keeping the household in order and taking care of the children to have time to pay attention to what's going on in our country or the world. Unlike you, I think most women wouldn't even bother going to the polls even if they could vote. They'd much prefer to be doing the things they're good at anyhow."

"That's your usual nonsensical self talking again, Angelo. I knew you were capable of spouting drivel loudly and frequently so I guess I should have expected as much from your big mouth now. Isn't it about time for you to saunter off to Raffaele's house or one of your other friends and leave us alone to talk without your annoying idiotic comments?"

"Ciao, mia cara sorellina. But don't forget to get moving on setting a wedding date before all the best ones are taken. The whole town is beginning to wonder if it ever will happen before you turn gray!"

Michelino had held his tongue all during the exchange between brother and sister. He knew it would be wise not to interfere with family relations even though they had been of the flippant kind. Still, he was left with Angelo's departing words rattling through his head. "You know, Antonia, we should use this period of relative calm to move ahead with our plans. Who knows how long it will last. We've lost momentum with all that's been going on in town and beyond. The summer is a good time, maybe even next month? I think we could be able to pull it off in a few weeks' time if we put our minds to it."

"I've been thinking the same thing but not quite as soon as June. There would not be enough time for us to prepare properly. And people might wonder if something was not right in not making an earlier customary announcement. What about July or August? That should allow for a sufficient interval if we make clear our intentions soon." Michelino put a finger to his lips and paused for a moment as if seriously pondering what he should say before answering. Having kept things in abeyance for so long, any time they could secure the church for a specific date in summer would be to his liking.

"The sooner the better is what I say. I'll look for dates in those months that suit both of our families and let you know what the choices are when I learn them."

"Your hesitation had me worried there for a few seconds. But I should have known by now you are sometimes a great kidder." Maybe her brother's words had worked to wake them up, that they actually been a positive motivation in spurring them into action. With the exception, that is, of Angelo's stereotypical misogynistic and gratuitous voting remarks.

Michelino did spend part of the next two days consulting with family members to fix a summer wedding date that could accommodate relatives and friends. Once he had identified two possible Sundays, one each in July and August, he proceeded to talk with the church for availability. His bride to be had been right. Sundays in those two months had already been booked. There were plenty of Friday and Tuesday dates available, as could be expected. Many people still believed—firmly holding onto old superstitions—to wed on a Friday was bad luck; it risked the wrath of evil spirits. And Tuesdays were still mostly avoided because of something to do with wars and fighting affecting the lives of newlyweds. So, going back to his and her parents for guidance on what to do next, it seemed a weekend day would still be best. And although Saturdays were considered the best day of the week for widows to remarry—at nineteen Antonia was exempt from that category—a Saturday date was still the choice of the elders. It was back to the church again for Michelino Conte where it was decided the date would be the first Saturday in August, if it was satisfactory to Antonia. She was ecstatic and even surprised at what Michelino had managed to accomplish quickly after so much procrastination. She also mused that the sound of church bells ringing on the 5th of August 1911 would be for them and for them alone on their special Saturday.

It was less than hour after the news had been shared with their parents that Angelo rushed out of the house. Her brother looked back once at the doorway when Antonia asked him where he was going to in such a hurry.

"I have to see Raffaele about a certain matter. This is exciting news, Antonia, and about time. I won't be away long." The last part of what he said she took with a grain of salt. When her brother got together with his good buddy it was never for a short time.

"Raffaele, *mia amico*, it looks like there is finally a winner of our little wager. I can see in your eyes you've already heard the news too. Don't you think it's time to settle our accounts? The date chosen means my sister will still be only nineteen when they walk down the aisle together."

"Well, it was nearly a victory for myself you must admit. And it does sort of look like you will be right; but I'm not giving in yet. Until I see them become a husband and a wife with a ring on her finger with my own eyes, I'll be holding off throwing in the towel."

Days sped by without any changes affecting the wedding plans. Then the two cousins dressed in their Sunday best, albeit on a Saturday, sat side-by-side as the church filled with wedding guests for the big day. And then, after so much waiting, it was suddenly over. They glanced at each other, as if to silently acknowledge the culmination of a long-awaited journey just as the resplendent couple in front of the altar exchanged their first kiss as newlyweds. The bride was handed a plate containing flower petals and coins as she and Michelino passed through the church door, which was then with dramatic flair flung onto the steps, shattering it into at least a few dozen pieces. A southern Italian tradition to keep evil spirits at bay had once again been fulfilled while rice bombarded them from all sides.

There was one more traditional ritual to be performed by the bride before wager settlements were to be made. Attendees, no longer following the wedding processional order randomly walked to the town square. And children now freed from instructions to behave with decorum and silence when inside the church sprinted in front and alongside the newlyweds shouting with glee. Somehow they were able to produce an endless reservoir of rice from their pockets to shower over heads and shoulders of Michelino and Antonia Conte. Then Antonia came to a stop and sat down on a chair magnificently adorned with flowers and leaves that had been specially placed close to the piazza's center. Turning to one side with a coy sidelong smile, she hiked her dress just high enough to remove a frilly paper garter from her right thigh. Tearing it into small bits with the assistance of her husband who stood by her side, she then cast them all about her. Those able to secure a bridal trousseaux fragment were thought to be destined for good luck. Raffaele, regrettably, beaten by the quicker feet of the young children failed to obtain a single scrap for himself. The moment had come; he had no further excuse for giving Angelo his due. He really didn't mind. The match uniting Antonia and Michelino had made the friendship between the two cousins even tighter. At any rate the true winners were his brother and a newly gained sister-in-law!

***

Bagnoli Irpino, Campania, June-July 1914

Then fate intervened. War had started in earnest in 1914, but the signs of it coming had been present long before. If they hadn't yet touched your life personally, it was because they were easy to ignore while carrying on with daily routines. When the threat of a war was mentioned, the usual "it can't happen here to us" response was the order of the day. With so much turmoil throughout the continent—empires declining, consolidation creating friction, conflicts breaking out, new alliances being formed—it seemed like Europe was in disarray rather than the opposite. Not exactly falling apart at the seams, not yet anyhow, but rumblings of discontent were everywhere and the atmosphere was different. Growing unrest, especially for those living in the more economically precarious and heavily populated southern regions, was obvious. For those in denial, they could only continue to shelter themselves from reality for so long.

Harbingers of change did not escape the Conte family in the mountainous Campania region. The rural south was aware, just as much as northerners, that forces over which they had no control were tightening their grip on daily lives. It seemed to be only a matter of time—probably not that long—before Italy and her people would be plunged into a chaotic abyss as well. Michelino and Antonia felt compelled to prepare for the inevitability of war when they learned the Italian military itself was already doing so. Word had filtered down even to the southern hinterlands that the Italian army could be repositioned to deter the threat of incursion of hostile forces at the northern Italian border as a precautionary measure. Then the final match was struck that lit the fire: on June 28th Archduke Franz Ferdinand and his wife were assassinated in

Sarajevo.

The odds of Italy being drawn deeper into the conflict rather than remaining in a defensive stance relegated to northern borders only became too great to ignore. And a twenty-three year old Michelino Conte would be prime cannon fodder.

"What do you think, Antonia, could I be called up even though we have a son now? I've heard that in the past a family to support didn't seem to matter much. Fathers were conscripted the same as single men. Nothing officially has been announced about Italy's position but I'm sure it will be soon. I'm not sure of what's the best thing to do for our family."

"If I remember right it didn't seem to matter if you had children or not. Military service was compulsory for all males at the age of eighteen. Period! No exceptions. I don't think any change in a policy that's been in place for such a long time can be expected. But maybe it's too soon to worry about it, *cara mia*. Maybe we should just look after the inn and our little Antonio and let things run their course a little longer before making any hasty decisions. After all it won't be long now until he has a baby brother or sister and that's what should be our focus of concern for the next few months."

Michelino had listened carefully to his wife. She was usually correct when it came to tough questions and answers. Unlike many other Italian men, he often deferred to her judgment without taking it as an affront on his masculinity. Postponing a major decision that involved uprooting their family seemed like the right thing to do. But when the news came the coastal force over the mountains in Apulia was indeed being redeployed northwards, they knew things had become serious. To Michelino's thinking, there seemed to be no plausible reason for procrastinating any longer when it came to putting his family in jeopardy. He was needed alive and at home, not in the line of fire. As for choices, the one in front of his nose came to him immediately. Only a few in Italy had the advantage of delving deeply into another culture as he done. Michelino's prolonged sojourn to America prior to their marriage had given him a strong connection to the country and its sensibilities.

"There's no question now of waiting any longer, Antonia. We must act as soon as we can. The time has come—sooner than I thought—to face our choices before they are gone."

She could see by the way he held himself and the fire in his eyes it would be useless to argue. Besides she knew what he was thinking and had also come to the same conclusion after hearing the latest news. The risks were too great; it was time to roll the dice and act on the plans set aside when they had married back in 1911. A life-altering plan was essential and agreed upon before the evening was over, a plan to make sure their family would not be subjected to the whims of war. In America, they would be safe from whatever transpired in Europe. It was a Central European affair, regardless.

"We must leave—for the sake of our family we must leave, Antonio. But how should we proceed? What should we do first? This is all happening so fast my head is spinning; I can't think straight." Her weary body sank into a chair, too tied in knots from anxiety in making such a decision to say anything more for the moment.

She recovered soon afterwards and by the time evening was over they had hashed out a tentative plan of action. They would arrange to give the small tavern and inn for overnight guests they had started to his parents when Antonia emigrated. It was crucial that Michelino be the first to leave for America on one of the next ships from Naples. He was the one in immediate jeopardy, and they would join him there later as soon as opportunity presented itself. As for the cost of the fare, Antonia was sure her parents would help to make up the difference from what they had put away. But first things first, with only three months to go Antonia must remain settled as calmly as she could be in Bagnoli until the delivery of their second child. There was no question in either of their minds it would be too hazardous to risk a voyage in her condition.

Time would also be needed to recover from the birth and for their baby to be robust enough to make a long voyage. At least several months would be necessary. Her parents would be by her side to help all they could. Alfonso and Maria Teresa Conte could also be counted on and Antonia would be surrounded by a score of other relatives as well. His parents were also living and financially better off than hers, but they would probably place unpleasant stipulations in order to gain their assistance. For sanity's sake, it would be better not to involve them at all, although they could usually find a way of intruding where they didn't belong if they chose to mettle in the affairs of others.

In any event it would be only a few months at most, they thought, certainly less than a half year, before they would be reunited as a family in the distant land so many before them had embraced. The few months apart would also give Michelino time to get established and have as much ready as he could in advance of his family's arrival. Lessons he had learned from his previous visit to America over seven years ago were mulled over. This time he would show more patience in navigating new territory and have more realistic expectations. It was also significant that his age—a significant impediment the first time—would no longer weigh against him in finding decent employment.

Ready or not, the embarkation date for Michelino came upon them. Antonia with their son Antonio at her side watched the soon to be father for a second time blow kisses to them as the SS Sant' Anna inched away from the Naples pier on July 14th, Bastille Day. He had left only two weeks after the assassinations had occurred in the Bosnian city. And two weeks later, on July 28th, just as they thought would happen, Austria-Hungary declared war on Serbia. So it was from different sides of the world Antonia and Michelino witnessed the First World War become a reality.

At the outset Italy maintained neutrality, as it had promised to do earlier, even though for several decades it had been allied with the empires of Germany and of Austria-Hungary. But pressures built for the nation to take a stand, to either join the Central Powers—formerly called the Triple Alliance—or the Allied Powers, during subsequent months. The prime factor ultimately tipping the balance to the latter was Italy's opportunistic demands for annexation of ethnic Italian areas located on the other side of the northern border, around Trentino in Southern Tirol. These demands also included the Austrian Littoral and its major city of Trieste. Rejected by Austria-Hungary, these objectives were eventually agreed to by the Allies made up of Great Britain, France and Russia. Italy became a member the Allied Powers by taking advantage of the possibility for territorial expansion and in hoping for a favorable war outcome. And on the 23 of May 1915, Italy officially entered the war.

Preparations had been going on for so long now that it was not a surprise the country would eventually become engaged in the conflict. Programs of recruitment and cultural indoctrination had been happening since August of the previous year. The Conte family had been wise in their decision to move expeditiously. By the beginning of 1915, the need for labor and increasing war requirements had resulted in travel restrictions reducing the number of emigrants from Italy to a drop in the bucket compared to the numbers of pre-war years.

THE TIES THAT BIND ~ ABIDING FATE

PARTINGS

Newark, New Jersey, 1911-1918

Pre-war years had brought forth four healthy children to Frank and Lydia Paulone in a span of ten years. But there had been tragedy along the way. If the second born child, a son had lived, there would have been five, but he had died after only a few months. His death had crushed them yet they were determined to not let it keep them from trying again, God willing. And enlarge the family they did: James, Mildred and Louis joined with Daniel to give Frank the family he always wanted. But it was Lydia who devoted herself to making sure the needs of the children were met at home on a daily basis. She had made sure they thrived during pre-war recession and even when prices were rising and food supplies limited in the early post-war years. Lydia had also begun a job at a factory to supplement their income.

Juggling outside work with household tasks, meal preparation and schooling demands left little time to complain about other things both little and big, her relationship with her husband among them. Concern for her children was a necessary distraction in shining the spotlight elsewhere than on problems in their relationship. Frank usually returned home after work late, and by that time dinner had been prepared and finished, dishes washed and dried, schoolwork completed, musical instruments practiced, baths taken, teeth brushed, stories read, little bodies were about to be tucked into bed. On top of that there were clothes to be washed and mended, the floors swept and scrubbed clean, and the straightening and organizing that had to be done during the week. Dead on her feet, she climbed into bed as soon as the last tasks were completed, fighting to stay awake to read a few pages before the lights were turned off. Frank, already sound asleep and snoring would be up and off to work before she rose the next morning to start another day's routine.

In 1920, around the time their youngest child entered his sixth year, cracks in their relationship began to appear again. Louis Paulone himself was by no means the reason of a widening rift between Lydia and Frank. The children were all in school during the week giving Lydia a window to think about her situation—their situation. Other than the children what had their marriage really meant? Frown wrinkles and graying hair of a woman still young in years did not compare favorably to the fresh-faced wedding picture on the mantelpiece of a nineteen year old Lydia standing next to Frank. It wasn't so much the physical change, which could be partially be attributed to motherhood, rather it was the mental strain of the gradual erosion of their relationship image that the mirror reflected when she got out of bed to cook breakfast for the children.

Her husband returned home from work grumpier and grumpier everyday it seemed to her. She tried talking to Frank when there was an opportunity, tried to get at what his feelings were about her and why his outlook on life had become so cynical. Was it her that made him unhappy? Or, perhaps the noisy children that aggravated him? Or had they just become different people from who they were at the beginning? Conversations between them had become few and far between, and even when one had begun, it sometimes ended with misunderstanding on one side or the other or both. It was like they belonged to different worlds at times and what they had in common when they married had withered away. She had changed too, she knew, and probably must accept part of the blame, but it was much easier to place the onus on her husband.

If it were just the two of them, that would be one thing. She could choose to continue to live in a brittle relationship or she could end it, either way without injuring others. With their alienation from each other she could cope but when Frank neglected their children, save with his obsession for their playing musical instruments, it was irresponsible in her estimation. He seemed reluctant to show real affection, unwilling to give an inch and made no effort to understand the thinking of teenagers on the rocky road to adulthood. The children, forcibly, complied with their father's demands for obedience, of course, practiced their instruments with regularity—or at least gave the impression of doing so—without daring to protest. But did authoritarian rule really translate into a true caring for their happiness? Of small consolation they were not the only families in their predicament. Some of their friends shared the same problems with fathers or mothers whose priorities were meting out discipline rather than showing love even if it was there and lay hidden.

Flecks of gray speckling his mustache and beard did not

mean Frank Paulone had mellowed. Nor had middle age changed his strictness with regard to his family. The distance between them that had lengthened over the years showed no signs of shrinking now that middle age had been reached. She couldn't say that it had recently become greater either. A wall between them had been built and its continual existence for so long meant it was sturdy enough to have thwarted any attempts in knocking it down. Efforts to do so failed time after a time until Lydia had accepted the futility of trying to regain a semblance of their early lives together. What she could do, though, to compensate for incompatibility, was to concentrate her attention and energy on her children. She could also look for solace in the company of friends. However, Lydia Paulone was not the type, however, to share personal matters, and certainly not her marital difficulties, with even good friends. All the same it didn't take any special awareness to gather things were not as they should be but her friends were too circumspect to ask.

***

New York City & Newark, Autumn 1921

It was one such friend, aware of Lydia's need for diversion, who asked if she would like to join her on a weekday excursion to the New York Public Library. Rarely able to get away even for the short trip to Manhattan, Lydia's first inclination still was to decline. But on second thought it might be possible with her children all in school during the week so she decided to accept the invitation. There was the kind of chill in the air and coloring in leaves that made you feel alive on the autumn morning when they left after she had packed her children off to school. By taking the Hudson Tubes under the Hudson River both ways she could be back by the time they came home and well before her husband too. Other than transportation, there would be little cost involved—the the library was open and free to everyone. And she deserved a break from the routine!

    Lydia couldn't wait to start exploring as soon as they had walked up three flights of stairs, past the two lion statues standing guard, between the columns and through the oversized doorway. The scale of the entry and the size of the rooms took her breath away. The number of volumes indexed in the massive card catalog—rows and rows of drawers placed prominently in the middle of a great room—was also mindboggling to contemplate. She ignored trying to thumb through them for the moment preferring to just walk alongside the shelves. She stopped in front of an enormous volume with the word "gazetteer" engraved on its spine. What could a book with such an odd word in the title be about? Lydia began to lift it from the shelf but the weight of the hefty tome made it slip from her grip and fall with a loud thud to the floor. Feeling a little embarrassed, she bent over to pick it up, but a tallish young man standing nearby beat her to the punch. "An interesting choice", he casually remarked as he handed it back to Lydia. "I like gazetteers too. They're great for seeing if some very out of the way places are included in it. Almost all of the ones I've looked for are actually there."

    "So that's what a gazetteer is used for. Such a strange word, I've never heard of it before."

    "You're right there. It is a strange name for a book that's really just a geographical listing of places. I looked the word up one time because, the same as you, I was unfamiliar with it. If I remember right, it comes from the French. And the word gazette relates to newspapers since it was initially a compilation of place names intended for use by journalists."

"Wow, that's a roundabout way for naming something. Thanks for the explanation. This is my first time in such a huge library and I'm sure there's going to be a lot more like that book." Lydia and the youngish and slightly overweight man—no more than thirty years of age she guessed—chatted for another few minutes, until Lydia's friend caught up to them and interrupted. "Come on Lydia, there's plenty more to see and do here before we must make our way back to Newark."

"Sorry to have kept you. Sometimes I can't help talking too much," he apologized and then turned to go. Lydia vigorously shook her head that this was not the case at all, and she also said as much. Stopping himself, he moved a step closer to the pair of them again.

"Did I hear you say you're going back to New Jersey? That's where I'm living as well. I don't usually do this sort of thing, but maybe we could get together there for a coffee, to talk about libraries, strange books or anything else. My name's Ed, Edward Bennington, that is." Lydia looked towards her friend for guidance and received a tiny nod of approval. When she told him her name and where she lived, it turned out Ed had relatives living only a few doors down from Lydia's address on Nursery Street. A day and a time and a corner coffee shop known to both of them were set for meeting on Tuesday the next week. On the way back home, Lydia questioned herself out loud as to whether she had done the right thing. Her friend answered for her: "Why not?" Ed was a probably a bit lonely and Lydia Paulone needed an outlet from life at home. It seemed harmless enough in any case.

It may have started out harmlessly. But the first meeting led to a second and then to a third and then the new friendship began to take on the guise of something more than that. In truth, flirting had sprung to life before they realized what was happening. Once they did, neither of them made the effort to bring it to a halt either. Early on Lydia had learned Ed was a native New Yorker and a veteran of World War I. He spoke a little about life in the military but not in great detail. Yet, it wasn't until their third meeting that she thought of asking him more about his life before the war.

"There's really not much good to tell about it. Maybe we should leave it just at that," a frown forming on the usually happy face he had when they spent time together.

"But it's part of who you are. And it doesn't do any good to avoid talking about things that help us get to know each other better. Here we sit sharing a cinnamon bun so why can't we share the more difficult times we've had as well?"

"Well, as I mentioned before, my parents were born in England, in a place called Hammersmith. It's part of London, I guess. They came to America about three years before I was born. At first we lived in a rented flat in one of the poorer working class Manhattan neighborhoods, on Amsterdam Avenue in West Harlem. My father worked as a ticket agent at Grand Central Station."

"That doesn't sound so bad; I grew up in a very ordinary part of Newark as well."

"If it had stayed that way, you'd be right. That's only the beginning of the story. Not long after my thirteenth birthday, in 1907, my mother passed away. Within months my father had died too. My sister, my younger brother and I, all three of us were suddenly made orphans. My older sister was actually born in Leicestershire, England. She was five years older than me and the luckiest one of us all. Her wedding date had already been set when our mother died and she went ahead with it anyway. It was pretty sad with no parent alive to give her away. Her husband was also from a working class family."

"So what happened to you and your brother then? Were you able to live with other relatives? Thirteen is too young to live on your own. And a younger brother, you said. How old was he?"

"Lester was only eight when they took him away. Social workers were at our door before the week was out after dad died. They focused on Lester first since he was the youngest. He was placed in an institution housing orphans and served as a reformatory at the same time. It was on the other side of the Harlem River. There were hundreds of inmates, as they called the children living there, at a place called the Children's Hospital of Randall's Island. It was not that far from where we were living, just off the eastside of Manhattan in-between the Harlem and East Rivers. As soon as he was eighteen he enlisted in the army and in 1918 went off to the war. About that time we lost track of each other for awhile."

"And you, Ed, what happened to you?" He took his time in telling her his own story. He didn't want to have to repeat it agaon. He rarely mentioned anything about those bleak days to anyone, preferring to keep them buried deep in the past where he thought they should stay. That Lydia was an exception meant a lot. Ed had made sure they didn't find himself at home when the social workers came back the next day after Lester had been taken away Then for the next six weeks or so he lived on the street, finding places to sleep he never had noticed before. The police caught up to him one day and held him until they learned that he was supposed to have been sent to an institution as his brother had been. A different place was chosen for him, further from his familiar Manhattan, and further from the risk of flight if he had been placed with his brother close to their old home. The New York Juvenile Asylum in the village of Greensburgh, Westchester County, New York became the place of his "incarceration", as he referred to it, since all of the three hundred or so young people there were also termed inmates. And for all intents and purposes he was indeed a prisoner. Located twenty-five miles north of New York City on the Hudson River, this facility was more appropriate for someone with his past record of disappearing.

"There's something else you should also know about me: I'm not really a World War I veteran in the usual sense of the meaning. I joined the National Guard in 1916 then was sent down to Pharr, Texas where I became part of the punitive expedition against Pancho Villa during the Mexican Revolution. That's how I got the scars on my right hand. Then the next year the First World War started, but I had already been discharged from the army by then. I guess my flat feet—good enough for fighting the Mexicans—were unfit for the Germans."

"Gosh, I would never have guessed you had such a hard time growing up. Mine was not the happiest at times, but after hearing your story, I've got nothing to complain about. Unlike your situation, which was not of your own making, I was a bit too independent thinking and that can bring about problems when you have very restrictive parents. And it really did. But more about my story next time. It's getting late."

"At least, Lydia and you have idea now of why I'm like who I am. I hope it doesn't make you look at me differently from now on!"

Not only did it not change her opinion of Ed Bennington, the fact that he had been so open and honest with her about the circumstances of his upbringing had made her respect him even more. She tried to remember if she ever felt that way with Frank. The twelve years separation between Lydia and her husband, inconsequential when they had met, had eventually become a divisive factor in constantly having to deal with a husband who had a crotchety old man's crustiness as time went by. His fifty-one when compared to her own thirty-nine years made her feel almost like one of their children instead of a spouse on equal terms. Was she meant to suffer too from his strict attitude towards childrearing as her children had done? How could Ed Bennington, after undergoing what he had growing up, seem to be so normal, so understanding, so attentive in comparison to her husband? Frank Paulone may have been like that in the beginning but he was none of those things these days to her mind.

From that point on her attachment to Ed became stronger each day even after Lydia talked a little about her husband. Having already gone from flirting to the romantic stage, their relationship grew even more intense over the next few months, until their unmentioned meetings seemed to be more like trysts. Yet, when Ed Bennington asked her if she would ever consider leaving Frank so they could be together permanently her answer to him was a firm no. She could live with feeling guilty in falling in love with Ed, but she could not hurt her children she had explained. But that too was to change not long afterwards. Purely by accident, Frank had spotted them huddled together one day at a local park. It had been bound to happen sooner or later. He restrained himself from confronting them then but when Lydia returned home he was ready and waiting for her. Livid, he did not spare her, by the choice words he used, the gestures he made, or the rage he displayed. It didn't matter that Frank was justified in his accusations; what mattered now was she knew someone else was waiting for her, someone who really cared about her.

Frank slammed the door behind him on his way out and she thought about everything for hours. There seemed to be only one clear path in front of her so she made up her mind. It was time! Done! Daniel almost fifteen, James eleven, Millie just seven and Louis three would have to understand someday. She would miss them every minute of every day. She had stuck it out for a long time but they weren't babies any more. Next morning while Frank was at work she packed a few belongings then walked out the front door and to the park to rest there until Ed Bennington would return home from work. The page had turned and a new chapter in her life had begun.

PANDEMIC

Bagnoli Irpino, Italy, October 1918

With the entry of the United States into the war in April 1917 the chances for a favorable outcome for Italy at the end of the conflict had looked more promising with each battle fought and won. Italy's progressive flip-flopping to serve its own best interests had started with the Triple Alliance of Germany and Austria-Hungary pact before the war then shifted to a position of neutrality and finally had ended with a commitment to the other side, the Triple Entente. There was no turning back again with the country showing its mettle in fighting alongside France, the United Kingdom and Ireland, the United States and Russia. The latter bowed out of the conflict in signing an armistice with the enemy near the end of 1917.

If nothing else, the engagement of the massive Royal Italian Army and the huge number of battlefield casualties it suffered primarily on the northern Italian Front were living, and dying, proof of the Italian nation's allegiance. Germany had begun its large-scale offensive in March of 1918, but already it looked like a lost cause. German forces were determined to carry on in spite of the apparent futility of doing so and were heavily engaged in the Meuse-Argonne clash on the Western Front in France. The battle had started in September and was still fiercely fought as a last gasp during the present month of October. Even with Germany's predicted defeat, it was no time for complacency in the world.

The waning war of bombs and bullets had been replaced with one equally as harmful in terms of casualties but even more insidious, one that was invisible and as lethal as weapons: germs. The first concerns with a new and rapidly advancing disease, identified by the older name of influenza or flu, had occurred while the German attacks were still raging. At first the severity of the contagion seemed not much different than before. And as the weather progressively warmed at the beginning of the summer season, it had mostly faded out too. As usual, deaths of the elderly and infirm were higher, but in reality the rate of mortality was not much different than previous years. Nevertheless, there was a measurable discrepancy in the seasonal numbers falling ill, which demonstrated a marked difference in how virulent and contagious it was. But there was no reason to panic, for most recovered completely within a couple of weeks.

Then the month of September arrived and along with it came a second wave of the infectious disease This time the mutated version of the disease was more virulent and much more lethal than the milder version of early 1918. Those who contracted the autumn variety of the flu often fell seriously ill and for many, death quickly followed. The three days or so it typically took to shake off the main symptoms of the illness during its less potent first wave had become three days of severe sickness and then on to an early grave with the second instead. To make matters even worse the pandemic was widening each day. Inexplicably, it was the younger, more fit and female segment of society who bore the brunt of the sickness. Women between infancy and fifty years old were most susceptible to contracting the illness.

Yet, the majority, even among females, remained uninfected or managed to recover if they were. But for those who were the sickest, and the number was not insignificant, there was nothing much anyone could do to help. There were no medicines providing a cure, none even to alleviate symptoms and suffering. And it could no longer be considered a normal year when bodies were piling up at the town mortuary faster than caskets could be made. The only way to avoid the Spanish flu, as it grew to be termed, was to avoid contact with others. But how could distance be kept when relatives and friends gathered at the bedsides of the ailing, attended funeral after funeral to bury the shrouded dead, waited in crowds for war rations, subsidies and in breadlines, and weary veterans returned home bringing the disease along with their military kits?

Bagnoli Irpino, only one of many small towns scattered in the foothills, was no different than the many others in its isolation from the majority of the population. As secluded as they all were, none of them were able escape the transmission of influenza. Townspeople had received word that certain cities and larger towns had been supplied with masks and were also using quarantine measures to combat rapid spread and contamination. While Bagnoli would never be far enough away from cities such as Avellino and Naples to be left unexposed to the danger, it would also never be near enough to its large brothers to benefit from the same government health support they were given.

"Another one has left us and two more are knocking on death's door," Maria Teresa Conte announced to her family sitting around the kitchen table awaiting their evening meal. Death would not normally have been a topic for family dinner conversation, but flu had changed all that. The accumulation of deaths condensed into a two-month period was shocking to a town where everyone knew everyone else and, in many cases, actually was related to each other through intermarriage. Migrants from medieval times had settled in Bagnoli bringing with them a few dozen surnames. A relatively few additional surnames had been gradually introduced at various times, of course, but for generations the names of early settlers had remained predominant. Bloodlines that had been sewn together and continued to be shared had created a network of personal and family ties that were part of the town's very fabric. And these interconnections were the perfect vector for rapid spread of the epidemic in their little of the Valle del Calore.

Antonia Conte felt overwhelmed and exhausted by it all. Funerals were occurring at two times the rate of past years. Entire families were preoccupied like never before with the threat of falling ill. A war in its final throes of mayhem, an outlook for increasing poverty and a husband off in America were all too much for any average person.

"Mother needs to lie down for just a little while. Antonio, look after your sister for a short time while I take a nap for a few minutes. If you need to, you can always wake me. But *nonna* and *nonno* should be back soon."

"Of course, mama. Don't worry about anything. We'll be fine. You just rest." Children seemed to be growing up faster than normal nowadays. And Antonio, though only six, was proud to be able to take care of a four year old sister even though Maria Conte could be quite bossy for her age. He realized they should play quietly while their mother slept so he placed sheets of scrap paper and a few broken crayons on the kitchen table. If their grandparents returned before she woke up, he would shush them right when they came in the door. They had gone shopping at the market, as sparse as the offerings were these days, and to run a few other errands.

"C'mon Maria, let's get the pick-up sticks. She was a bit young for the game of concentration and steady hand, but she had become tired of drawing and they needed something else to keep them occupied. Antonio was a good teacher; she watched him carefully and was starting to get the hang of it. And when it was her turn she studied the pile from every angle before attempting to lift one clear without moving the others, showing off her competitive nature at an early age.

Sure enough, their mother was still asleep when their grandparents returned. In place of speaking to warn them, the children closed their eyes and rested their tilted heads on hands folded prayer-like to get their point across. But Antonia Conte semi-awake had also heard the door open and was about to get up anyway. It would not be for long. As soon greetings were over, she plopped down again on the nearest chair. It was so unlike their energetic daughter who rarely stopped moving usually. And there was a paleness that was normally not there. She just seemed to be so fatigued. Something was definitely wrong. Why had they failed to notice these signs before they had left in the morning? Perhaps Antonia had been pushing herself too hard in looking after her children while trying to do so much around their home. She was always trying to spare her aging parents, who had slowed down considerably as they entered their seventh decade, from more burdensome tasks. What could they do to help her now?

"Sit still, Antonia," her father said when Antonia began to lean to forward on the arms of the chair in order to help herself up, "these baskets and bags are light as a feather and we can manage them ourselves."

"Are you sure? They look very heavy and you must be tired after walking home in these winds we've been having. Strange, they've already been blowing hard enough for the trees to lose their leaves already although it's barely the beginning of October."

"We're fine, *mio caro*, absolutely fine. In fact, we were thinking on the way home that we wanted to cook something special for dinner. It was worth going today since we were able to get our allotted ration of meat for the month. A proper meal will go a long way in making us all feel healthier. Let us take our turn in the kitchen." She was about to open her mouth to object when they added: "Not a peep, Antonia. There's no two ways about it. Rest a little more and we'll get started." And after those firm words, they started unpacking the groceries. The little story they had ad-libbed in jiffy to keep Antonia from exerting herself any further seemed to have worked.

With most of the young male farmers away serving in the military, agricultural production had shrunk so much by 1918 that even the basic grains needed for pasta, polenta and bread were at a premium. Older men and the wounded returned from the war were left to till the soil as best they could. And women and children were also seen at work in the fields much more these days than before the war. But even as a whole they were unable to match the production of previous years. The outcome: increasing penury, especially for the more remote rural families. Everywhere you looked, hungry faces stared back at you.

Antonia Conte was ready to lie down again as soon as she had swallowed the last bite of food she was able to get down. She wished she could have eaten more, to show her worried family she was not feeling poorly, but her appetite had vanished.

"I'll be all right. I'm having one of those off days when I feel a bit tired. I must not have slept well last night. I just need to close my eyes again for a little while. In case I'm not awake later when you go to bed I'll say goodnight now." She had lied. She was not feeling at all normal, not even a little bit. It had started while she was walking home after visiting her cousin the previous evening: two sharp pains in a row hitting the center of her back like nothing she had ever felt before. It was as if someone had stabbed her with a knife that had penetrated deep into her body. So bizarre. Then today she had been feeling so weary she had begun to wonder if there was a connection.

Within minutes Antonia was fast asleep again. At first she slept so deeply that nothing could disturb her slumber. Not even the loud roar from the motors of the planes flying low overhead could wake her. But sometime later a rising temperature broke through the walls of her sleep. Delirious, Antonia watched herself, like she was a spectator from a distance, travelling lickety-split down train tracks. At first the speed that she was going was thrilling but then something else happened: the single pair of tracks suddenly split into two separate sets, each set veering in a different direction. Her speed continued to accelerate as she saw the parallel rails and railroad ties of the second track unfold in front of her. Then the second track lifted off the ground and shot into the air. She soon realized her own had done the same and she was now airborne as well. The paths of the two tracks diverged more and more with each passing moment, but she could still see them both constantly changing directions, going high in the sky then swerving downwards again. Finally, she flew off the train track altogether, floating through the air in slow motion. And that's where her delusions stayed until the whole sequence repeated itself again. Even if meant crashing to the ground she wished it could be brought to an end.

"Who is it? What are you doing?" she moaned in trying to push the hand holding a wet cloth on her forehead away.

"It's all right, Antonia, calm yourself; it's just us, your parents. We heard you almost shouting and you're drenched in sweat. We must cool you down. It's too dangerous to be so hot." For a minute she did become quiet. Then with eyes glazed over she began tossing so violently from side to side her parents were forced to restrain her fearing she would tumble onto the floor if they didn't.

The worry written all over his wife's face was not something her husband had ever seen before. But if he had looked in a mirror he would recognized the same expression on his own. "We better stay by her side during the night. We can take turns, let's say changing every two hours or so. I'll go first. You should lie down now and try to get some rest before it's your time."

"You'll let me know if the fever breaks or there are any other changes. Wake me no matter what, Alfonso" Maria Teresa instructed so vehemently there was no chance her husband would dare to disregard them. And an hour and a half later he did wake her. Antonia's fever had changed into chills, and through her shivering and chattering teeth she was complaining of being terribly cold. No matter how high the pile of blankets her father placed over her it seemed to be not enough. Now neither of them would leave her for the rest of the night. In fact, they no longer felt tired, worry having supplanted the need for sleep. In the early morning hours Antonia began to wheeze and her efforts to breathe became more labored each passing minute. They could wait no longer; one of them must fetch the doctor and do it now.

Dr. Domenico Leonardo Cione arrived back with Alfonso less than thirty minutes later looking almost as haggard as most of his patients did during these unparalleled times. Bulging black bags under his eyes and hair uncombed in a tangle, the doctor did indeed feel very weary for at his age he should have been retired. But how could the one and only doctor in town snap close his black bag for good and call it a day when the need was so great? Before he went to bed his medical bag was placed beside his shoes which were under his coat hung on a peg near the door ready for the next call. But therein lay the problem: there was only one of him to go around, one of him to serve so many in town and throughout the outlying rural areas, just one old-time doctor born and bred in their own Bagnoli Irpino. And when he spoke of diagnosis and treatment, it was with the warm Neapolitan dialect, like the other natives, but made all the richer by its unique silkiness.

Antonia's parents knew of the friends and neighbors Dr. Cione had helped to recover and also of those who had failed to respond to his efforts. They were reassured by little things he did with care, like the confident way he used his stethoscope and the gentle way he sponged their daughter's forehead. But Antonia had grown worse, with coughs coming from deep within her chest, during the half hour before the doctor arrived. He heard them as well as soon as he did and it was only a minute or two after examining her that his opinion had been formed. He was direct and somehow kind at the same time when he gave his pronouncement after guiding Antonia's parents to the hallway for privacy. It was his belief that she might live until morning. In listening to her lungs he was positive pneumonia had set in, and the rattling sound meant it was already at an advanced stage. At this point only a miracle could help stop the progression and there was nothing more he could do. As soon as the doctor had left, Maria Teresa and Alfonso fell to their knees and prayed for a miracle. Two hours later they thought their prayers had been answered when Antonia opened her eyes and had the strength to sit up a little in the bed.

Her eyes wandered around the room and then she started to babble. "Where is he? I saw him only a minute ago. Where did he go? Make him come back! I have something to tell him; we're going to have a second child. He'll be so happy when he hears the news." It was said with such clarity she seemed almost like her normal self again. "Michelino, come here. You'll be so excited when I tell you the news," she continued with urgency in her voice. "Sit down beside me, please," were the last words she ever spoke in calling her husband to her side. Antonia had then slumped back down on the mattress again, flat on her back but this time with one arm dangling limply over the side. In this position, and with an audible whoosh of exhaled air, at eight-fifteen in the morning on the 4th of October 1918, their wonderful daughter had departed her earthly home. If only Michelino Conte had been there for real instead of oceans away, maybe, just maybe it would have been easier to say goodbye. It could only be hoped that his spirit running through her confused mind had been of some comfort to her in the end.

THE GREAT WAR

Mahoning Valley, Ohio-Pennsylvania, 1914-1918

Michelino Conte was too busy simply adjusting to life in America again at first—after an hiatus of almost seven years from his first stay in 1907—to worry much about his wife and children back home in Italy. After the ship had arrived in New York and he had again passed through customs at Ellis Island without a problem, he had proceeded directly to the train station and waited for the first one which would take him closest to Brier Hill in Ohio. He was already familiar with the city since it was where his sister and her husband had lived on his former trip. In fact, Michelino was staying with the growing Clemente family at the moment until he found a job and a residence of his own. He had already begun in earnest to beat the pavement for work opportunities although still regaining his land legs and adjusting from constant travelling. For now, Michelino wasn't particular about the type of employment. At the age of twenty-three, he was young, eager and ready to take on anything.

Job openings it seemed to be plentiful, even for an Italian immigrant whose English-speaking abilities were not that great. Underage for much of the time during his first trip to

America, Michelino had been unable find himself at a workplace where he would have become more fluent. Still, he regretted he had retained so little of what he had picked up and hoped it would eventually come back to him at some point. The first jobs he found were in local stores, helping in opening and closing routines, pricing items, stocking and straightening the shelves and sweeping up at the end of the day. It was the kind of labor most anyone could do, but he was grateful to have it as a start because it made him feel more connected to his surroundings, part of the community and pulling his share. But a better prospect soon came Michelino's way while walking home on the same route he took every day. A help-wanted sign in the window of a building with a red and white and blue spinning pole in front had caught his attention. He knew it was a barbershop but wondered what kind of job it would be exactly. Maybe they were only looking for a janitor, window cleaner or something else so he stepped through the door to inquire. He didn't need another job of this kind and if it was anything but barbering he would walk out the door and continue on his way again.

But the owner of a one man barbershop was looking for a second person to work as an apprentice barber part time to start since he was trying to grow his business. He wanted an apprentice specifically, the owner explained, because he couldn't afford the wages of a journeyman until he knew a two-chair shop would work out. Although it would be nothing like his tavern and lodging business in Bagnoli, part-time work sounded good to Frank since he could continue working his custodial shift in the evening. The combined number of hours could be handled for someone with a lot of extra time on his hands and the extra money wouldn't hurt. He had dabbled a little with haircutting in Bovino but lacked essential skills and would be fortunate to have training from a professional.

In the beginning he would carefully observe techniques used by the owner and become familiar with the tools of the trade. Then he would practice on the owner himself and any other non-paying guinea pigs willing to take a chance on a novice. Two mirrors would be used to cut his own hair and when he was finished he would be wearing what he had learned in his new trade for all to see. The green light from his boss would be needed before Michelino would be allowed to take on full-price customers. And even then he would be supervised closely for a few weeks. It was only after demonstrating an aptitude for cutting hair as well as mastering shaving methods—no bloodletting these days—that he would be assigned a few regular hours a week to the second chair when more than one barber was needed at busier times. He would still be carefully monitored, but if all worked out a regular schedule, even working alone at times, would be allowed.

Within a year it was evident Michelino Conte had the talent for the profession; a steady stream of return clientele even asked specifically for him by name. He had proved to the barbering world he had what it takes for hair and face grooming. And he also proved to be adept at casual chit-chat—actually thoroughly enjoying it—essential in providing a relaxed and trustworthy atmosphere for customers. Idle conversation also ended the use of Michelino as his first name for it was far easier to be remembered as Michael or just Mike instead. A lot could be learned from customer-barber exchanges. Soon clientele were so numerous his boss and Michael had as much work as they could handle even in a two-chair shop. Hours of work fluctuating during weekdays and on Saturdays amounted to a full-time position and suited Michaels's bachelor-like lifestyle to a tee, at least until his wife and children were able to join him from Italy. He gave his notice to his other employer since he no longer needed supplementary work to fill his day and make ends meet.

Though he was thriving in his new occupation he was often downcast from missing the ones left behind in Italy. When would he ever see them again? There was dread the conflict in Europe could be a long but there was also some optimism that it would be a short one, possibly even over within the year. In any event, at the moment it was an impediment preventing Michael's family from leaving the country, and would probably remain so until there was an official end to hostilities. Only then, he believed, would his wife, two year old son and the daughter he had never met be allowed to sail to America.

With no reported progress in bringing the war to a close the rest of 1914 passed in the same way. German offensives in France and Belgium had resulted in the slaughter of a massive number of soldiers and citizens from those countries which was not a good sign. Russia's large army participation might yet turn the tide against the Germans but that remained to be seen. Then the fighting drug on and it had become four long years without peace. Not only in 1914, but in 1915, 1916 and the first months of 1917 battles were relentlessly fought. Then America entered the war in April of 1917. For most of time the Great War had occurred primarily on European lands but then it spread to a much lesser extent to the Middle East, Africa and Asia. The United States, although officially neutral and a non-participant until 1917, had been providing supply support to Britain, France and other Allies all along. No American troops, however, had been sent to bolster the military effort. But by late 1917 America U.S. troop involvement had begun, and in 1918 the American Expeditionary Force was fully present on the ground, shifting the odds of victory in favor of the Allies.

The war seemed to be winding down, according to what Michael read and heard in-between snipping an errant strand of hair or lathering and scraping an upturned face. It hadn't been that way at the beginning of 1918 when Germany's might still predominated and a cloud of pessimism hung heavily over the chances of Ally victory. But then the tides turned with America's entry making the difference during the summer. The retreat of the German Army in July of 1918 seemed to be a sure sign the fighting was finally about to conclude.

Movement of civilians out of Italy by ship had been on hold from almost the beginning of the war. Before it could resume again the sea needed be free from threats of attack and made safe for passage. Assuming it would be open to travellers again sometime in the near future plans were already being made by Antonia Conte in early 1915, four months after the birth of her second child in the previous year. The excitement of a family once again reunited in the letters exchanged could be felt on both sides of the Atlantic. But they had also put Michael in a bit of quandary of what he should do in his part of the world. He had learned by word of mouth some days ago of the impending retirement of the owner of a well-situated and much-loved barbershop in the nearby city of Sharon. After contacting him he was told the sale of the shop would be announced during the following week. Would it be the right time for taking the risk of giving up a stable job at a Youngstown barbershop to move from Ohio across the border to Pennsylvania or should he wait?

***

    Chills had rippled up and down his body when Michael Conte read that the Sant' Anna—the very same ship he had taken to America in 1914—had been sunk. The Sant' Anna had been converted into a troopship by the French in 1915 and a German U-boat had sent it to the bottom of the Mediterranean in May 1918. Maybe the war was not almost over after all, like everyone had expected. Certainly the seas still remained unsafe. On top of that the Russian czar and his family, which had been arrested in 1917 during Russian Revolution, were murdered by the Bolsheviks in July of the same year that the Sant' Anna was no more. And that was not the end of the bad news in what was turning out to be a very eventful year already. The latest headlines also captured the story of a new virus that had been spreading across nations like wildfire since March. Although it was something different than the usual seasonal ailments, recovery from this form of influenza—a word of Italian origin—seemed to be normal though. But it was just one more tale of woe to add to an already gloomy five years.

    The metal flap of the mail slot snapped shut with a loud bang as the envelope fell to the floor. Michael Conte was sitting at the kitchen table nursing a cup of coffee in his hands when the sound had made him jump for some reason although he had heard it dozens of times before. There was something different today about the delivery or something different about himself that morning. The cup began to quiver and the coffee sloshed about until he placed it down on the table. On a normal day he would have been curious enough to go to the door to see what the postman had brought. Today, he stayed seated and looked vacantly down at the floor; he had slipped into a kind of stupor, even forgetting to finish his coffee. It was tepid anyhow and he wouldn't have enjoyed it. But eventually he got up from the chair and walked the few feet, bent down and picked it up. He noticed right away the Italian lira stamps in the corner, but the handwriting of the address was unfamiliar. One thing for sure, it wasn't his wife's. The contents were short and to the point: on the 4th of October 1918, Antonia Conte had succumbed to influenza after a short battle. Antonia, the love of his life, his steadfast supporter as he prepared for their life in America had been only twenty-six years old.

Michael Conte's world had crumbled around him in an instant.

He read the words again and again not wanting to believe them. How could this have happened when they were so close to being a family again? If it was true, and it must be true, what did anything matter now? It was as if a dark curtain had dropped over him, shutting out everything else. And it lasted and lasted. The curtain only began to open a month later when the war to end all wars finally came to an end. Before that, he had lacked the motivation to even to write to his children or their grandparents in Bagnoli. But even a half broken man must pull himself together again. The pain his children must be going through was the same as his own as the grieving widower. Probably it was even worse in having to watch their mother die in front of them. It was time to put thoughts of himself aside and think of what could be done about Maria and Antonio. Half-orphans, they had no parent to look after them Italy, and their grandparent's responsibility had become even greater. But how could they fit into his life in America without their mother, his wife, while he worked and they all lived in a tiny rented flat? His brain ran in circles searching for an answer until it was absolutely ragged.

    A visit from his brother-in-law the next day reminded him of the barbershop for sale in Sharon. Aniello Clemente wondered whether or not Michael had done anything about it one way or the other. Because of the shock he had nearly forgotten all about it. "You should look into it, Michelino." He was still referred to as Michelino and not Michael by Aniello and Antonetta. His sister had dropped the letter "i" in Antonietta for ease of spelling and pronunciation. "We know you and what you are going through, but it would give you something else to focus on and would do you good," his sister added. "You have to get on with your life, and take care of your children sooner or later. We don't have to tell you that your situation has already gone on way too long here."

    Something new to focus on, she had said. It couldn't hurt and actually made sense. At that very moment he made his decision. He would move forward; any reservations he had over timing were cast to the wind. Even if it turned into nothing at least making the effort would help to take his mind off other things. Chances of an offer being accepted with the way things were going in his life were practically zero anyhow.

    But he was wrong.

    The retiring owner liked him personally, and to his surprise the conservative amount of what he thought he could afford was conditionally agreed. Without the total amount in hand to purchase the barbershop outright, a deal was struck between buyer and seller to pay the remainder of what was owed over time after making a down payment. Monthly installments would be made for a two year period at the end of which time the shop would be paid for in full. There would be no interest charged. Both sides believed it was manageable based on business expectations for barbershops, which were almost an essential service in a revitalizing post-war economy.

In December, just before the Christmas holidays, he moved from his flat in Ohio into another in South Sharon, as the former Borough of Farrell was now called, a boomtown chock full of immigrants some fifteen miles from Youngstown. And in Sharon the birth of the Cozy Barbershop became a Mercer County reality. It was a big step to take in leaving the close proximity of relatives whom he saw often and had depended on for friendship and support in Ohio. Nevertheless, the move had served the purpose of switching his focus and lessening the grief over the loss of his wife. Still, what to do about Antonio and Maria plagued him every day. From what he gathered in letters received from Bagnoli on a more irregular basis now, they were coping well for the present. In spite of sharing the same bloodline and bearing the same Conte surname, relatives from his side often did not see eye-to-eye with those from his wife's. At least he had made a decision, right or wrong only time would tell. A lot depended on which direction a now war-free country would

CALLINGS

Martinsville and Indianapolis, Indiana, 1921-1925

Eldest child Daniel Paulone had reached the age of seventeen in 1920, with an eleven year gap between Louis, the youngest in the family, and himself. He had less than a year of high school left until graduation and couldn't wait for it to be over so he could be on his way to a new life. It was time to free himself of his father's inflexible methods and harsh discipline. Enough was enough. For Daniel, though, it had nothing to do with his father's insistence on practicing a musical instrument; Danny needed no encouragement to do that. The thing he was most grateful for at home was the gift of music his father had given him. Indeed he could be found cradling a violin in his arms whenever he had a spare moment. The sounds coming from the bow sliding over the strings spoke to him like a conversation. And Danny, who had been a rambunctious and talkative small child, had replaced other relationships with a religious-like devotion to his best friend made of wood. Taciturn and moody now, the young man about to seek his fortune looked forward to becoming his own master.

And so it was with his violin case strapped on his back

that Daniel Paulone in his eighteenth year set off from home. A letter confirming his first engagement for a stint with string quartet in New York City he had safely tucked away in a coat pocket. There had been tears streaming down his mother's cheeks when they met on the street to say goodbye, but in her heart of hearts she knew it was best for him to leave home as she had done before him. He had tried to keep farewells to an undramatic minimum. Besides, the inexpensive room in a boarding house he had found was not far away. What the world had in store for a talented musician eager to carve out a niche for himself he was ready to find out.

Daniel Paulone wasted no time in opening his atrophied wings. There were a stream of musical engagements to dive into when his short tenure in Manhattan ended that would take him to places many of which he was familiar and others he had never heard of before. New Jersey had been his compass for so long it felt like going to another world when Pennsylvania, Ohio and even more distant Indiana beckoned to him. Before he knew it more than a year and a half had whisked by since Newark had been left behind and Daniel Paulone had proved to himself that he could make it on his own and was proud of it. He was not leading a life of luxury by any means. All he required were the essentials—enough food to keep him fit as a fiddle and a roof over his head to keep his strings dry wherever he landed next.

Maybe it was an air of confidence that had stood out most to the avid listener in the audience one evening in Martinsville, a small town about thirty miles southeast of Indianapolis. In any case, she felt compelled to personally thank the violinist for the beautiful music he had just played.

"Where did you learn to play the violin like that? You

look so young when I see you close up, if you don't mind me saying so."

"Thank you for the compliment—if that's what it was meant to be," he shot back on the spur of the moment to the girl as youthful as himself and with the most gorgeous, twinkling blue eyes he had ever seen.

"I'm sorry if I misspoke. You were really good and I enjoyed it so much. That's all I really wanted to say."

"I know that's what you meant. I was just teasing you a bit. I don't know what got into me since we've just met. Here I am taking liberties with someone kind enough to tell me of their appreciation for my music who I don't know at all."

"I'm glad I didn't offend you. I can't imagine being so accomplished so early in life. It would be impossible for me to be at your level even if I thought I had any real talent in that way—and I don't."

"Everyone has something they're good at and I'm sure you do as well. Maybe I can make up for my poor attempt at a joke if you'd like to join me for a cup of coffee or something at the place right next door? I'm always famished after playing and we could learn a little more about each other. By the way my name is Daniel, Danny for short, but you probably knew that from the program they handed out when you entered." Sybil Reeves, his newfound admirer and potential new friend, accepted his invitation. And the two young people soon learned they did indeed have much to talk about.

Small talk about this and that changed to the more personal when Sybil let drop that her mother had passed away some years before. Her father, still alive and healthy, had remarried and a second wife had brought three children with her from her previous marriage who were now, of course,

Sybil's step-siblings. They found common ground when they shared that both of their fathers were of the overbearing type, which had made it hard to live at home. They parted that evening as newly made fast friends. The next day Danny left for another concert venue and Sybil returned to her residence in Mooresville. But before they parted, they agreed to see each other again in two days. She looked forward to seeing this interesting and handsome musician of more than average height and so lightly complexioned that his Italian heritage he had mentioned failed to reveal itself.

Over the next several weeks musical commitments took him to Shelbyville, Bloomington, Terre-Haute, Plainfield and Spencer, the last the town in which Sybil had been born. Then the tour ended in southern Indiana with a final concert in Indianapolis, the capital city. Each time that he had a day or two off in-between performances in the Hoosier state, he travelled back to Mooresville to be with Sybil. It didn't take long before they had fallen completely in love. Then Daniel, the violinist prodigy five months shy of turning twenty, proposed to the eighteen soon-to-be nineteen year old Sybil on a late afternoon. Marriage to anyone had crossed neither one of their minds before they met, still there must have been a subconscious readiness to wed with the right person for a commitment to have been made so quickly. And what better place to marry than Martinsville where they had first met? It was conveniently located among the group of small towns in which he performed and held special meaning to them both. Neither Daniel nor Sybil seemed concerned about their parents' participation. Daniel never talked about his mother anyway and his father was no longer part of his life. Only his two brothers and sister still at home in Newark sparked a hint of enthusiasm when they were mentioned. Sybil, for her part, was equally disdainful of her father's wishes whatever they may have been. So within three months of having first laid eyes—and ears—on each other they went ahead with their plans alone. And on the 19th of May 1923 Daniel and Sybil became man and wife.

That eldest son Daniel had been away from home for nearly three years and had taken a wife somewhere in the hinterlands of Indiana without informing him beforehand might have given his father at least a moment of pause to ask himself why that was so. Then Frank Paulone found out that Daniel had not spoken to his mother either, the woman who was still Frank's wife in law only having left her husband and children some three years before. So both parents had learned of Daniel's marriage after the fact. Lydia believed her estranged husband to be the main reason for why neither of them had been contacted to take part in Daniel's wedding. And she made him aware of her beliefs on a Saturday after visiting with her children, making the point that the marriage had been planned and was not a spontaneous elopement. There had been time to inform them but instead they were intentionally excluded. It barely seemed to faze him. No longer part of the home ménage, what Daniel decided to do with his life was beyond his control and apparently beyond his interest as well.

Work called again and honeymoon days were short but sweet for the newlyweds. Not even the sacrifices required in starting out on the very modest salary of a musician could break their romantic bubble. They just took it in stride. Financial worries were a normal part of building a life together and they looked forward to meeting the challenges head-on. Some changes, nevertheless, could improve how they met those challenges when it came to quality of life issues. Travelling from small town to small town to play music and frequently staying overnight no longer was the best option for Danny. It made sense that a city offering a variety of musical events and organizations and businesses would be the best place to find employment so they would be able to spend more time together and before they seriously considered starting a family. Job openings in a large city such as Indianapolis came about often and would give Danny the chance to work for a single employer mostly in one place.

    Danny took the lead in directing their search to find properties close to the city center having already become familiar with several areas in Indianapolis from concerts he had performed there. They figured living close-in would be the easiest for giving access to the best Indianapolis had to offer, including a large job market and access to public transportation. They were fortunate enough to find and rent an apartment they liked within the week. That had been the easy part for Danny. Almost immediately Sybil was hired as a clerk in the office of Strong Brothers, a plumbing business within walking distance. Danny, conversely, struggled to find permanent employment. Without formal musical education and professional training to bolster his resume and no matter how well he played the violin, the criteria set by the established orchestras in the city was not met. Rather than leave them in a financially precarious situation after weeks of rejection, he resorted to manual labor, something he was not particularly cut out to do but was readily available. By combining handyman and other physical jobs with sporadic evening concert dates from a variety of smaller musical groups he was able to do his part in making ends meet. It was disappointing in terms of career expectations, but he wasn't too concerned about the state of his hands when blisters and splinters took their toll.

Although they were still only in their early twenties and had stable incomes stress still managed to enter their lives at times. Their apartment on North East Street in Indianapolis was affordable and convenient but a bit cramped even for the two of them and would be even more so if they were to start a family. Living on the fringe of one of the seedier parts of downtown also could be disturbing at times. Just last Thursday while walking home from work Sybil had encountered the same down-and-out derelict guy she had seen before. Perhaps a bit drunk, he had touched her arm to stop her. Nothing serious had taken place but still it might have done. Fresh in her mind, Sybil used the incident to talk about where they lived:

"Twice this week I've felt afraid just walking down the street, Danny. The skid row vagrants seem to be moving further into our neighborhood or our neighborhood seems to moving further into skid row. I know moving again is always a hassle, but would you really want our children living around here? I don't think you would and I certainly wouldn't. Could we think about possibly moving somewhere else?" she implored with a look in her eyes as irresistible as the day they had first met after his concert in Martinsville.

"I'm glad you brought it up. Moving has been on my mind too and I'm ready for some peace and quiet. We've put up with a lot of city racket for long enough now and we could also use more greenery around and less endless concrete and pavement. Today, when I was landscaping on the Westside, I came across a small development around where Washington Street becomes Rockville Road. You know, just after crossing the White River and passing the hospital for the mentally ill. One of the cottages had a "For Rent" sign in front of it. The area is not that far from where we are at here and still within the city limits, but it's almost like living in the countryside. It would be a place where our kids could be kids, playing outdoors with the other children in the neighborhood; and it seemed so peaceful." Sybil was surprised he spoke with such enthusuasm in his voice for she hadn't seen him so animated in a long time.

"I guess we're not quite ready to start a family yet. But just for the sake of our own sanity and safety I'm glad you feel the same way as I do. Let's go to see it tomorrow morning if we can. I hope it's still available by then."

"Better yet, we might be able to call. I remember seeing a phone number on the sign. If I can get a hold of the fellow I was working for today, he might be able to tell me what it is. He said he only lives a mile down the road from there." As if the stars were aligned in their favor, the number was obtained and an appointment was made to visit the small cottage first thing the next morning. Rockville Road was a main thoroughfare, but the cottage was set back well away from the road with a small stand of trees as a buffer. They loved it right away. They loved that it was away from the noise of the city, the trees that would shade them during the heat of Midwest summer days, the privacy it afforded and they loved that the rent was less than what they now paid. In a little over a month they would move and put city living behind them. Access to the city center would still be easy for Danny once he became an employed musician again. And by bus it was a straight shot to Sybil's workplace too.

The new home they had chosen was everything they thought it to be with one exception: a perfect place to raise children needed children to raise. As soon as they had settled they had decided it was time, yet despite their efforts for nearly two years there were none. Thrilled as they had been in moving away from the city, living in the suburbs had begun to lose some of its luster. Perhaps they had been jinxed in moving to a larger place before a child was actually on the way. Timing and pressure could have been the problems, and timing again could also be the solution. Before the week was out a letter arrived in the mailbox addressed to Daniel Paulone with a Church of the Nazarene return address written in the top left corner of the envelope. It had to be about the musician job Danny had spoken to her about a few weeks ago. She didn't think she recognized the church name, though. As soon as he returned from work and had hung up his coat she handed the letter to him then waited for his reaction. Danny didn't appear that excited over the contents after he had read it to himself. "They're interested in my musical background but apparently have some questions about religious persuasion and so forth."

"But is there an actual job or is it just in case of a future opening? Sybil wondered.

"They're looking to hire a musician so there's definitely a job, I'm not sure what and where it would be exactly. It's all a little vague so I don't know if it's worthwhile to write back. But I guess I will answer them and see where it goes from there."

He had given an impression of disinterest but a door had just opened that would remain so for the rest of Danny's life.

Raised a Catholic in a hybrid religious family—his mother a Protestant—an invitation to attend a Nazarene revival meeting as part of the application process for a position with this unfamiliar church was accepted. And it turned out to be a life changing experience. The atmosphere of something greater than himself could be felt in the joy, the enthusiasm, the laying on of hands, the singing and everything else he witnessed that day. He loved every minute of it and returned home a newly converted man, transformed by the Holy Spirit. Along with his admission into the church came an offer of the post of evangelist musician. But first he must undergo training, licensing and credentialing in the ministry of music at the Nazarene facilities in Illinois.

A settled life in one place would become a thing of the past once preliminaries were completed and Daniel was officially launched on his new career. Although he would not be travelling on horseback, as circuit riders had done a decade or two earlier, he would be called upon to serve churches and participate in revival meetings in a group of different states of the union in his role of an itinerant musician and preacher. Playing sacred songs on his violin and mandolin while preaching the gospel and seeing a bit more of the world suited Daniel Paulone just fine at this stage of his life. Not so much for his wife, though. Such a peripatetic profession came at a price: Sybil much preferred the more permanent less nomadic lifestyle which she thought they had intended to continue children or not.

HOLLOW YEARS

Sharon-Farrell, Pennsylvania, 1919-1925

A tumultuous 1919 did not restore confidence to Michelino Conte in his life of living alone in Sharon. The Great War had indeed ended on the 11th of November 1918—a month after his wife had died in Bagnoli—when Germany signed the Armistice along with a simultaneous ceasefire. Soldiers were returning to the United States in droves but many of them not always to the farms and small towns they had originally left. The draw of finding a job in the cities had become a lure not easy to resist in light of the dearth of work in a country relying more and more on mechanized agriculture. Steel companies located in Sharon and other parts of the Shenango Valley, which had boomed beyond belief during the war years, now found themselves scrambling to adjust as supply outpaced demand during the early post-war period. After living through the fevered pace of war production and then its sudden cessation, there was a need for returning soldiers and local workers to find new sources of employment opportunities. This was particularly true in the town of Farrell, which had changed its name from South Sharon a few years before. Steel expansion brought about by the war years could still offer an avenue for the future—or could not—but for the present it was stagnant. Eggs all in one basket would be a foolish choice in any case.

 Strikes in major industries, including steel, had affected Michelino Conte's outlook as it had many others around him. The uncertainty over the direction things were taking was just one more worry to add to his grief over the death of his wife. He felt like his life was caught in a downward spiral, taking him deeper into a black hole. And as always there was the question of the welfare of his children still living across the watery divide. How could he allow them to be brought to a country at a moment when the economy and political situation appeared to be so precarious? The American Federation of Labor had backed industrial actions at several steel mills just in the last few months in Ohio, where he had formerly lived, and in other neighboring states. The Great Steel Strike of 1919 had ended in 1920 with the failure of the AFL's attempt to organize the giant United States Steel Corporation located only a few miles down the road in Pittsburg. But not without leaving a trail of damage seriously affecting many ensnared in the aftermath.

 The impact of the US Steel strike was not confined to the city of Pittsburg alone. The company's involvement in mergers, consolidations and acquisitions within the established steel industry in Farrell had also left its mark. The Sharon Steel Company and Sharon Steel Hoop Company were part of this group, and the threats of sustained unrest and long-term unemployment continued in the local area. And they did so until 1923, the year when the Westinghouse Electric and Manufacturing Company had been established and built a plant in the Sharon District. The end of the recession of 1920 and 1921 combined with Westinghouse's reshaping of local steel industry into the manufacturing of electrical transformers promised better times to come for the Shenango Valley through industrial diversification.

There was, however, by this time an additional obstacle upsetting plans for Conte family reunification. Riding a wave of anti-immigration sentiment, a quota system on immigration had been passed into law in 1921. Early attempts at reducing immigration in 1917 had failed to have the desired outcome; mandatory literacy tests, the passing of which were required for over sixteen year olds to immigrate, had been insufficient to stem the tide enough. According to the current government, more effective measures were needed. Another bill was passed to restrict immigrants to no more than three percent of the total foreign born already in the United States based on the population counted in the 1910 federal census was intended to further reduce overall numbers. The new law that came into force in 1921 was time-bound, however, expiring after three years in 1924, at which time the push to limit immigration persisted as strong as ever. The open door was shutting but still needed another nudge to further reduce the number of newcomers admitted.

The new American Immigration Act of 1924 had the desired effect and the number of foreigners immigrating went into a notable decline. How was this achieved? By reducing the percentage of immigrants to two percent from three; and by basing population figures on the 1890 census taken twenty years earlier when the total population was decidedly smaller. It amounted to a clever manipulation of the weaker earlier law. The new law favored those of British descent due to their much longer settlement in America, and places like the southern part of Italy saw a drastic drop in admissions to America when compared to the recent past. There had been some dissention when a percentage system was initially introduced and became law back in 1921. The 1924 legislation appeared to be only a minor adjustment to its predecessor, which allowed it to be passed without opposition. The open door had closed a little tighter still.

It was clear in Michael Conte's mind his children were going to have to jump through additional hoops if they were to become a family once again. His record of supporting himself for years and the fact that he was in the final stage of becoming a full-fledged American citizen should mean something. And since he was the only living parent of Antonio and Maria, he thought his chances for gaining approval for them to join him were better than average despite the harsher regulations. Then it was reported passports would soon be required to enter America. Demanding official documents when neither visas nor passports had been necessary in the past was just one more detail to be ironed out. But still he hesitated in giving the word to begin the process for their immigration. Even more needed to be done to ensure everything was in place and leave no questions over his ability to provide for them. Any concerns officials might entertain about his children becoming wards of the state could have devastating consequences in view of present relocation sentiments.

During the immediate post-war period barbershop clientele had remained stable for the most part. The expected surge in numbers from a swelling population led by returning soldiers had failed to materialize. But by 1923 demand for men's hair services was on the rise again. Already another competitor had opened a barbershop a few blocks away. And a second was about to do the same near Sharon's border with Farrell. His own haircutting operation had prospered in the first half of the decade and Michael had increased the number of chairs and hired more barbers. It was as if history was repeating itself from the beginning of his career when he was an employee and the shop owner had done the same thing. But even after expanding his shop there were more clients than could be accommodated. The idea of opening up a second shop was tempting and the timing seemed right but it involved greater risks. So far, in working alongside barbers at his current shop there had been no challenge to his leadership. Two shops would be a different ball game. Michael could not be in two places at the same time so close supervision would be out. It would be another test of his business acumen and management skills, but if it worked out his family would be much better off. It was a tough decision but in the end he decided it was worth the gamble and threw caution to the wind.

 All the same, there was just one more thing on his plate he wanted to do before hoping his children would be sent to join him. A real house, not the small flat in which he was living, would be ideal for the three of them if he could afford it. Almost a month passed after the opening of the second shop before he wrote to inform the folks in Bagnoli about his current situation. In the last letter he had fallen on the excuse of setting up the new shop for another delay in having them come. There was always something that got in the way. But what if they knew the real reason for Michael's tardiness in writing again was fear of their reaction to further postponement in order to find a suitable place to house them all. Maria, the younger of the two he thought would be more likely to handle it better on the surface. Even in America he was aware of her tough-minded reputation. But underneath this façade, she would be even more devastated than her brother, who might be more likely to show he was upset. He thought his assessment was true when he read between the lines of the letters they had previously sent. After all it had been five years since his mother had died and nine since his father left. But there was no question they would both at least inwardly feel even more downcast than he did.

Michael did write his letter and posted it in the mailbox on the corner. Their grandparents responsible for the raising the children were in agreement for once when they read it. Michael was not wrong in how he predicted his children's reactions, only he had forgotten to consider the feelings of those who watched over them day in and day out. Not only the children felt the disappointment of another postponement, all of them did. And the unspoken thought that was in the back of their minds moved to the forefront: Michelino was never going to send for them and Antonio and Maria would remain in Italy for the rest of their lives. And from then on they took great care to not mention their father as much. Nothing would be gained to be constantly reminded of what might have been. It was time to focus on the present in Bagnoli Irpino, on family, friends, school, church, talents and even the more mundane, like chores.

So a plan was hatched to transition from unrealistic expectations to embracing the life they were leading in their Italian home. Maria was asked to help in the kitchen and with housework more regularly. She was also given permission to join the church choir as a means for expressing her love and talent when it came to anything musical. Antonio, not to be overlooked, was also asked to lend a hand in cooking and actually enjoyed it. The warmth of the oven made the kitchen a cozy place to be during the cold weekend days of winter when they would likely be spending most of their time indoors anyway. His enthusiasm when there reached its pinnacle when there was baking to be done and it showed in the results. Sometimes a new twist on homemade bread was brought to the table and all knew Antonio must have created it. These distractions seemed to be working; Maria and Antonio were more content, happier, at least on the surface. Daily routines were helping them to forgive if not forget. It was what good doctors would have prescribed as the best medicine to cure heartaches.

Michael had not been so fortunate. Deferring the reunion with his children again had left him feeling exposed. At the barbershop he was not the usual voluble person who stood behind or to the side of his customers. In keeping with his mood he only listened to what they said with one ear open. And he nearly missed hearing when Fred O'Malley, the real estate agent from a few doors down, began to describe a property he had viewed earlier that morning.

"You know, Mike, I haven't come across one like this for quite a while; an older home that's in good condition and in Sharon too. No doubt it needs some updating here and there. But it doesn't appear anything major, like walls, roof, pipes or foundation, would need to be replaced or repaired. The house has already been inspected and passed muster with a few minor recommendations. The rooms are spacious and the floor plan seems logical to my way of thinking. Best of all, it's in one of the better parts of the town. An older woman is selling it and I have the impression she might be eager to see it done soon." Fred moved his head just enough to catch Michael's eyes in the mirror, wondering if Michael's had listened at all to what he had said. A brief suspension of clipping and the raising of Michael's left eyebrow were the only signs he might have gotten a little rise out of him.

At any rate Fred thought he had. And given the dreary disposition the barber had been displaying since he had seated himself, it was enough to continue. "She's older and after holding on for so long it seems like she can't get rid of it fast enough. And she already has a retirement place in mind, according to one of the other realtors who was there this morning. But nothing is written in stone. But as they say in the business, she seems motivated." This time Michael had both ears open and went as far as sliding over to the counter to lay down comb and scissors, ready to make some kind of comment. But, in truth, he had already disregarded most of what Fred had said. It smacked too much of a salesman promoting something that was never going to live up to reality, a bit like selling used cars. Still, he wanted to show interest.

"Do you have any idea yet of what the asking price might be? And what's the address? Do other potential buyers already know about it?" he asked in a rather flat voice. The string of questions at least reassured Fred that he wasn't wasting his breath.

"I really can't say anything yet about what the price may be. But I think if you're interested you should take a few minutes to go over and see it. I could turn out to be well worth your time. I could try to arrange a visit this afternoon if you could make it. I can read your mind, though; you think it's just idle barbershop talk to pass the time. But I promise it's not a bunch of malarkey and I'm serious. For someone like you who has told me you were looking for a house in the right place at the right price, I really do think you should see it soon. Just go over and take a look at it because if you don't others will and it won't last long. I'll try to get you a price after you have had a peek."

Still a little wary, Michael was convinced enough that he would go to see it and they agreed to meet at the home at three o'clock. It would be a late lunch hour and his colleague could hold the fort down if it happened to take a little longer. The house was all it was cracked up to be and right away he let Fred know he was very interested in it. Now it was all about the price.

"I'll stop by your place this evening to tell you what I've found out if that's okay."

"Thanks, Fred. I am definitely really interested. I already can see in my head where things would go and the changes I'd make to turn it into a real home for my children." Just after the dinner hour Fred made good on his promise to let Michael know what he had learned.

"I can't believe it. I think I could actually make both the down payment and the monthly mortgage amount. Let me have some time to let it sink in and to double check my finances, but I think by morning I'll be ready to take the plunge. Just give me overnight to wrap my head around such a big decision."

"Understood, but let me know first thing one way or the other as soon as you can. If it's yes, then we should put an offer in writing right away."

Short as one night may be, it was too long. A couple had

made a full price offer on the evening of the day before and it had been accepted. Hesitancy had lost a great prospect but a lesson had been learned for the future. And as fate would have it the future came quickly. Three weeks later Fred contacted Michael again. Another house in the same neighborhood as the one that had been sold from underneath him had just gone on the market. This time it was Michael who pushed Fred to take him to see it within a couple of hours. It was equally appealing and already priced. Prepared in advance this time, he was positive it would be within his budget. A stretch at the beginning for sure, but he believed in the potential growth of his businesses and the profits that would come with it. Michael made an offer without needing further reflection this time. It was accepted within the hour and a contract was signed all before he went back to work smiling from ear to ear.

Within the span of a month—following eight long years in Farrell—he had become a proud homeowner for the first time in Sharon. Some of the remodeling he planned on doing himself and for the more specialized work he would take it one step at a time, hiring help and starting projects as finances permitted. Talking with tradesmen while they sat in a chair waiting to be shorn was a good start for finding the right people at the right cost. And from the purchase in 1923 until well into 1925, the interior of the house was transformed by many skilled hands into a beautiful home fit for a family—his family. It had been a long road from arrival in New York on a hot and sticky July day in 1914 and ten years later becoming a naturalized citizen in 1924, but the new home in Sharon helped to make it all worthwhile.

Christmas holidays at the end of 1925 came and went a little less depressing than they had in past years. There was truly something to look forward to in the coming year, for the last piece of his plan had fallen into place. On New Year's Eve, he was finally ready to send for his children and, if all went well with the authorities, to bring them to America. As wintry and bleak as this 31st of December in Pennsylvania could be, it was spring-like hope that buoyed his spirits. And tomorrow the top of the new calendar hanging on the wall would boldly announce **1926**!

TRIALS AND TRIBULATIONS

Newark, New Jersey, New York City, 1921-1925

Daniel Paulone had left life in Newark behind him in 1921 and at eighteen had struck out on his own. Less than two years later he was a married man. Major changes in Daniel's short life to this point had come early and with deliberation. Now it was up to his two brothers, one in his early teens and the other seven, as well as a sister of eleven to negotiate living in a single parent home without him. Nothing changed as far as their father's unrelenting attitude in exercising his patriarchal command over their lives, just as he had tried to do with Daniel. Jimmy and Millie continued to collude when they could, covering for each other when deviating from the rules. Louis occasionally sided with his older siblings but just as often followed his own path. Daniel never had much reason to join them when he was still living at home. The eldest child he could do little wrong in his father's eyes. The unfairness was annoying to the others but seniority usually came with perks.

Raising three children had not left much room for non-essentials on a barber's income even though business was good. The last four years had been financially painful with food and clothing prices mounting in relation to greater demand and a growing population. From the years 1916 to 1920 inflation had been particularly hard to stomach when it attained its apex of seventeen percent during the middle two years. Still, it seemed unjustified their father could be so miserly even if they had some understanding of the situation. A few pennies to spend like the rest of the kids on the block would have been nice. There was a golden lining for Jim, however, in having a father who was tightfisted. How could he, a young person with no special skills—other than the ability to play a flute and piccolo better than most—earn some pocket money on his own?

    His first job when he was eleven had consisted of shoveling snow off the sidewalks of neighbors during the winter. That had helped for a while but it was summertime now. There must be something else he could think of to do but what? One afternoon on his way home from the store he noticed wildflowers growing in patches of a vacant lot. The answer had popped up right in front him! Simply pick some, make bouquets and then sell them door-to-door. At first the new venture was successful, but then the supply dwindled as the sunshine disappeared. Scouting for other places where flowers might be more plentiful led nowhere fast during exceptionally cool weather in the middle of April. Any flowers daring to show themselves did so slowly and thinly, the others waiting for temperatures to climb before peeking out.

    Disappointed but never discouraged another idea came into Jim's mind when watching chimneys continue to billow smoke even in the midst of spring. The last wintry storms that had passed through may have kept flowers from blooming but they had also left a need for wood to keep homes heated after the winter months had passed. Near his home there was a factory on a hill that produced wooden boxes. From the road, leftover scrap wood could be seen piled in the yard when Jim passed by. Why not ask if he could have it for free. He would be doing them a service in getting rid of the wood waste at no cost to them, he thought, as the chilly winds blew right through his sweater. They would be happy to see it gone from their property and they were. So, bright and early on a Saturday morning while pulling a red wagon behind him the collection began. It would be the first trip of many during the day, each one with wood remnants piled as high as they could be without spilling, or even worse, tipping over completely and dumping the whole load, as had happened once when he had been overly ambitious.

When he got home with the final load, Jim chopped the larger pieces into a size to fit wood stoves then filled a basket with the kindling. Like with the flowers then came the door-to-door selling phase, which he went about with confidence. He knew he had something they could use and at a good price so convincing them to part with a little money for a basketful should not be that hard. Many of those he met seemed to actually enjoy talking to an enterprising young man. Beginning a business venture—spurred on by a penny-pinching parent—was something he liked doing and had been good at so far. Maybe the makings of a natural salesman had been passed down from some distant ancestor and could be used to his advantage again sometime in the future.

"Why are you looking like the cat ate the canary?" asked his sister when he came home pulling the wagon behind him. "You see the empty basket in front of you, Millie? During the last few hours that basket was filled with wood at least a dozen times. Now come a little closer and listen to the jingling sound coming from my pocket. Do you hear the noise all those coins are making? We'll no longer be the laughing stock, the ones that always pass by George's corner store without stopping. So what are we waiting for; let's get going. It's our turn today to buy candy like the others always do." She didn't need to be asked twice; holding hands, they made haste in walking the four blocks to get there.

    Not only had Jim Paulone demonstrated to himself that he had a salesman's gift of the gab but he learned he was a bit of a risk taker too when it came to playing the odds. On the spur of the moment one day he entered a shop with a "Going out of business" sign hanging in the window. Everything was discounted, even the lowest priced items including a wide variety of candy. Another light went off. What if bought most or all and then resold it to the other kids at a little higher price than he paid but still lower than it would then at the local shops? The markup would still be lower than at George's, their closest store, for instance. Everyone would be happy; they would enjoy a bargain while he made a tidy profit. Even so it was a gamble since he would have to spend most of his kindling sales money to buy a large quantity and then there might be a refusal to buy the candy for some reason. Should he rely on his recently tested powers of persuasion in hoping that they did? Of course he would!

    Taking the road less travelled became a pattern for Jim to follow going forward. It came to a head when at fourteen, only two months into his first year of high school, he decided he had enough of formal education. During tough times— unemployment rising, veterans returning in droves, Spanish flu wreaking havoc and other factors leading to recession in

1921—Jim had decided spending his day in a classroom was a waste of valuable time which could be better used in earning his keep. It was like treading water when what he really wanted to do was to start swimming in the stream of the money-making life happening all around him. Jim Paulone was by far not alone in becoming a school-leaver after completing the eighth grade. Not only other friends he knew were cutting their schooldays short, but it was not uncommon to consider eight years of schooling to be sufficient nationwide.

His father, of course, was very displeased—nothing could please him other than toeing the line —and in a fit of temper ordered him to leave. By morning he had cooled down and allowed his son, who had spent the night wandering the streets, to return home. Jimmy had thought the few dollars he earned from odd jobs might improve the atmosphere at home but had been sadly mistaken. That his mother had gone to live with another man was set in stone and would not change. Neither blaming his father for her leaving nor his mother for the same thing would bring her back. That Frank Paulone had for a while made an effort to try to pick up the pieces and reestablish a cohesive family was to his credit. But his old dictatorial habits couldn't stay suppressed for long and he fell back into trying to keep Jimmy, Millie and Louis under his thumb once again.

Later Jim described his father in his own words:

"He never lost his accent, always talked in broken English, as people used the broken English at the time. He always talked about being honest, etc. He tried to save money, but somehow the banks he trusted always went broke. In those days we had no protection when a bank went broke. You were out too. My father had a temper. One time he hit me in the head with a barber cup. He took me to the hospital. He told me to say I had a fall. He was a good father in an old type way. When I wouldn't go to school he threw me out of the house. I walked around all night. I had trouble with my glasses at the time. I could not see the blackboard in school. My father was very strict. Very tough. That's why I practiced two or three hours a day on the flute."

Jim, undeterred by his brief expulsion from home, had put the episode behind him the best that he could. Time passed by, life went on and the children grew into adulthood. A new idea was needed, something on a grander scale, to help with household expenses, and to keep him occupied and out of trouble. When Jimmy asked his sister if she could think of anything to do, put on the spot, nothing immediately came to mind. But after reflection, Millie thought it best to remind him of the imagination he had used in drumming up money-making undertakings a couple of years ago.

"Do you remember, Jimmy, how you gathered kindling wood and later used the money you made to buy and resell candy you bought at a low price? I know if you thought of doing that you can put your mind to it again and come up with something else as good or even better. You're smarter than us all when comes to the business making money."

"Those were different days, Millie. People had a little money in their pockets so they could afford to spend little of it on a good deal. Nowadays even good deals are beyond the reach of most folks."

She continued to encourage him in her usual calm and flat

intonation: "You will soon think of something. You always do. Right now, we should find somewhere to cool off from this hot weather. We need to get out of this stuffy house. Let's go outside and find a shady tree to sit under. You'll come with me, won't you?"

Jimmy had an inkling of what that really meant. Millie had taken up smoking over the past few months and she wanted to light one up out of the way of prying eyes. "You go. I better take a walk to see if it helps clear my head. Maybe the sun's rays pounding down will bring some light into it." On the corner around the block the ice cream cart that always appeared when temperatures soared had made an appearance again. For a few cents he could indulge his cravings for something cold and sweet and maybe that would help. But then again why should he waste his money when a cone from this cart always tasted mostly like water? If you're going to sell this kind of ice cream then make it good ice cream. So he passed by giving barely a glance at the vendor. Whether it was the hot weather, Millie seeking out shade at home, or a vendor selling an inferior product, something clicked in his mind as he wiped away the sweat on his brow for the tenth time. What if he could duplicate the first and most delicious frozen custard he had ever tasted on a trip to Coney Island? It was many years ago now but he had never forgotten it. If he could match that quality and sell it at an affordable price, the other neighborhood vendors would be no competition.

Returning home, he told Millie about his brainstorm. With her signature tightlipped half smile she nodded her approval. So he got to work. Main ingredients: milk and cream with the addition of, unlike normal ice cream, egg yolks. Egg yolks were necessary to make it dense, unlike most ice cream that had air whipped into the mixture to give it greater bulk. And they also had the added benefit of keeping frozen custard colder for longer during lengthy summer days. Soon he was experimenting with the quantities of the ingredients. Another key in achieving the quality he desired lay in the proportion of cream and milk used—in the butterfat level. Ice cream, he learned, had often ten percent or less of butterfat; soft ice cream even less. It was determined the ideal percentage of butterfat to achieve superior quality hovered around fourteen percent. There would be the added cost to figure but it was an easy decision to make. In order to beat any rivals, his product would be one hundred percent quality!

Not only did Jim want his frozen custard to be first class, he would accept no ordinary cart to sell it from either. He thought he had enough saved to buy a self-contained unit that could hold extra ingredients he might need while out on the street during a day. A cart that could be pulled by human effort for short distances and could also be attached to a vehicle for hauling further away would be ideal. Within a few days he found one for sale but only meeting his criteria halfway. It would need modification to give him all he wanted. To cover the extra cost he would ask his sister to see if she would be willing to make an investment. Dependable Millie emptied her piggy bank without batting an eye.

Two weeks later the work had been completed and the cart was ready to operate. The proud owner stood to one side while Millie took a photo. On the front of the cart printed in large letters with frosted edges read: **Frozen Custard** and in even larger lettering the price: **5¢.** To distinguish his frozen desert from others, in small handwriting above the printing and just below the service window was written: ***This is not*** *average ice cream*. A natural gift for buyer/seller psychology served him well as business boomed. His territory for sales—anywhere he could roll his cart to in the city of Newark that seemed promising for customers.

Maybe it was too good to continue in the long run. Moving his cart through the neighborhood of Mount Pleasant one day he crossed Branch Brook Park into Upper Roseville. The North Ward felt like home with its Italian bias, and the affluence of Forest Hill even further north was not a bad day's work either. Having just set-up on Springdale Avenue a car pulled up and stopped along the curb about fifty feet from him. Three men in suits got out and sauntered over. From their body language they weren't only looking to buy something cold and delectable. After placing their order, they began asking him a series of personal questions: Where are you from? What's your family name? Why are you selling stuff in this neighborhood? How long have you lived in Newark? And so forth. Then they told him he had a very nice cart in very good condition, and they hoped it would stay that way. One of the other men added: "Business must be good—while it lasts." Then three frozen custard cones, one after the other, were dropped with dramatic flair on the sidewalk in front of the cart. Without paying! "We don't like them. We don't like you in our neighborhood. We don't like you in Newark. We don't even like you," the main spokesman of the three mumbled out with a familiar accent. Then they slowly went back to their car and left.

Jim Paulone wasn't born yesterday. He had just been paid a visit by the local Italian Mafia, and they had clearly made their point. Illegal alcohol and gambling weren't enough for them? Really, was it necessary to banish a frozen custard business to control their territory and keep them busy? Didn't they have something more important to do? Going after the little guy must have come from boredom or plain old stupidity. Perhaps the scuttlebutt going around that Prohibition would be ending soon, and along with it their chokehold on liquor supply, had something to do with it. At any rate he was an easy mark; he pulled the curtain down over the sales window and trod home as quickly as he could pulling the cart behind him.

But there was also another reason it was time to wrap up his custard business in Newark: he had developed a strong mistrust of the police. A few months earlier he had been downtown on 14th Avenue when he tried to stop a man roughing up a young woman. Police arrived just after the man had left and had assumed he was the assailant. For daring to protest his innocence, one of the officers hit him on the ear so hard it rang for days afterwards. On another occasion he had also been made to spend the night in jail after he had been accused of being a communist agitator, apparently based on his looks and speaking up for himself when confronted by officers during the Red Scare panic of the times.

Jim had made up his mind. It was time to move on, to start making use of his musical skills. At fifteen going on sixteen he was tall and broad enough to pass for older. A job in New York City, if he could land one, would be far enough away from Newark troubles that he could breathe a little easier again. Two days later he had his first regular job in the music industry working nights in a burlesque theater in Manhattan. The pay was good, the work steady, the people interesting, the audiences receptive, the management appreciative and he could return home every night with money in his pocket. All the years of practicing the flute had finally paid off. And before he knew it, almost three years had gone by working at the same job.

SHIPS IN THE NIGHT

Newark, New Jersey, July-August 1926

    Given the restrictive life at home and the variety of work experiences already under his belt at such a young age it was hardly unexpected that Jim Paulone chose to emulate his brother in leaving the family fold as soon as he could. He wanted to free himself, exactly as Danny had done, from an overbearing father and his fits of bad temper, a combination which was not all that uncommon in patriarchal Italian families. But equally compelling was an adventurous streak to strike out on his own to see what the world had in store for him. Undoubtedly, earlier forays in earning money in small ways had helped to develop self-confidence.

    It was a self-confidence that only became greater with the attention he received from young women. Handsome—some might say devilishly so—tall and dark, Jim seemed to define the stereotype so often found in romance novels. The goal of obtaining his freedom and independence had been set and the young man was ready to test the waters when the right opportunity presented itself. And just such an opportunity came along two months after celebrating his nineteenth birthday. An advertisement in the Newark Sunday News had caught his eye as being something entirely different. Several positions were available for musicians to join the orchestra onboard a ship, one of which was for a **flutist**!

The SS Leviathan was a ship almost everyone had heard about and its background was well-known since she claimed to be the largest and fastest steamer afloat. The Leviathan had started out in 1913 as the SS Vaterland in Germany, but was appropriated while docked in New Jersey after America entered the Great War. In Hoboken the ship was converted and renamed to serve as a troop transporter, eventually carrying thousands of soldiers safely to Europe. Refurbished and converted back to civilian use following the end of World War I, in 1923 she made her maiden voyage in a new guise and had been cruising the seas ever since. Jim had read somewhere recently about the Leviathan's pianist who also served as director of the band, a man named Nelson Maples, who had a good reputation in the musical community. Thinking back, hadn't his sister—whose instrument was the piano—practiced playing some of same popular pieces Maples was said to have recorded on the vessel?

Auditions for the ship's orchestra were to take place in Manhattan in July. All positions must be filled and contracts signed by the end of the month and successful candidates must be ready to set sail in August 1926. These were the required stipulations. He could do this! First thing would be a trip to the big downtown music store to see what sheet music they had in stock for the kind of tunes they would be playing shipboard. Modern music—music you could dance to—was purchased and practicing began with a new sense of purpose.

"What's that you're playing? Where on earth did you pick-up such stuff?" his father demanded from the doorway to the kitchen. Not usually at home so early in the day, Frank Paulone had returned from an appointment at the dentist in the late afternoon. Surprised to see him, Jimmy quickly inserted his body as a shield between the music stand and his father's line of sight. "It's something I heard on the radio and I wanted to see if I could replicate it. It's good to try something that's popular right now just for the sake of seeing how hard it is to learn to play. I know it's not the same league as Flight of the Bumblebee but still interesting enough just the same." Raising both arms above his head and rolling his eyes in disgust in pure Italian style, Frank turned to go back into the kitchen while managing to murmur a few final words as he did: "I'd much rather listen to Rimsky-Korsakov any day."

He would have to be more careful in the future when he played music more suitable for dancing the fox trot, tango, or even the Charleston, than listening quietly to a concert performance. It would be much safer if Millie was around practicing the piano at the same time. His sister would warn him if their father was within listening distance as he did for her when she needed a break. Of all the Paulone children, Millie was the least attached to her instrument. Jimmy did select his opportunities with care and became familiar with a number of tunes of the popular genre while Millie was on the lookout. And he felt he would have a step on those who hadn't done the same. Two weeks later, on the 26th of July, Jim's time to audition in Manhattan had come. His nerves had stayed steady when he had played and he thought it went well but you never could be sure. Told to wait in the foyer with the other candidates until all of the auditions were completed, the anxiety in the room was tense. The names of those tentatively selected would be called to be brought back into the audition room for an interview. When he heard his own name everything else went blank for a moment.

A decision to accept or refuse an offer of employment would need to be made on the spot, it was explained, due to the short interval between the audition and when the Leviathan was due to depart. A pressure-filled moment for some but not for Jim as he filled in the blanks and penned his signature on the North Atlantic contract placed on the table in front of him. In doing so he had lied about his age in stating he was twenty-one instead of nineteen in order to meet minimum age hiring regulations. It was a necessary little white lie and would be his secret to keep. A whirlwind of four days would whip by, the only ones orchestra members had to meet together and rehearse before they were to leave for England on July 31st. The Leviathan should arrive in England about a week later after embarking from New York Harbor. He was told on the way over there would be just one port of call in Cherbourg, France before reaching Southampton. His new employers had been quick to emphasize prohibition laws banning alcohol would be strictly enforced under the command of Captain Herbert Hartley. Even after leaving American waters and on the high seas the Leviathan would remain a dry ship.

But now the hour had arrived to face another kind of music; Jimmy must tell his father of what he had intended to do. He was dreading the worst, however Frank Paulone's reaction was just the opposite; he was not angry in the least and thought the chance to join an orchestra on a ship—or on land—was what his son should be doing with his life instead of dallying around with stuff unrelated to music. His grand plan for instilling a musical regimen in his children had paid off handsomely! Two of his four children had now launched themselves into the world of work on the back of the musical instruments they had mastered: Danny with his beloved violin and Jimmy with his woodwind friends, the flute and piccolo. Frank's worry that his son would find another harebrained scheme to make money had come to naught. He was now a professional musician on a prestigious ship, the Leviathan no less, and it looked as if a lasting career as a musician would be off to a good start. Only Millie and Louis would need his attention now in hopes that his two youngest would also follow in the footsteps of their brothers.

***

North Atlantic, France, England, July-August 1926

    Stepping on board the much-heralded ocean liner for the first time was an eye-opening experience for Jim Paulone. Elegance and substance oozed from all quarters: the lobby, state rooms, dining areas and entertainment venues. The orchestra set up early for its opening performance night in the Ball Room as couples started to arrive, seating themselves at tables closest to the dance floor. Their choice of attire was something to behold. Having remarked earlier in the evening how well-dressed the passengers were, he still hadn't anticipated such a range of unique feminine clothing—glittered, bejeweled, feathered and headbanded in keeping with the Roaring Twenties, or as the French called it *Les Années Folles*. How could such elaborate costumes been packed in normal size suitcases and come out looking totally unblemished?
    Bedecked as they were, couples in legion glided around

the ballroom with an ease of movement matched only by their sense of style. There were reputed to be eighteen hundred passengers or so onboard, and every dancer among them made a lasting impression at nine o'clock when the dancing got underway. The all male musicians of the orchestra had been given instructions they were to be formally dressed in white tie and tails in keeping with the elegant atmosphere of evening concerts. And it was true, elegance oozed throughout the night. For less formal, daytime musical events, black tie suits should be worn. Casual suits for more nattily dressed occasions should be saved for when they were on shore.

The musicians sitting around a number of tables that evening ready to dine studied the menu choices with enthusiasm. For Jim, he couldn't wait to tuck into the selection that had his mouth watering when he read: "Boiled Brook Trout, Sauce Niçoise, Boiled Potatoes, Roast Sirloin of Beef, Southern Style, and Pudding Milanaise, Strawberry Sauce for dessert." A menu fit for a king! Between courses there was time enough to peruse the booklet containing all the important transatlantic crossing information simply entitled "Passenger List – United States Lines." Jim read twice over the section headed: "**Orchestra**: The vessel carries a first-class orchestra which will play daily at the under-mentioned times and places." That would actually be him! The oboe player sitting next to him had leaned over to tell him he had heard that Edith Bolling Wilson, the wife of deceased President Woodrow Wilson, was supposed to be on board accompanied by her brother. She was purported to be on her way to attend the League of Nations assembly in Geneva and would be spending time in England as well. Jim was prepared to perform in front of any and all comers. Famous or not, he always gave his best.

Performances were held at different times and in different places on the ship, including the dining and social halls; but his favorite venue was the Winter Garden. This capacious room was decorated as a tropical paradise, with full scale replicas of palm trees placed here and there, large bouquets of real tropical flowers, wicker-framed sofas and armchairs and a cozy stage befitting a small size ensemble like their own. Jim felt like he could stay in the warm and inviting place all evening long—and would even sleep there if he could!

On the crossing's third night he saw Captain Hartley watching from behind the railing surrounding the Ball Room dance floor. Clean-shaven and dressed immaculately in an all white uniform, he stood straight as an arrow. Jim was glad they had been forewarned against alcohol consumption in view of the Captain's imposing military-like appearance. Although the Italian in him believed in the benefits from a glass of wine during an evening meal, he would hate to undergo a reprimand from this man! But it was the fourth night that turned out to be the centerpiece of entertainment for the voyage. Along with a concert program presenting both classical and popular music, there would also be vocalists, readings and a comedy scene from a short play.

On the morning of the sixth day at sea, Jim woke to find the Leviathan had already moored at the pier at Cherbourg, the only stop the ship would make on its way from New York to England. He rose and dressed as quickly as he could to get an early start to the day. Musicians had leave to explore Cherbourg or, if they preferred, travel to Paris instead. They were to return to the ship by the dinner hour, which would be immediately followed by the evening program. A few passengers would be disembarking for good in Cherbourg, as it was their final destination, and new ones would be boarding to join the cruise. Before he had left home he had promised himself to take every advantage to see and do as much as he could. It would be a long day but a trip to Paris could not to be missed! Special direct trains were ready and waiting at the Cherbourg port to transport him, a few bandmates and others to the City of Light and back again in a hurry. Fingers were crossed they would be up to the task.

    That evening, Jim, Cyril and Salvatore regaled the table with the glories of the Eiffel Tower, the Luxembourg and Tuileries gardens, Montmartre and sites in-between they had rushed around to see after they rejoined colleagues who had remained onboard. And, naturally, there were the many beautiful *mesdemoiselles* they had seen along the way, which grabbed the listeners' attention the most. The days at sea passed quickly even though the ship's speed was held to an average of twenty-five miles per hour. The Leviathan had the engine power to go faster but that would be contrary to the idea of a leisurely cruise leaving time for the enjoyment of the onboard experience. An array of entertainment, great dining and relaxation in abundance was the order of every day on the Leviathan and it should never be given short shrift.

    Jim Paulone and his shipmate musicians were, nevertheless, looking forward to seeing what England was like. And the wait wasn't long after weighing anchor in France, crossing the English Channel and passing by the Isle of Wight until the outline of Southampton came into view. Trains leaving from the Southampton Terminus, just as in Cherbourg, would provide conveniently rapid transportation for anyone going to London. But before visiting London he had something else on his mind: a stop at the Croydon

Aerodrome in Sussex. Jim was at the age where taking risks was sought rather than avoided and he hoped to take a joy-ride in a biplane. A number of surviving biplanes had been redeployed for civilian use following their action in WWI and more had been manufactured to meet the demand of the new flying craze. Magazines featured photographs of celebrities climbing into planes and waving to spectators below to promote interest, and air shows drew crowds to witness biplane maneuverability while emphasizing their record for safety.

The publicity had done its job and the biplane fad had struck Jim's fancy too. After consulting train timetables, it looked like the easiest and surest way to get to the town of Croydon would be to take the special train from the terminus in Southampton to London then double back. England's only international airport was only ten miles from the capital city. Soon, on his very first day in England, Jim was seated with one other adventurous spirit and the pilot in an Avro 536 ready to soar into an overcast sky. Before they were airborne the pilot had obtained their agreement to perform barrel rolls and loop the loops. Jim, an old hand at riding the Great Racer roller coaster on Coney Island, was impressed but undaunted.

A next, tamer adventure took place the following day in London. Having read works by the famous author Sir Arthur Conan Doyle about the fictional detective Sherlock Holmes, Jim intended to visit the London restaurant at which Holmes, his sidekick Watson and the author himself had all dined. He knew the restaurant actually existed and not merely a figment of the author's imagination because of its notoriety. Sightseeing would have to wait. As soon as the train arrived he walked out the station door and took aim for Simpson's-in-the-Strand located inside the Savoy Hotel. It would be expensive but he would have a meal no matter what the cost. It was his one chance to walk in the footsteps of the famous British sleuth and the man who created him and nothing was going to get in his way. He had even dressed himself in the morning in a manner as to fit the occasion. When he was shown to a table, it was a dapper-looking gentleman standing tall in a flat-crowned and wide-brimmed boater made of straw that they saw. The hat was partnered with a white bow tie and the same dark suit he wore for more informal performances on the ship. When the waiter asked him for his order, he chose the traditional carved roast beef complete with Yorkshire pudding and trimmings of course. It was the dish the place was known for, so how could he not?

Three days to explore the riches of London were hardly enough. His ship had arrived in Southampton during the early hours of August 7th 1926 and was due to set sail again for New York August 10th. He strolled through Covent Garden, down Regent and Oxford Streets, across the Tower Bridge and through the magnificent parks, toured the Tower of London and viewed art works in world class museums. It was all that he could manage but enough. In the short time he had been away from home he had sampled some of the best of what France and England had to offer. He hurried back to the ship with two hours to spare so as not to cause undue stress on himself and everybody else concerned. One thing for certain, Jim Paulone would take home with him a wealth of exciting memories from his sojourn overseas. Unforgettable were the quarters of Paris, soaring in the air above Croydon and three days of site-seeing in London, crowned by springing for one of the city's best and most costly meals at Simpsons. All these experiences while he had gained invaluable professional experience as a musician playing with a prestigious orchestra on a famous ship.

Jim Paulone was already looking forward to using his new credentials to make a name for himself in America when the time came. But he was conflicted about just when that should be. As long as his employers were satisfied with his work on the Leviathan, he could continue working as a musician seaman probably on the same ship or a different one operated by the United States Lines. It would be a disservice to his employer's expectations and he might be living at home again if he chose to end his contract. He could possibly do what his brother had done and join an itinerant orchestra. But rather than working always in other states like Danny, he could stay with his father when performing in the Newark area and find a room when on the road. But unlike Danny, Jim Paulone had no intentions of falling into an early marriage. Not yet twenty, there were too many girls looking his way, too many things to do and too many places to go without tying himself down to one person.

Eight days later, on August 16th, Jim Paulone was back in New York City. And he hadn't the foggiest notion that at virtually the same time on the same sea destiny had already been hard at work.

***

SS Conte Biancamano, Atlantic Ocean, August 9-18 1926

In the same month of the same year a lavishly adorned Italian ship taking Maria Conte to New York had nearly crossed paths with the Leviathan with Jim Paulone onboard. The SS Biancamano with Maria, but without her brother Antonio, had left the port of Naples on August 19th; the Leviathan had docked at New York Harbor three days after that. Only three days of separation or it really would have been ships passing each other in the night. Only three days and destiny might have been given a push in fulfilling its charge, even though it probably wouldn't have meant that much to the two young people travelling at the time. Eight years separated two young people—an ocean of time in itself when she was eleven and he nineteen—so a brief 1926 encounter may have been only something vaguely remembered later in life anyway.

    Maria Conte easily made new acquaintances on the ship even though she lived with the sadness of having left behind her brother in Bagnoli Irpino. An infirmity of the eyes had prevented him from sailing with her. With her vivacious outgoing personality, casually chatting with others no matter what their age was never a problem for her. Without parents she had grown up faster than her years would suggest. Her age and name had been erroneously noted on the ship's manifest as twelve instead of eleven and Marianna in lieu of Maria, but she had already acquired a facility for interacting with those senior to herself. And relating to other passengers was made even easier since "South" was how the majority were categorized in the "Race" column. In other words they were from southern Italy just like herself. She was engulfed in a sea of compatriots all communicating with Italian accents not unlike her own and all with a culture entirely different than northern Italy. Indeed, as long as she could remember it was as if there were really two Italies.

Angela Fandolfi and Francesca D'Agostino, the former from Bari and the latter from Airola, had already become quite attached to the young Maria's enthusiasm. Together with a third voyager, Rosa Cerasuolo, a friend from Bagnoli well acquainted with Maria's musical abilities and aspirations, the coterie of four were looking down to the floor below one late afternoon listening to a pianist. Leaning on the balustrade, they marveled how his playing resounded through the main lounge underneath the impressive dome and skylight overhead.

"I've told the others how you love to sing and what a terrific voice you have when you do. Why don't we see if the pianist will accompany you in playing one of your favorite songs? It would be a shame for the people listening right now not to have the enjoyment of hearing your wonderful voice. Just something short, you know," Rosa suggested while wrapping her arms around Maria's shoulders for encouragement.

Maria shook her head as she said no. Then the other two recent acquaintances pitched by adding pressure.

"I really haven't had time to do any singing for a while; too many other things going on when I was trying to get ready to leave."

"You're always humming something, though, and staying in practice that way. You can do it. I know you can, just like I've heard you singing all around Bagnoli. And then you can tell everyone you sang on a steamship on the way to America!"

It didn't take a whole lot of coaxing to convince Maria to sing almost anytime, anywhere given the chance. Like a mini hurricane the three females approached the lone and vulnerable pianist when he had stopped playing for a short break. He smiled a little you-must-be-kidding type smile when they made their proposal. But after realizing the girls were serious, he asked Maria to sing a line or two from any song she liked. He was convinced it wasn't a hoax in hearing her unfaltering range of pitch and attention to phrasing. Given her short stature, the pianist had her stand on a table to sing, which suited her perfectly. The voyagers who had remained after the intermission were soon joined by others who had heard Maria in the corridors as they passed by. Drawn to the music like moths to light, no one who listened was disappointed. Maria, who had fixed ideas on the direction she would be taking in the future, was even more certain now.

There would be no other occasion to exercise her voice for the benefit of entertaining the passengers, a luxury liner which spoiled to no end those who could afford it. The third class passengers, the vast majority, were not allowed in first and second class areas, reducing the possibility of an audience for an encore performance. Maria hadn't thought about singing on the ship, but it had been a golden opportunity and her father would be the first to hear all about. As New York drew a nautical mile closer each day, her thoughts became focused on meeting him and nothing else. She hoped he still looked like the photo she had kept by her bedside in Bagnoli. She wanted to recognize him from the very first instant he came into view.

Even if the two ships transporting Maria Conte and James Paulone on the way to New York had been at sea on exactly the same days, the routes they had taken were different. Starting out in Naples took an extra day, the crossing to New York taking nine days instead of the eight it took from

Southampton. But given a crystal ball to look into the future, that the two ships should occupy the same ocean during the same month and year within days of each other in the span of a lifetime seemed like more than a little coincidence. To the fortune teller, it would be enough to imply that fate had intervened in bringing two passengers to meet in another time and place.

REUNION

Sharon, Pennsylvania, November 1927

Antonio Conte did not have to wait for very long after his sister had sailed away without him in August 1926. Within a month all signs of Antonio's eye ailment had disappeared. His problem was not the more serious infection of trachoma but a form of conjunctivitis, treatable with the simple regime of frequent rinsing with warm water over the next few weeks. Avoidance of other contaminants, including touching the eye area, was advised, and making sure all redness had cleared was necessary to regain normality. Antonio's urgency to find another departure date to New York was felt as much by his relatives who were eager to see the family made whole again in America. The Biancamano, the same steamer he had been booked on before with his sister, was scheduled to leave again from Naples on October 30th. It seemed fitting he should be on that ship and no other.

Antonio Conte would need to show that he would be accompanied by a parent or a responsible adult in charge of his welfare since he was under sixteen. Alternatively, he could provide documented proof an adult with proper authority would meet him when he arrived at Ellis Island in New York.

When asked about occupation on his first attempt at leaving Italy, he had answered barber, in thinking an actual trade might allay any concerns over his age. He had been a minor then and was one still. But since he was dependent on a guarantee from his father instead of a chaperon to permit departure this time, he had decided to label himself as student, which he actually was. And when he arrived at the port in Naples and met with customs officials, that was the occupation printed on the ship's manifest along with his other details. It was then his nerves took over and got the best of him in trying to look as confident and serious as the agent's expressionless face.

"I believe everything should be in order, sir. You can see there are no health-related problems now," he proffered without being asked in hopes of speeding things up a little.

"You're correct there, young man. But what do you mean by saying now?"

"Well, you see there was…" he began then hesitated for a split second in realizing his error "… I was supposed leave with my sister but there was a problem with my eyes. But they are completely better now according to the doctor."

"I'm glad to hear that. But there is a note about the fare. It seems there should have been a payment by now. Do you or someone else know why there hasn't been?"

Any trace of confidence had just been wiped away. All he could recall was being told that the old ticket from the earlier voyage could be exchanged at no cost for a new one. He was pretty sure it had been clear to the ticket agent who booked him onto this ship. "I didn't have to pay again because I missed the earlier sailing in August for medical reasons."

"Do you have anything in writing about it? If not, I will

have to speak with the chief purser." Antonio shook his head. "Wait here then and I'll be back shortly."

When he did return it was with an even grimmer look than when he had walked away.

"I'm afraid I have bad news for you. Since you have no proof with you of what you say, and the purser can find no record about your former ticket, either the passage must be paid now or you can wait for another sailing. Since you are a student you should talk it over with whoever's responsible for seeing how things can best be arranged.

"Unbelievable—this can't be happening to me again!" Antonio grumbled. Of course neither he nor his relative who had come with him had the amount of a fare on them. What could be done right now? Not much! How could one agent tell him his former ticket would be honored for a future voyage and another claim to know nothing about it? He did receive one piece of information before he left dejected again: an appeal to the shipping line could be made by writing a letter explaining all the details. But for now it meant a second long trip back to Bagnoli.

A letter was written in due course to Lloyd Sabaudo, the shipping company operator located in Genoa, without much faith that the confusion would be rectified. Amazingly, the response turned out to be favorable. The return letter even went as far as apologizing for the inconvenience caused to him along with enclosing a reimbursement of the original fare paid. Once again another departure date was found and booked. Not a believer in the third time's the charm cliché, this time a different line was intentionally chosen, one that was much older and with a proven record of successful crossings under its belt. The description in the brochure noted the ocean liner SS Patria had been built in France and first went into service in 1913 for the Fabre Line. Later, in 1920, it began transporting emigrants from ports in Marseille, Naples and Palermo to New York City. The two Biancamano ship fiascos made the Patria the best choice to avoid bad luck in a third attempt at joining his father and sister in America. It had better be the best because neither Antonio nor his grandparents and uncles and aunts in Bagnoli could withstand any further useless travels to Naples that might fail again to see him off.

Antonio Conte reverted to being barber again for passenger list purposes as he had done in the first instance rather than in naming his occupation as a student as he had done for the second. It made more sense since his father had done some barbering in Bagnoli before the war and it was a true trade. His father was now the owner of not one but two barbershops. If the custom agents in New York had concerns over employability during his entry, he would say he was going to work with his father in the family business. Any preparation that might tip the scales in his favor was always in his mind when having to undergo an immigration interview.

Antonio, "barber" from southern Italy, was once again in a queue on November 18, 1926 waiting to be questioned by an official who had the power to grant or deny permission to board the ship. A rapidly beating heart was put to rest by a quick arm gesture indicating he could move forward. An urge to run and not walk up the gang plank was hard to resist. Uncharacteristic as it was for Antonio Conte to do anything in haste there would be no dawdling on this particular occasion. It was hard to believe that after all the other obstacles he had encountered before it had been so easy this time. Soon he would be able to relax, but for now it was his turn to elbow his way forward on the deck to lean against the rail for his last adieus.

The ship managed to arrive in New York intact and on schedule despite some blustery days typical for mid-November on the Atlantic. What was the most memorable part of the voyage for Antonio? No question, it was the number and variety of dishes served at meals. Of course he ate the Italian cuisine with gusto, but there were many fine French recipes to sample as well, courtesy of travelling on a vessel owned by a French company. Obviously there was a need to satisfy the palates of passengers who had boarded at French and Italian ports. A week of temptation might easily have led to the perils of over-consumption for a fourteen year old with an interest in cooking and a hankering for everything appetizing, But Antonio possessed a metabolism that seemed to keep any discernable weight gains in check. He was in heaven and lacked self-restraint. And it didn't go unnoticed by fellow passengers who shared his table. Ice cream for dessert was always on the menu and on warm evenings it was expected Antonio would order a second helping. But whispers began in earnest when he requested a third and bets were made he would never be able to finish it all. In the end his fellow diners were stunned by his capacity to devour such a quantity without batting an eye, as if it was the most normal thing to do.

Antonio had other things on his mind as he squeezed into a barge transporting a full load of passengers to Ellis Island. Butterflies in his stomach had returned, just as they were in Naples. Would these officials find something wrong and refuse his entry to America? But by a miracle the first step was soon over and gone without a hitch; then it was on to the

Registry Room. Doctors poked and prodded him for common ailments such as cholera and tuberculosis—his eyes were given extra attention for residual infection—and when they were done no problems with Antonio's health had been detected. Next, he was directed to a waiting room where he was to stay with several others until the responsible relative or guardian would meet him. A guard was stationed at the door to make sure immigration laws were strictly enforced. Within minutes his father and sister, who had also been biting their nails, were told Antonio Conte was ready to be picked-up and released into their custody.

"It's about time, Antonio. What took you so long? Did you take the long way around," were the first words of his sister while squeezing him to death.

"You know me, Maria," he began, "I'm not like you—I take my time at everything but get it right in the end. But it has been long and I'm really hungry," he complained with a sparkle in his eyes showing nothing had changed between them. Then it was their father's turn. Michael pulled Anthony to him, pumping his hand and hugging him long and strong before finally releasing him. "My son", were the only words he spoke but were enough.

Antonio, mentally exhausted from the ordeal was not given much time to pull himself together. It would have been nice to be able to at least get his bearings before beginning the next stage of the journey. The overnight train eastward would be long, more than eleven hours from start to finish. There would be one gigantic difference, though: Michael, Maria and Antonio would be travelling as a family for the first time ever. Regrettably, it wouldn't be the recently-introduced Pittsburgher with its luxurious Pullman sleeping cars. They would have to doze as best they could while sitting up in rather cramped quarters. Bendable children would find a way to sleep anywhere. The tedious journey would be survived somehow and soon forgotten about afterwards.

The next morning Antonio was taken to the Conte house on Sherman Avenue where Maria took over. It was like she had lived in the steel town of Sharon all her life. She showed him each room, giving extra time to the kitchen to explain all the modern features. Michael Conte had no chance of participating if had any thoughts of doing so. To be honest, her father really didn't mind letting her take charge. He knew he had a lot of making-up to do for all the time lost before his son would feel at ease with him.

"Well, what do you think? Does anything about what you see remind you of Bagnoli?" Not waiting for his answer she went on: "To me, the countryside between Montella and Bagnoli is a little bit like here. And maybe Laceno too, although there are forests all around." In the short time they had been apart, Antonio was surprised to hear that English words had already crept in when his sister spoke to him in Italian, words he had certainly never heard before. Expanses of well-maintained very green grass were a good indication of a bountiful rainfall compared to the dryer and higher elevation climate of Bagnoli. In the quiet neighborhood only a few trees separated houses from streets.

"You're like a sponge, Maria, in soaking up the language of the natives so fast. You were the one who could emulate the voices of the singers on the radio when we finally got one. No matter which language was sung, French or English or even German, you seemed to understand what they were saying too." Michael couldn't restrain himself any longer from barging in: "You probably already know the first Italian radio station only began broadcasting not that long ago in Rome, so we weren't that late in getting a radio. But by the time Italy had radio entertainment it had already been in Britain for a few years. Guglielmo Marconi, an Italian who was living in England at the time, was the inventor. Obviously a brilliant man, but he was also the one and the same who became a card-carrying member of the Fascist Party cozying up to Mussolini along the way."

The two of them could depend on each other in adjusting to the new environment, which was of great help. New schools with an ethnic diversity never encountered in their homogeneous little town in Italy were attended together. And then there were new friendships, and potential enemies, to discuss ad nauseam. Even Sharon itself, with its steel industry mindset and population of twenty-three thousand, was like living on the moon compared to home. Why were there so many blast furnaces belching out smoke from an assortment of mills. Michael knew his local history and explained. Following a coal mining era, the mills had prospered since the end of the First World War causing a rapid growth in population. And the Sharon Steel Corporation in Farrell, the town that had its beginnings in the 1860s and the same one in which he had previously lived, was at the forefront of the iron and steel industry in the Shenango Valley. When the newcomers went about town it was like endless talk of mills by men with besmudged faces everywhere.

SURVIVAL

East Coast, The South, New Jersey, 1927-1936

His arrival back in Newark had put Jim Paulone in a quandary. Something had changed with his father that seemed to have shaken his role as of head of the family. Perhaps it had to do with his wife's abandonment of the family some years ago or more simply because he had reached an advanced age. In the past when the children behaved in a manner that met his disapproval, he acted quickly and with an iron hand. But now he looked disinterested no matter what was happening around him. Perhaps it really did have mostly to do with Lydia leaving him and fear his children might do the same. She never visited them at their home, but met Jimmy, and one or both of his younger siblings, on weekends occasionally, which always left them sadder than they had been before she came. As for Jimmy, he thought he was cross-eyed from crying so much after she had left home for good.

Millie, the only female in the family, had helped fill her absence at first, but at sixteen she could not be expected to continue to be his main support. Thirteen year old Louis was even less prepared to do so. As for Jim, before he left on the Leviathan he had assumed duties of cooking meals, a task which actually gave him a sense of satisfaction. But now returned he wrestled with the choice staring him in the face. Should he honor the contract he had signed and ship out again in a few days time or was it his responsibility to stay and help a single-parent father and his siblings still living with him? In the end he chose the latter. There might be regrets later in making the decision to terminate the seaman's agreement but he felt it was the right one at the moment. Although he had been bitten by the travel bug he wasn't worried over finding something besides visiting foreign lands to keep him busy. Times were still prosperous and jobs for an experienced musician should not be difficult to find.

Larger theaters in Newark and New York City and around the country were hiring musicians to provide musical accompaniment to silent screen films. The live performances played from orchestra pits located in front of the screen were essential for adding drama and color to the moviegoer's experience. Highlighting moods through tempo changes and synchronization with the unwinding story could generate a wealth of emotional responses to scenes that might otherwise have fallen flat without music. And an engaged audience helped to guarantee a film's success in both fulfilling its narrative and keeping the bottom line in the black. Jim was hired at a cinema in Newark but after a few months quit over poor direction. Still itching to do more exploring, he decided to look for work that involved going to new places.

And to new places he was about to go. The contact he had made with a Newark employment agency had meant a job doing silent movie work again but this time out of the local area. He was informed by the agent to start packing his suitcase to get ready for an extended stay down south if he accepted the placement. A signed contract including an all expenses paid trip on the Comus—a Morgan Line steamship operated by the Southern Pacific Company plying between New York City and New Orleans—would be leaving in a week. He jumped at the chance, and after a four day cruise along the East Coast, the slow-paced life of the Big Easy was there before him. Moving from city to city he soon lost all track of the number of boarding houses in which he stayed. It was all part of the adventure so he didn't really care. More importantly was the appreciation and respect shown by audiences and management alike for his gift of improvising and interpreting cue sheets, a skill many musicians lacked. From his experience in Newark he had known what to expect. He was also proud to be making enough money to send some home to help with household expenses.

New Orleans' special charm seemed to hold a particular allure to young men. The very first thing he did after working his first night was to head to the French Quarter. On Bourbon Street he ordered and consumed in record time a dozen of the city's finest oysters for a single dollar! And there was still enough time afterwards to explore the nightlife on Canal Street along with the pretty girls everywhere that went with it. All said and done, silent film work was another feather in his cap to add to a dance music repertoire and concert work experience. Though contract commitments included travelling to other cities in Louisiana and Mississippi, Jim was always the happiest when he returned to New Orleans. His favorite southern city among them all had certainly cast its spell on him! But with the last few months spent in Shreveport, and after a year and a half on the road, the novelty of being on the road had begun to wear off.

Then, in the middle of 1933, news from home came to him in two parts. The first concerning his sister was expected. Millie had gone ahead and married a fellow named Paul who hailed from the state of Georgia. She had mentioned him once before at home but when he had started to ask a few questions she had promptly shut him down. Millie wasn't about to let anyone become too involved in her affairs even it was her dear brother. "His real name is John but he goes by the middle name of Paul. That's all you need to know for now. And that's between us. I don't want father catching wind about him before I'm ready." It was true, there would be repercussions. Frank Paulone still thought of her as a daughter needing his guidance and protection and all the more so when it came to the young men prowling about! Like her brother, Millie thought her father had mellowed a degree or two after their mother had left. And everything should be done, they had agreed, to keep it that way. There should be no cause for reigniting old ways, if possible. Only the worst reaction could be expected if he were to learn by chance that Millie was serious about someone without first having gone through paternal vetting and approval. As long as she lived in a home with her father, it would always be like that; traditional Italian values were ever-present when it came to a daughter's suitors.

Jimmy had heard from time to time she was still seeing Paul. Yet, it was hard to believe that Millie, only twenty-two, could now be the spouse of a drug store clerk only a couple of years older than herself. Whatever southern charm he possessed, it had certainly worked in captivating his sister. A non-Italian whose roots were in Statesboro, he was apparently content, or at least reconciled, to remaining in Newark. Jim looked forward to meeting Paul; he wanted to get a sense of his character, and to see whether or not he had a good head on his shoulders. Millie was not short on spunk but very young and might have been a little impetuous in seeking escape from a father's dominance.

The second piece of news three weeks later left him reeling and anything but joyous. His younger brother Louis had gone to join older brother Danny in Lewis County, in upstate New York, for few days in late May. Danny, now wearing the official moniker of Rev. Daniel Paulone, had been visiting the Church of the Nazarene in the town of Lowville for the past two weeks in his capacity as evangelical musician. With very warm weather at hand already in late May, Danny and Louis were invited for a picnic at Whitaker Falls near Martinsburg and about seven or eight miles from Lowville. The gorge, rugged, precipitous and wooded on either side, comprised a series of three waterfalls in the Black River Valley.

Rev. Seamans, the pastor of the local church, had decided to hike down a short path to swim in a pool formed in a bowl in the rocks of the Roaring Brook, a tributary of the Black. Seamans' four year old son and Louis had accompanied him, the others, including Danny, remaining behind at the picnic grounds. Already wearing his swimsuit, the pastor slipped into the pool from one edge. He took only a step or two before sliding off a stone into deeper water and hitting his head on a rock outcropping. Dizzy from the blow he was also seized by leg cramps from the freezing water. He tried to reach a place where he could find footing again while shouting for help. Louis ripped off his shoes and jumped into water otherwise still fully clothed.

It was a brave effort but a completely foolish thing to do

for Louis could not swim! He disappeared beneath the surface before having any chance of reaching the man. The exhausted and frozen pastor sank to the bottom as well, and both he and Louis were gone. Four days later the headline of an article appearing in the local newspaper, the Journal and Republican, describing the tragedy read: **DOUBLE DROWNING AT WHITAKER FALLS**. Louis, unassuming but handsome in appearance, photographed with a bible in his hand, serious in his studies, accomplished clarinet player, their baby brother had drowned at the age of eighteen. Jim's southern digression had come to an abrupt end and he left for home as soon as his suitcase was packed. He took the same Comus steamship back to New York, this time travelling in lower class to save money. He nearly met the same fate as his brother in doing so. So violent was the gale off Cape Hatteras that his cabin mate had pleaded with Jim to contact his relatives should he die and Jim lived to tell the tale. It was a very close call but the ship somehow held together and weathered the storm with no human loss.

Jim Paulone was unsure of what he would do next after Louis' funeral apart from spending a few days with his father to help console him in his grief over this latest blow. It might help to dampen Jim's sadness as well. Jim Paulone was never one for letting the grass grow under his feet for long, though. During breakfast one morning he spotted an announcement in the newspaper for someone interested in joining a military-style band. Not just any band but one where all of the musicians were mounted on horses—a cavalry band no less! There were several positions currently vacant in the thirty-two piece band and one of them was for a flutist. It would be paid employment with the added benefit of full board wherever they performed. This was something he hadn't done before. Fancy riding a horse—someone would have to give him lessons since he'd never been in a saddle before—while playing music! He had seen pictures of mounted military bands and could imagine himself looking good dressed in a fine uniform with campaign style hat on his head.

He didn't have to use his imagination for long as he was accepted into the cavalry group almost immediately. The minimum one year commitment suited him at this stage of his life. His qualms of lacking any kind of riding skill were soon allayed. It was more of a question of how well trained horses walked slowly and stood still with music blasting in their ears. There would be no galloping about with musicians astride only mild mannered steeds. Jim's adventuresome side had provided him with more than enough self-confidence to manage what was yet one more musical experience to add to his portfolio.

As it had been with silent movies during the early years of the 1930s, bands of this kind were also vulnerable to innovation. Mechanization and motorization had eroded the use of animals on farms and in the military to where horse drawn plows and mounted bands were vanishing. Those that remained owed their survival to reasons of nostalgia. At the end of year his latest endeavor had finished along with the band itself. A country still mired in the economic doldrums of the depression looked for new ways to keep citizens employed.

One such program, part of the New Deal of President Franklin D. Roosevelt, focused on those in the musical business. The Federal Music Project under the aegis of his Works Progress Administration had started in 1935 and Jim was quick to jump aboard during the first year of operation. It was a new paid opportunity to perform before larger public audiences again, audiences which attended for free or a very low cost to encourage music appreciation for the masses. The job required flexibility with an array of orchestra types and sizes, including chamber ensembles, concert and theater bands performing at schools, amphitheaters and before small civic groups. Jim returned to live at home again since most of the venues were in Essex County. It was a welcome change after trooping around the East Coast for months.

Most of the performances were recorded on transcription disks, which were then distributed to local radio stations in Newark and New York City. He could now call himself a recorded artist! The WTNJ radio station broadcasted from Newark and simultaneously on WNYC on the other side of the Hudson River in Manhattan. Upon hearing his son playing one evening over the wireless air waves on WTNJ his father was so thrilled he would have leapt to his feet if he could. He had slowed down considerably after the death of Louis, but had given a hint of his old self on this occasion. Frank's rejuvenation didn't last long; he had returned to his despondent self by the next morning. Only a visit by his daughter and her husband living only a few blocks away seemed to lift his mood a little. Still childless Millie, while working as a waitress in a Newark restaurant, was able in her off hours to spend time each week in trying to make him happier.

There was another benefit attached to living at home in New Jersey again. For ages Jim had wanted to study with one of the foremost flutists and piccolo players in New York to further hone his skill. Financially speaking, this had always been out of the realm of possibility. But now the WPA Music Program included a component that paid for professional development opportunities of musicians aiming to build their career by achieving standards of musicianship at even higher levels. And he was finally able to arrange for private lessons from the celebrated professor who taught at the Julliard School of Music in New York City. Each day he thanked President Roosevelt for the good fortune of having paid employment and for the chance to learn from the best at Julliard. His 1930's odyssey had finally reached a conclusion, or so he thought.

DEDICATION

Sharon, Pennsylvania, New York City, 1926-1935

Adjustment to a new life in Sharon after leaving Bagnoli Irpino would be a trial by fire for the young Maria Conte. On the 7th of September, the day after the Labor Day holiday and a month and a half before her twelfth birthday, she was in school. Only ten days after setting foot in New York City in late August 1926 she had been cast into the fire. At first she thought her father had been cruel in making her start so soon. He explained that compulsory school attendance was required by state law so there was no choice in the matter. Besides, it was the best way to make new friends, learn English quickly and to begin adapting to a foreign culture. Michelino Conte was convinced his determined daughter could handle it. Marie Conte—she had already dropped the "a" in exchange for an "e" as a gesture to her new American identity—entered the elementary school classroom a few blocks from her home as a fifth grader.

Normally assertive, the first to step forward or to raise her hand in class, it was clear from the beginning that was no longer the case for Marie Conte. Patience would be needed since she realized she was in over her head. Language was the monster barrier. She possessed not even a sketchy knowledge of English. There was no chance of understanding history and civics or grasping mathematical concepts. The elements of grammar so fundamental in writing a language would be incomprehensible since they were not taught in a way non-native speakers could learn. Her father and teachers conferred and concurred; to give her time to achieve essential basic proficiency in English she should be moved back to the fourth grade.

The change to a new grade level almost immediately led to good results. Marie Conte had the aptitude for becoming a quick learner of spoken English in spite of starting from zero. Her teacher remarked that she was one of those fortunate individuals who possessed a natural talent for foreign language learning. On top of that, she also had the ability to perfectly imitate the accents of others. Her father, conversely, arriving as an adult in America and without the advantage of immersion in an English-speaking school, had been slower in picking up a new language. Michael Conte had been in America for over ten years but at times he was still at a loss in finding the right English word and fell back on body language to get his meaning across. It was the same thing he did when speaking Italian anyway so it came naturally to him. But Michelino Conte never lost his Italian accent.

From the beginning Marie had promised herself there would be no trace of her heritage when she spoke and she was passionate about achieving that goal. So much so she practiced speaking in front of the mirror while watching her image pronouncing words she had heard at school or on the radio. There was a downside to devoting so much energy to learning to do one thing, however: Marie continued to lag behind in some of the core classroom subjects at a time when she should have been ready to transition to the next level. Without the necessary progress she would be held back at the same grade another year. It turned out it was the right thing to do even though she was unhappy at first. By end of the school year both her English and subject mastery were at grade level or above. Junior high, the next stage, presented no problems and was finished in June 1933. Summer vacation provided a break then it was on to high school. The final three years of public education at Sharon High, was entered in September of the same year.

On some days the expense of keeping his two children fed, clothed and educated on a barber's income during an economic crisis seemed nearly impossible. Antonio, like his sister, had also altered his name. He was now going by Tony to friends and family or Anthony for more formal occasions. He had enrolled as a student at a local college at a later age than most having undergone the same educational delays due to English learning as his sister had. Unlike his sister, though, he had kept a distinct Italian accent as his father had with no regrets. College costs were modest with Tony living at home, but for his musically gifted and ambitious daughter, managing educational expenses in the future could be another thing.

During the first few months of her freshman year at Sharon High Marie seemed to be on a mission to join every singing and drama group. And at home, the sight of her singing her way around the house was not an uncommon occurrence. Quite obviously this was what she loved doing and was meant to do and intended to do. One evening Michael gave a short cough to announce his presence, interrupting her while she was doing homework. She questioningly looked up at him, hoping that this wasn't going to be lecture for something she should have done or done wrong.

"You know I've been thinking about some things lately. Since everyone in town knows how much music means to you, it might be a good idea to study the piano more formally with professional help. What would you say about taking lessons from a piano teacher?"

"Are you kidding? I'd say yes of course—and then I'd say let's start today! It would be like a dream come true. Piano, singing and music—that's what I'm sure I want to do with the rest of my life. But can our family afford it? Private lessons must be really expensive."

"We'll find a way. That's not for you to worry about. Good music teachers are facing the same difficult times we are. I'm sure they'd rather work than stay at home. I suspect there would be some flexibility in what they charge when presented with the right argument. But you would have to take advantage of every moment to get the most out of it. Then it would be more than worth any sacrifices we have to make."

"I promise you not a moment will be wasted. I wouldn't let you or myself down. If for any reason it doesn't work out as it should, I would definitely stop. You know I'll always do my best."

"That's what I thought you'd say. From what I've heard, and from what your brother says too, I think you have what it takes to go a long way. You should take the next step; and after that perhaps there will be more steps I hope."

"There will be, just you wait and see!"

A piano teacher was hired in Sharon soon afterwards at a price they could afford, at least for a while. Fortunately, Michael Conte owned his barbershop business, a decision made years ago, which had given him a financial advantage many other barbers didn't have. The newly hired teacher was let go after only three lessons, however, not without a little drama as she left in a huff. Criticism was her strong point it seemed, serious and sour she lacked the capacity to encourage when complements were needed and deserved. She also showed up late two out of three days. It was as if accepting a moderate rate meant lessons could be delivered half-heartedly.

A second teacher prospect was located in Youngstown. This time, with greater wisdom, a single trial lesson was arranged before engaging him for a longer period. His piano playing was solid, and it was also in his favor that he insisted upon keeping interruptions to a minimum. An hour private lesson went by quickly and should not be wasted while teaching his new protégé. Marie progressed steadily under his tutelage which continued throughout her freshman year of high school. But her musical endeavors were not limited to the piano; she was delighted to find the Mirror, her high school yearbook, listed several of her school-related accomplishments: she sang in the glee club, participated in interscholastics and won voice competitions at high schools in Farrell and Sharpsville. Recognition was also given for her selection, with classmate Lena Ferrari, for Girls Voice at the 10th annual county round-up to be held in Sharon in 1932. All of this just in her freshman year!

   Freshmen on course to graduate in 1935 were specifically highlighted in the same yearbook:

> "The class of '35 has proven to be a very outstanding and promising one. The higher classes call us green, but we don't mind that, for we have proven to be true blue to the ideals of

Sharon High School."

Followed by:

"Also we found that there is talent displayed both in voice and dancing. Who could fail to see that…Marie Conte and… possess these artistic abilities."

Marie's musical activities continued unabated during her sophomore, junior and senior school years. During a lesson she would frequently accompany herself by singing the lyrics to a piece she was playing on the piano. Her teacher couldn't help but be impressed by the purity of her voice. The answer was negative when he asked if she also had a voice teacher, but she also told him that singing was her true interest. In listening to her sing several more times without the piano, he was persuaded she had a gift and encouraged professional voice training. Marie was persuaded too and so was her father after speaking with her teacher. At school, music was often part of theater productions and she captured almost all of lead singing actor roles in musical plays Sports club and the French and Spanish clubs rounded out the rest of her time. Language clubs especially, she thought, would serve her well for the kind of career she was planning for herself.

During the first quarter of her senior year, at the time when applications to colleges and music schools were submitted, Marie was forced to make a decision on how to answer questions of age. She would be older than other high school graduates and had concerns her age would be viewed negatively by college admissions offices. Eighteen would look better than twenty on applications, she thought. When attending grammar and junior high schools it had seldom come up that she was older than the rest of the kids. In fairness to herself, she had completed the same curriculum as the others who finished high school. The extra years spent on learning English had been necessary in order to do just that. There was really no unfair advantage there. If a college administrator challenged her that would be her answer.

    Prompted by her voice teacher and high school advisors, Marie Conte was bound and determined to go to the next level of music education. Two music schools stood above the rest and they became her focus. Both the Curtis Institute and the Julliard School of Music were well-known and had excellent reputations. Curtis had the advantage by its location in her home state however the city of Philadelphia was only slightly closer to Sharon than Julliard in New York City. Also, worthy students merited free tuition if accepted at Curtis. But then again what musician hadn't heard of Julliard's famous school of music? Marie certainly had and almost as soon as she set foot in America. And what's not to like about New York City? Could any musician ever regret going there to study? She made her decision: applications would be sent to both schools but Julliard would be first choice. There was one glaring stumbling block: tuition at Julliard was not automatically covered like at Curtis. Scholarships were given based on merit and on financial need. Julliard would be a dream beyond her reach without granting of a near full scholarship.

    Her father gave his approval to her first pending financial support from the college. He had no doubts about her abilities, perseverance and diligence. But New York City, so large and so potentially dangerous in many respects, was a concern. At the very beginning of high school Michael had laid down the law that there would be no dating allowed and so far boys had not presented a problem. It was probably the one thing he was most strict about. There would be time for that later. Well, later was now and trust in his daughter's instincts was all he had left should she be accepted.

Marie told her father she had learned that Julliard's admission guidelines required an audition as part of the acceptance process. There were guidelines to follow depending on musical emphasis. Although she hoped to continue with the piano, her principal aim, of course, would be as a vocalist. She would respond by practicing even more now if he knew anything about his daughter. An appointment with the college for the beginning of March was confirmed. Only two months away, preparation with her teacher began in earnest. Portions of three works were selected: two operatic pieces, the first sung in Italian and the second in French—a bit of a risk—and a third of a more popular style and in English, to illustrate her versatility to the judges.

Marie Conte had read countless times the admission criteria needing to be met in addition to the audition. Could she satisfactorily accomplish all that was expected of her even before acceptance was considered? A high school diploma she would certainly have in her hand. No problem there. Artistic training by an established and recognized voice teacher she had fulfilled. And no one who had listened to her speak could dispute her fluency in English, and her non-native language was delivered without a trace of an Italian accent in it. Every opportunity to perform had been seized, which should demonstrate her singing ambitions and talent if Julliard were to make inquiries. And if anyone was asked, they were bound to say that Marie's capacity for disciplined and sustained practice was part of her make-up. That she had sung alongside other musicians and actors would be taken, she hoped, as a strong indicator of teamwork performance.

All in all there should be no question of Marie's dedication to the world of music performance. Be that as it may, there was one academic requirement needing to be addressed and that was mathematics. Dealing with numbers, formulas and theories was a consistent weakness throughout her school years although she had been able to improve to grade level during the summer between her sophomore and junior years. But the increasing difficulty of advanced math in junior and senior years had resulted in a standstill. It could only be hoped that there would be some leeway given to an Italian immigrant who came to America only a few years ago.

Was it enough for a highly selective music school to consider Marie Conte for admission? Many other applicants must have similar or even better qualifications. It dawned on her while taking a break from practicing one day that the make or break difference could very well depend on a combination of the live audition and on personality when she was interviewed. All other things being almost equal, a talented musician who also showed charisma might just be the key in influencing the minds of those making final decisions. She would be prepared, she would spare no effort and she would leave her best impression. And she would be cordially serious. But could she really be herself in such a context? Already a professional persona was beginning to emerge, a stage presence if you will. She would just have to let the chips fall where they may with regard to her credibility.

Her brother saw her looking into her bedroom mirror as if in a trance when he peaked through the crack in the door two days before the Julliard audition. Tony started to turn around, not wishing to disturb her meditative state. But before he managed to leave she stopped him.

"Come in and stay a moment. I need someone to talk to. I don't think I know what I'm doing. I mean New York, the Julliard School, leaving my family behind. It seems too much change at one time. Maybe I should give it up—cancel the audition. They probably won't accept me anyway."

"What are you talking about? I've never seen anyone more ready to go to college. You've done everything you can do and more to get there. Remember when we both were at the port in Naples about to get on the ship together to leave for America? When the authorities stopped me from boarding because of my eyes, well it didn't keep you from going. You were fearless then in leaving without me because you knew I would follow as soon as I could. I'll never forget what you said to me just before you walked up the gangway—you said we'll be waiting for you. Well, we will be waiting for you to become a famous songstress too. Dad and I will be right by your side all the way along your journey. You're the one with all of the artistic talent in this family. So let's not have any last minute nerves, please!"

"But it's so far away. What if something should happen to Dad or you?"

"You can't worry about things like that, Marie. Something can happen to anybody at anytime anywhere; no one can be around all the time when it does. We'd be more worried about it if you were not to pursue what God gave you the talent to do. It would be terrible to see you hanging around home or going to a job you didn't like. Who wants to live with a frustrated sister? Besides Mae, the lady Dad met at the department store in Sharon and has been seeing ever since, looks to me like someone who could become even more a part of his life. I've spoken with her more than once and she seems like a really nice person. I'm sure you already know all that. And I think she has the effect of taming his tendencies to be overly strict around the house sometimes, which is a really good thing for this family!"

"That's true; she is nice and does seem to be good for Dad. She has a daughter named Isabel about our age who's been living with her grandparents on the other side of Pennsylvania, in Lancaster. She's a little older than us and finished high school already. Supposedly, she's in college somewhere, if I remember right what Mae said. But do you think it really will last with Mae, Tony? I hope it does."

"She was married before but divorced for many years now. Her ex-husband passed away just last month Dad said. I guess it must have been after the divorce that Isabel went to live with her grandparents. At the same time that's when Mae went back to live with her own parents in Sharon while she got back on her feet. Lots of sons and daughters and other grandkids, I think about nine in all at last count in that household. The older boys work at the tin mill, you know, the one with the long name, the Mercer Works of the American Sheet and Tin Plate. Mae's mom has really had her hands full since her husband passed away but she couldn't say no to her own daughter."

"It might be just the right time then for Dad and Mae to become a bit closer then."

"I wouldn't be at all surprised to see them married some day and maybe even soon. But you should get started now. Warm up those lovely vocal chords because I want to hear you sing at least one of the audition numbers once more before dinner."

The fateful appointment day seemed to come about faster around than any other day in her life, certainly much faster than she felt she was ready. More time, just a little more time to polish that one phrase in the French piece; just one more session with her instructor; just another review of the outfit she would wear; just a day or two more to gather herself together. But it was not to be. On the next day she left on the long trip to New York City accompanied by her father. And after a restless night, during the late morning of the following day Marie heard her name announced and then was led to the stage of a small campus theater. Standing before her jurors she felt what it must be like to be on trial in a court room about to be grilled by an intimidating attorney. Somehow she managed to force a smile as she introduced herself but received nothing but blank stares in return. She clearly stated the songs she would sing and then began. Weeks of waiting for her moment seemed to be over in a flash. The jurors lifted their noses from notebooks when it was over just long enough to thank her and say she would be hearing from the college before long. On the way to rejoin her father, she couldn't help but wonder what they had jotted down in the notebooks on their laps. She felt she had done well; but feelings could easily lead you astray.

THE TIES THAT BIND ~ ABIDING FATE

FULL CIRCLE

Sharon, Newark, New York City, 1935-1941

Two Italian immigrant families in two adjacent states; a long, windy river and a mountain range separated them from each other. In Pennsylvania, on the western side of the Delaware River and the Appalachian Mountains, lived the Conte family; on the eastern side, in New Jersey, the Paulone family. Two families divided in the past by another mountain chain in southern Italy, the Apennines; families unknown to each other then and now. The driving distance between the Conte's in Sharon in Western Pennsylvania and the Paulone's in Newark on the eastern seaboard, for those fortunate enough to own a car, totaled a not insignificant three hundred and seventy-five miles. The less than fifty miles between the small towns of Bagnoli Irpino west of the Apennine range and Bovino, the Italian homes of the Conte and Paulone families, to the east paled in comparison. But the shorter distance did not come without difficulty; rugged terrain and winding roads served to partially nullify the difference. The hours required from Sharon to Newark might even be less than their Italian counterparts!

An offer of a place at Julliard had been made and Marie

Conte had accepted, with the proviso that she study math in summer school. Nine years ago she had boarded a ship and left her Italian home for a new beginning on American soil. Now twenty, she was ready to extend her world to another new environment. It would be her chance to shine, to showcase the musical talents and mastery of the English language in attending the most selective and prestigious specialty school in the nation. Very welcome was the response the Conte family had received from their relatives, the Melores. An invitation to live in a spare room in their Manhattan flat had been extended after they had been informed of Marie's imminent arrival in the city. Room and board with costs more favorable than the market rental rate they had expected to pay would be to both of their advantages. The Melores would benefit from having a bit more income while keeping an eye on the proper young lady they knew her to be; while Marie would find herself in a safe, hospitable and low-priced accommodation with friendly and trustworthy faces to return to each day after attending classes.

 But first things first, there was still another month and a half until graduation at Sharon High School. And after that, along with summer school, there would be three months to earn some money to supplement her father's support in seeing her through her freshman year at Julliard. Major changes were taking place in their household in the months leading up to her departure. For some time he had been thinking of ways to increase his income during yet another economic downturn. Michael Conte was expanding his Cozy Corner Barber Shop to include a beauty parlor for both sexes to be renamed the Fitzpatrick Beauty Parlor. Although Marie had been granted full tuition, his daughter would need financial help to cover all of the other expenses.

Then there was Tony. His twenty-two year old son, while employed, was not yet totally on his own feet in terms of making ends meet through his salary. Maria's father had all of this in mind when he decided he had procrastinated long enough in enlarging. In the past he had disregarded colleagues who had told him that a hairdressing business would bring in much more revenue than what the standard men's barbershop could do. But he had finally had taken the horse by the reins and had him galloping. There were carpenters, sheetrock hangers, plumbers, floor sanders and painters all contending to get the remodeling done as quickly as possible. Seeing the transformation taking place in the first few weeks had made him a believer. And when it was finished the reinvented barbershop cum beauty parlor was everything he had been told. He could have kicked himself for having waited so long to make the gender leap. The revenue generated from a variety of more costly services had already contributed significantly to his income.

There was an even more risky change that had occurred. The woman who he had been dating for some time was now his partner living full-time in their household. He hadn't been sure how it would work out after years of living alone, or with only his children, but he shouldn't have been bothered. Mae brought with her a warm personality and positive outlook that immediately fit in and seemed to be rubbing on Michael too. If anything, the atmosphere around the house had lightened from her presence. But mainly it was great to see the two of them happy together. It had been a long time coming since he had lost his first wife in 1918 and his children had become motherless. And they had also gained a step-sister! Isabel would also be welcomed into the family the next time they saw Mae's daughter.

Marie Conte's last few months of her high school years were more of the same. She sang whenever she was given the opportunity and performed the lead vocalist role in the springtime musical drama. But in truth, her heart was already halfway in New York City. As is often the case for young people heading in new directions, leaving home was probably felt harder by those left behind. In 1935 she was about to start on a new journey nearly rivaling her departure from Italy nine years earlier in 1926. So completely wrapped in her own thoughts, she was oblivious to the fact the household atmosphere had changed. She talked and they only listened as the day of departure neared. It was really only when she saw the tears in their eyes when they exchanged final hugs at the station that she fully realized both their sadness and happiness marking the occasion. But she wasn't leaving forever and all of them knew she would come home again. Hours later, she was again in New York City and at the Melore family residence—her home away from home for the next four years.

She adapted to the academic rhythm of college student life with ease. Out of bed, dressed and a quick bite to eat, she was ready for an early morning class, voice and piano later with the library and cafeteria in-between, practicing, practicing and practicing whenever she could. She had the knack for striking up casual conversations, which was important for making friendships on a certain level. However, it was a different story when it came to really good friends.

It was soon learned while most talented musicians understandably have a strong belief in their own abilities—and confidence in showcasing them when the right opportunities presented themselves—they are very competitive with each other as well. Jealousy even among "musical rivals" in her singing niche of lyric sopranos was evident. Be that as it may she would never let it keep her from always moving forwards when it came to the career she was intent on pursuing to the fullest. And for that reason Marie relied on family at home in Pennsylvania and the Melores in the city as those she could confide in, count on and trust. With very few exceptions this was how Marie Conte conducted her life while studying voice, piano, foreign languages and opera in graduate school classes.

One of the exceptions was the student she had met in the late afternoon in the Julliard cafeteria. It wasn't by chance he had placed his tray down on the opposite side of the table from where she sat for an unusually late lunch in the mostly vacated hall.

"I hope you don't mind my sitting here. I'm new to Julliard, and you look like someone who might be able to give me some tips for getting to know my way around this place," were his opening lines.

"Of course it's okay. You're free to sit where you want. Do you play an instrument or sing or do something else?" she asked of the tall, thin and dark-haired young man.

"I'm a flutist and piccolo player. How about you?"

"Piano, but I'm really here to develop my voice for classic opera and more contemporary music as well. In fact, I just finished a sight-reading exam this morning. But you said you were a new student?"

"You probably noticed I'm a bit older than most of the others. I'm not really a student in the sense that you probably are, in a regular degree program, that is. I'm taking private lessons at Julliard from a professor in one of the studios three times a week. By the way my name is James Paulone, but people mostly call me Jim or Jimmy when they get to know me."

"Mine is Marie Conte. Are you from New York?"

"No ma'am. I'm actually a Jerseyite from the other side of the river. And you?"

"Pennsylvania is my home. But Italy is where I was born."

"I'm half Italian myself. My father was born there but my mother was born and raised in Newark, my hometown."

"You do have that southern European look about you. I would have guessed both of your parents were from there."

"So I've heard; but my mother's people originally came from England and France, with maybe a little Irish thrown in for good measure."

"You were asking about Julliard when you sat down. I think the best thing I can tell you after two years here and another two to go is to be sure to take advantage of the school's reputation to make connections even before you've finished your training. That's what I intend to do in order get an idea on ways of finding employment. Oh, and also attend as many recitals and performances on campus as you can. In fact, I will be giving one next week on Wednesday morning. You're welcome to come if you'd like."

Who could refuse an invitation from such a lovely girl as this? Exact time and place were duly transferred and the two new acquaintances parted ways for the time being. The following week Jim did attend Marie's musical recital and waited for her afterwards. A few words were exchanged amid complements and then Jim had to run to his lesson, but not before arranging to meet at a coffee shop around the corner from Julliard to continue talking. He insisted they split a huge slice of cake while they nursed cups of coffee. Conversation flowed smoothly without the curse of musician one-upmanship sneaking in. Family and music predominated then eventually Jim was asked to tell a little about his personal story. He started with a few of his more recent escapades of the last decade, after leaving school and before coming to Julliard.

Then it was Marie's turn. She described what her life had been like in southern Italy as a young child. When she mentioned the name of the town she came from he was amazed to learn Bagnoli Irpino was not that far from his father's birth place in Bovino. Then it was Marie who was astonished. Non-stop for the next half hour she spoke of the people she knew from Bovino, even some distant cousins. It was hard to get over how in all of Manattan she had just met someone whose father came from a town in Puglia so near to hers in Campania. Why, the two villages were almost within shouting distance! Hardly, but close enough to be quite a coincidence. So excited by this twist of fate she almost forgot to mention that there were actually several families in Bagnoli bearing Jim's Paulone surname.

Coincidences did not end there. Jaws dropped even further when they discovered both of their fathers were barbers. Not only were they barbers but they were both barbershop owners! Her father Michael Conte had tried his hand at hair-cutting a little before arriving in America, she recollected, but had been open minded to what he would do in America while he was still in Italy. As for Frank Paulone, he had decided to become a barber within weeks after his ship had anchored in New York harbor.

"Tell me about your family, Jim. It sounds like there were a lot of children for your parents to handle."

"Not that many, not like some really large families, just the four of us in all. But it was not always parents plural that raised us. When I was about twelve or thirteen, I think, my mother left home. My parents hadn't been getting along for a long time and she met someone else. For my older brother Danny and me it wasn't as traumatic as it was for the two younger ones. My sister Millie, losing the only other female in the household, and little brother Louis not yet ten, felt it much more than we did. They were really crushed when she was gone. It was almost like she died."

"I can imagine your father must have been hit pretty hard too. A father bringing up children on his own, though, is actually something with which I can identify. There were only my brother Tony and me, but when we came from Italy my father had to take care of us from about the same ages as were your and sister. That was after Tony and me not having a father or mother around for years. She died in Italy near the end of the war after he had already gone ahead on his own to America. We ended up living with grandparents and other relatives in Bagnoli for a dozen years or so before we were able to join him here."

"It seems like we have a lot of common, including a lot of unhappy times we had to get through. But at least your father, I'm sure, is grateful to have his two children alive and doing so well."

"With four children in your family, hopefully yours feel the same way."

"Four once: now only three. My little brother Louis died four years ago. He was only nineteen. My father may have become resigned to my mother leaving her family, but I don't know if he will ever recover from the death of Louis. It seems my religious brother Danny and his zealot-like religious convictions played a part in it. I'm sure Dad has never completely forgiven him. The whole thing has really aged him. He was in the hospital a month ago, in December."

"Why do you say your brother had something to do with it—and what is it about his religion that's so bothersome?"

"It's complicated. But if you really want to hear about it I'll try to make a long story short."

"I do, I do. You've really have me curious to know more now."

"All right then, here goes. My older brother Danny even before he left home somehow got connected with the Nazarene Church. I mean fervently engaged. Of course we had been raised Catholic but this sort of Methodist-related church had got hold him and converted him into a fire-breathing disciple. He never stopped talking about it. Millie and I were too old to listen much but Louis, I guess, was more susceptible to his evangelical preaching about it. Eventually Danny's involvement with the Nazarenes grew to the point that he became a minister and he used his musicianship as a way to bring others into the fold. One of his duties was to tour some of the other Nazarene churches in New Jersey and New York. He asked Louis, whom he had already convinced in becoming a church member too, to join him upstate. The pastor of the local church had decided to go swimming near a waterfall and got into trouble. Louis jumped in to save him even though he couldn't swim. They both drowned."

"That's horrible. You all must have been devastated. It's really put me at a loss for words." And indeed Marie did become silent.

"For my father, it was the worst. He's never gotten over it, and although he doesn't say so, I know he blames Danny. To tell the truth Millie and I think Danny is at fault too. Why did Danny have to make Louis part of his kind of religious evangelism anyhow?" he lamented as tears began to well up in his eyes. "Anyway, enough about sad things, let's talk about music."

And talk about music, and many other things, they did incessantly that morning and many days, weeks and months afterwards. Once, when he picked Marie up at the Melores he had asked if the photo on the table in her room was of her mother. It was her turn to become teary-eyed when she told him it was and that she never went anywhere without it. Her death was clearly the defining moment of Marie's life. In February of 1937, Jim's father died, a month after the first lengthy conversation between Jim and Marie. He regretted that Marie never had the chance to meet him and made a point to introduce her to his sister and her husband not long thereafter.

Life became more intense during the final academic year of her studies at Julliard for several reasons. Gradually their relationship had evolved into a commitment, one which could only be solemnized once Marie had completed her degree. Pressure from final exams and papers, together with evaluations of vocal and piano technique, including a grand finale recital, made it out of the question to contemplate anything else. Jim too was feeling pressure but in a different way. Even though the lessons at Julliard had taken him to another level, longer lasting, more stable employment had eluded him thus far. And finding the kind of employment he wanted became his objective before taking their relationship to the next stage.

Then all of that changed when Jim was offered a job with the MGM Studio Orchestra in Hollywood for the filming of the Wizard of Oz. His selection as an orchestra member must have been due to his experience in playing with orchestras in silent movie theaters and recent professional development at Julliard, he thought. Regardless, it was a golden opportunity for someone with a diverse background and past musical achievements that fit so well with how movie studio work was done. He had learned about the opening from his teacher, and to spur him on he had written a letter of personal recommendation that Jim could enclose with his own. If he accepted the offer, he would need to leave for California within ten days, since filming had already begun. Musical accompaniment was to be recorded separately as soon as the first scene segments could be sent to the orchestra's studio room for synchronization. Without thinking twice Marie told him he must do it. It was the kind of job he could hardly refuse, one that could make your career. Besides, the job in California was only temporary and they could wait a little longer still.

In October of 1938 Jim Paulone packed his bags, flute and piccolo and left for the West Coast. He had been told recording would continue well into the next year, possibly as much as six months, so to be prepared for the long haul. As it happened the last sequences were not submitted to Herbert Stothart—the conductor who also composed the original score—and his associate Georgie Stoll, who also took the baton intermittently, until March 1939. In the same month Jim headed back home with invaluable experience tucked under his belt. He also brought with him a plethora of Hollywood stories with which to regale Marie Conte. She had graduated with flying colors three months earlier in June, and now freed from her packed schedule was ready to resume their relationship from where they had left off. Time passed quickly, until four months later they arranged to meet early enough at the cinema to be able to find the best seats. On August 17, 1939 the Wizard of Oz premiered in New York City at the Loew Capital Theatre and they would not have missed being there for the world. It had been only two days after its very first premiere in California at Grauman's Chinese Theater in Hollywood. Listening to the soundtrack more than watching the movie, they were thrilled each time Jim's playing soared enough above the rest of the instruments to stand out.

***

Just when high unemployment figures were trending downwards and there was optimism in the air news of another war threw a shadow over the country again. Germany had invaded Poland only two weeks after they had gone to the theater to watch the Oz film together. And two days after that, on September 3rd, Britain and France declared war on Germany. As disturbing as this was for some, Jim Paulone and Marie Conte kept it all in perspective and were not overly dismayed. Jim was living at home and working for the WPA Music Program again and also performing at concerts. And Marie, as determined as ever, had not let it dampen her enthusiasm to forge ahead in the operatic world. After all, hadn't it always seemed like Europe was in turmoil for one reason or another anyway? Maybe this time it would all blow over quickly.

Before long a whirlwind of musical engagements were sought after and booked. One day she was in New York, the next somewhere in New Jersey and then it was on to Pennsylvania. Marie brought Jim along to meet her family for the first time and to show him off while they performed at her former high school in Sharon. Their very first concert together would be presented as a special tribute to the support she had received during the years she spent at her alma mater. The concert was announced on page four of the Wednesday, September 27, 1939 issue of The Youngstown Daily Vindicator and the brief article lit up their day:

Sharon Soprano to Sing, Flutist to Play Thursday

Miss Marie Conte, soprano of Sharon, Pa. and James Paulone, flutist of New York City, will present a concert at 8:30 p.m. Thursday in Sharon High School auditorium. Miss Conte and Paulone are graduates of the Juliard School of Music in New York City. Miss Conte has appeared as guest soloist with the Newark Symphony Orchestra and has spent several seasons with the Chatauqua Opera Co.

Signing a contract with the Chautauqua Opera Company in Chautauqua, New York first had been a significant step for the promising young American singer. It meant Marie would have steady work for the entire next two operatic seasons with a widely recognized musical institution. She would be singing and acting under the direction of Albert Stoessel. Maestro Stoessel was a well-known conductor for both the opera and the symphony and he had been instrumental in building the new opera house. In tandem with the opera company, Marie was also a guest artist with the New Jersey Symphony Orchestra in Newark. And as well she had returned to her old stomping ground to perform as guest soloist for a "pop" concert with the Youngstown Symphony Orchestra in Youngstown, Ohio. A myriad of recitals in New York City filled up the rest of her time deep into 1940. Jim, meanwhile, was now inundated with work. He had been contracted to play with the Radio City Music Hall Symphony Orchestra. This was in addition to soloist concert work with the Essex County Symphony Band and performances from time to time with orchestras elsewhere in New Jersey and in New York. All of this while still trying from time to time to honor an ongoing commitment to the Federal Music Project.

But when Marie Conte won the "Artists in the Making" competition it was as if she hit the jackpot. Her singing and dramatic expertise when coupled with proficiency in both English and Italian led to a proposal for her own program on WOV, a radio station broadcasting out of New York. The station's programs were delivered in a foreign language to listeners who spoke the same language. WOV's Italian broadcast programs were daily from 7 a.m. to 6 p.m. and as a native Italian-speaker, Marie was hired to fill a time slot. The Italian audience was huge in the New York-New Jersey metropolitan area having the potential of reaching over a million Italo-Americans.

Marie and Jim had successfully launched on careers and were finally ready to take the next big step together. Everything came together just after they walked over Bow Bridge to the other side of the Lake in Central Park one morning. The 5th February of 1941 was chosen as the day and the marriage venue would be St. Joseph Church, the large Catholic Church located on the corner of Case Avenue and State Street. Their choice of Sharon, Pennsylvania for the place of marriage had been straightforward: it was the home of the bride-to-be and where her father, brother and Mae lived.

Marie's multiple cousins living in Niles a few miles away across the state line in Ohio and her aunt Conchetta in Meadville, Pennsylania would also be able attend. Brrother Tony would serve as the bridegroom's best man. Of course Isabel, Mae's daughter, would be coming, and Marie's best friend Virginia from high school days would be the maid of honor. Many other old high school friends would also be present. Millie would travel together with Jimmy to Pennsylvania although his brother-in-law Paul would be staying behind in Newark. A wedding breakfast was planned to follow the morning ceremony and in the evening Marie's parents, Michael and Mae now married for over two years, would receive relatives and friends at their Sharon home.

A rapidly changing global picture had not gone unnoticed by Jim and Marie even when totally wrapped up in all of their wedding preparations. In the larger picture, Germany had consolidated its invasion of Poland by conquering France, the Netherlands and Belgium while annexing Austria and Czechoslovakia along the way. President Roosevelt's policy of neutrality appeared to be about to collapse as it seemed inevitable America would soon join the fray in one way or another. Then, as if to make it even more likely, in October 1940 all men between the ages of twenty-one and forty-five were required to register for the draft. Jim, thirty-three, was one of them. The gloom hanging over Europe seemed to be contagious and the young musicians' strong beginnings after finishing Julliard began to fade. In March 1941 the WOV radio station had merged with two others, all on the same frequency. The new configuration resulted in a reduction of WOV's broadcast time to a few hours a day, which greatly impacted the programming formerly offered. Marie's program slot was eliminated altogether. Musical engagements also had become harder to come by for Jim and his Radio City Music Hall tenure had fallen onto shaky ground.

Even before the wedding took place the recent changes in world affairs had led to a rethinking of their futures. Maybe it was the right time for making a fresh start somewhere else although New York City would always be their special place. The prestige of working in Hollywood at the movie studios, and the very good salary that went with it, had stayed locked in Jim's memory. He was convinced there would be many more opportunities at the major studios, like MGM, Warner Brothers, Universal and Disney. But the idea of moving so far away did not resonate so readily with the newly minted Marie Paulone. The East was the only part of the country she knew. Family and friends lived there, and the big stage of New York City was where she envisioned herself singing in the future. Jimmy's argument that the size of Los Angeles and Hollywood's fame would provide plenty of opportunities to display her musical talents won the day in the end. But persuading her to take the plunge westward to California had come with the proviso: they would make New York City their permanent home afterwards.

Following the wedding events, the newlyweds left immediately on an extended honeymoon, proceeding southwards and heading first to the city of New Orleans. Jim was excited to show his wife his old haunts, including sampling a dozen of the best oysters in the world. Then turning westward to Louisiana they continued onwards through Texas, where they hoped to be lucky enough to hear a prairie chicken, that strange bird with a booming voice. From there they crossed the rest of the southern United States until reaching their final destination of Los Angeles. A two days' stay in a motel and then a small but cozy apartment was rented in the City of Angels.

The very next day Jim rose early in the morning to take care of business leftover from his previous visit out west. He had been very fortunate to be hired by MGM in the late '30s without membership in the musicians union. Because he was a temporary musician imported from the East to fill a critical vacancy on short notice an exception had been made. The same warnings had been issued several times that in order to continue working in the studios the union must be joined. No union card, no work in the future, in other words. They planned to reside in Los Angeles for the foreseeable future and Jim Paulone wasn't about to waste another moment before going down to the union hall. Once initiation fee and dues were paid he became an official member of Local 47 of the American Federation of Musicians in August 1941. And with his union card safely tucked away in his wallet he was ready to begin working.

Benefits from union membership were soon returned in spades by the number of jobs he lined up at the studios. Warner Brothers, Universal Pictures and, of course his former employer Metro-Goldwyn-Mayer all called him to work over the next few months. But when America entered the war in December 1941, he thought his studio work might be over before it had barely got started. Instead, it continued almost unabated for the next two years. Then in early 1944 he was asked to report for examination at the induction center for military draftees. Cross-eyed since birth Jim was disqualified from service and instead was assigned to work the nightshift at an airplane factory in Los Angeles.

Music industry work tapered down for Marie as her expected delivery date drew closer. She had become pregnant a month after reaching their new home. After waiting the first few months she told her brother the good news and he immediately told his wife there would soon be a new addition to the family line, the very first to be born in America. When Marie heard the excitement in Tony's voice for some reason a picture came to her of him standing on the dock in Italy when she sailed away so many years ago. Tony Conte, a truck driver for a bakery in Sharon, had married the daughter of the bakery's owner in November of 1941, the same year and at the same St. Joseph Church in Sharon in which Jim and Marie had wed.

***

Before Marie and Jim had exchanged the eastern for the western half of the nation, there had been one last thing Marie had insisted on doing. The Bagnoli Irpino Club in Niles—the town in Ohio in which many of her Italian relatives lived and worked—must be visited. The club had been loosely established in 1926, the same year that she arrived, and six years later, in 1932, it was officially formalized. Jim was happy to share in the pilgrimage to pay homage to her past life before they set out for California. One of Marie's cousins who was showing them around in passing asked Jim if might be related to the Paulone families in Bagnoli. There was even a Paulone who supposedly moved to Bovino to marry a girl there. Jim knew nothing about it and was a bit mystified by it all. Perhaps it was a kindly attempt at linking Marie's husband more closely to the proud Bagnoli community of Niles. It soon was forgotten about and it was time to go.

Seventy-five years later a recently added record in a genealogical database was stumbled upon by accident, a record lending credence to what had been mere speculation earlier in Niles. It was a typed and minimally extracted marriage listing for an Antonio Paulone who wedded a Maria Michela Petrini in Civile, Bovino, Foggia, Italy. Names of Antonio's parents matched what was already known about them, and a listing of "Household Members" contained the correct names regarding Maria Michela's parents. But it was Antonio Paulone's birth place that leaped off the page: it was Bagnoli Irpino! Could it really be correct that he was actually born in Bagnoli and not Bovino? Maybe it was simply human error in deciphering the original handwritten document, and the two towns both beginning with the letter "B" had been mistaken for one another? It happens frequently enough when transcribing hard to read penmanship in another language.

In the summer of 2017, Marie's granddaughter and her husband tried to get a definitive answer to lingering questions as to the true birth place of Antonio Paulone. Combining a holiday along the southern Italian coast and elsewhere in the Puglia region with a visit to the *Municipio di Bovino*, they found Bovino's town hall open with staff willing to research through registers for the original marriage record of Antonio and Maria Michela. On the seventh line following the name of Antonio Paulone were clearly written the words *"di anni quarantatre nato in Bagnoli Irpino*", aged forty-three born in Bagnoli Irpino! A second record for the birth of their son Francesantonio confirmed that his father had been born in Bagnoli. No further doubts remained: the actual heritage of James Paulone was half-Bovinese, half-Bagnolesi! And what's more, it was discovered Maria Michela had been married previously to a man who had passed away who had also been born in Bagnoli.

The family ties between these small Italian towns were inhibited neither by the mountain range that separated them nor by the different provinces in which they were located. And the ties between the Conte and Paulone immigrants stemming from them that had settled in Pennsylvania and New Jersey would not be broken either. Across mountain ranges beginning with the letter "A", the Apennines and the Appalachians, in American states adjoining one another, Pennsylvania and New Jersey, and of fathers who had found their professions in barbering, the young and ambitious musicians, Marie and Jim, had unwittingly taken the long way around in closing destiny's circle!

www.ingramcontent.com/pod-product-compliance
Lightning Source LLC
Chambersburg PA
CBHW032027290426
44110CB00012B/702